THE WRITING
OF NARRATIVE LATIN

BY

BENJAMIN W. MITCHELL, Ph.D.

PROFESSOR OF LATIN AND HEAD OF DEPARTMENT OF ANCIENT
AND MODERN LANGUAGES, CENTRAL HIGH SCHOOL
PHILADELPHIA

AMERICAN BOOK COMPANY

NEW YORK   CINCINNATI   CHICAGO

INTRODUCTION

THE only excuse that can be offered for another textbook on the subject of writing Latin is a presentation of the subject from a point of view differing somewhat from that generally adopted. In the present work the author aims to present the subject from the standpoint of English idiom, using material derived mainly from the first book of Caesar's *Gallic War*.

In using this book the pupil will have the principles of Latin syntax, applied to English forms of speech, before his eyes as he writes, without the necessity either of handling three separate books — composition book, Latin Grammar, and Caesar — or of making, with insufficient experience and on insufficient data, inductions which are usually erroneous. The sentences herein set for the pupil are based on principles plainly stated and copiously illustrated. There is no servile imitation of the language of Caesar, though the sentences are chiefly of a military character based on the principles of syntax exemplified in Caesar's work.

The working vocabulary comprises English equivalents for about 600 Latin words, with which the pupil has been made familiar in his first year; and he is supposed to be renewing daily that familiarity by reading the text of Caesar. The words have been selected as follows. 1. Caesar uses 364 words 20 times or oftener in the *Gallic War;* only 11 of these do not occur in Book I. Of these words 363 are employed in the exercises of this book. 2. The words used by Caesar between 10 and 20 times in the *Gallic War* number 316; only 48 of these do not occur in Book I. Of this second set of words 177 are employed in this book. 3. The remaining few words used in

3

the book, occurring less than 10 times in Caesar, are deemed
of special importance as representing common English words in
daily use, or as resembling closely their English equivalents, or
as connectives.   Only 4 words occur in Parts I and II which
Caesar does not use — the words for *to-day, to-morrow, yesterday,
pity.*   One word is used in a sense not found in Caesar, **stō** in
the sense of *cost.*   No word is found in the first lesson which
does not occur in the first six chapters of Book I of the *Gallic
War*, none in the second lesson which does not occur before
chapter twelve ; and so on in somewhat varying ratio, so that in
the first eleven lessons words found in the first book of the *Gallic War* are used exclusively.   After that point no vocabulary
restriction by books of Caesar is observed.   The first sixteen
lessons employ about 450 of the commonest words, to form a
working capital for the remaining lessons ; for it is the repeated
use of words which fixes them in the mind, rather than small
accretions memorized daily.   Furthermore, with all of these
words the pupil will have become familiar in the first year's
work.   This arrangement has been found to work well with
classes in which the book has been used in manuscript form.

To English synonyms special attention has been given.   Re-
sourcefulness is the one quality that is most often lacking in the
beginner's attempts to write Latin.   If the pupil can be made
to realize that it is by canvassing English synonyms that he can
best arrive at the Latin equivalent for a given English idea, a
great gain will have been made.   In the application of principles
of syntax, however, the pupil must distrust the English *form of
expression* at every step and must delve for the real meaning.

In Part II the story of the first five books of the *Gallic War*
has been cast in the form of easy exercises in connected writing.   In these the vocabulary is slightly less limited, though it
is still restricted to words of frequent occurrence in Caesar.
For more advanced pupils, to give practice in analyzing idiomatic English and in penetrating *form* to arrive at *meaning*, as
well as to illustrate the fact that the language of Caesar may

be applied to the narration of any military events, even those of the twentieth century, a brief sketch of the first stage of the Balkan War of 1912 is given in Part III. Here also, proper names excepted, not more than five or six words are necessary which Caesar does not use.

The primary object of Latin composition is to aid in developing sound reasoning fortified by memory. If in any way this object shall be secured or promoted by the present work, its aim will have been attained.

The author desires to express his obligations to many of his colleagues in the Public School system of Philadelphia for useful suggestions and material; to Professor John C. Rolfe, of the University of Pennsylvania, for advice and encouragement; and especially to Professor Charles Knapp, of Columbia University, who with painstaking care read the work both in manuscript and in proof, and contributed suggestions and criticisms of the utmost value.

BENJAMIN W. MITCHELL.

CENTRAL HIGH SCHOOL, PHILADELPHIA.

SUGGESTIONS TO TEACHERS

WHILE it would be presumptuous to do aught to hamper the individual teacher in freedom of treatment of the present book, it may not be amiss to indicate its design and to offer certain suggestions which, it is believed, will tend to secure the best results from its use. The book is designed primarily to cover the composition work of the second and third years of a high school course. It may even be used to cover the entire course of college preparation in this subject; for a student who has mastered the book is qualified, by adding to his vocabulary less than fifty Ciceronian words, to pass any of the examinations usually set in Latin Composition.

The writing of at least a considerable portion of Part I should accompany the reading of Caesar. Should the time allowed for Latin Composition in any school not be deemed adequate for the completion of Part I during the second year of Latin study, the book may be used in either of the two ways indicated below.

I. Thirty lessons may be completed in the second year, leaving the remaining ten lessons, with Part II and possibly a portion of Part III, for the third year. Part III may be completed, and the book reviewed, during the fourth and last year of secondary school work. This method will postpone until the third year the difficulties of indirect discourse and of the more complex English non-finite constructions.

II. For teachers who feel that the student must in his second year handle the laws of indirect discourse as instruments of production, certain sections may be omitted during the second year, together with the sentences based on them. These sections

7

have their numbers printed in light-faced italic type, and the sentences concerned are grouped together after a dash at the close of the several exercises. The sections thus marked for omission are: 31 (printed for reference only in the earlier instruction, but to be mastered thoroughly by degrees), 113, 114, 135, 136, 137, 141, 156, 166, and Lessons XXX, XXXIII, XXXVIII, XXXIX, XL entire.

The use of the book throughout the course secures constant practice in prose writing during the reading of the *Aeneid*, and attention to the *general principles of syntax* rather than to the peculiarities of style of individual Latin authors.

CONTENTS

PART I

9

PART II

PART III

ABBREVIATIONS

abl. = ablative
absol. = absolute, absolutely
acc. = accusative
adj. = adjective
adv. = adverb
affirm. = affirmative
coll. = collective
comp. = comparative, comparison
conj. = conjunction
dat. = dative
dem. = demonstrative
dep. = deponent
dir. = direct
encl. = enclitic
exc. = except
f. = feminine
fig. = figurative, figuratively
fr. = from
fut. = future
gen. = genitive
impers. = impersonal
impf. = imperfect
imv. = imperative
ind. = indirect
indecl. = indeclinable
indic. = indicative
inf. = infinitive
interrog. = interrogative
intr. = intransitive

lit. = literal, literally
loc. = locative
m. = masculine
(n.) = noun
n., neut. = neuter
neg. = negative
num. = number, numeral
obj. = object
pass. = passive
perf. = perfect
pers. = person
pl. = plural
pos. = positive
poss. = possessive
prep. = preposition
pres. = present
pron. = pronoun
ptc. = participle
q.v. = which see *(quod vidē)*
ref. = reference, refers
reflex. = reflexive
rel. = relative
sing. = singular
subjv. = subjunctive
subst. = substantive
superl. = superlative
tr. = transitive
(v.) = verb
w. = with

THE WRITING OF NARRATIVE LATIN

PART I

LESSON I

THE SENTENCE. THE CONCORDS

1. A sentence in its fullest form consists of (1) subject; (2) objects, direct and indirect; (3) verb; (4) the modifiers of each. These modifiers may be words, phrases, or clauses.

2. The subject of a sentence is in the nominative case; the direct object is in the accusative case; the indirect object is in the dative case.

a. The indirect object is the person or thing to which or for which a thing is done, toward which a thought or feeling is directed, or to whose benefit or hurt a state or condition exists.

b. In English the indirect object is usually expressed by a phrase with *to* or *for;* but if the indirect object immediately follows the verb, the preposition is omitted. Thus, *he gave a book to him* or *he gave him a book.*

3. Tenses.

Tense forms in English, in simple and compound sentences, are represented in Latin by the tenses expressing in part the time in which the action lies (present, past, or future), and in part the nature of the action (continued or completed). Thus, *the troops are coming now* represents an action going on (continued) in present time and requires in Latin the present tense;

the troops are coming to-morrow describes a future action and requires the future tense. *The army has been disbanded* represents completed action in present time and requires in Latin the perfect tense; *the army has been marching all night* represents action continued in past time and requires in Latin the imperfect tense.

a. An action begun in the past and continuing in the present is expressed in Latin by the present tense.

He has long been an enemy, **iam prīdem hostis est.**

b. The historical present is a present tense used for a past, to secure vividness of style. It is regularly used in newspaper headlines in English, and often in lively narration in Latin.

Caesar ordered (*orders*) *the cavalry to set out*, **Caesar equitēs proficīscī iubet.**

c. An action begun or attempted is sometimes expressed in Latin by the imperfect tense.

The enemy tried to keep our men from gaining entrance to their works, **hostēs nostrōs intrā mūnītiōnēs ingredī prohibēbant.**

d. Tenses which refer to present or future time are called **Primary** tenses; those which refer to past time are called **Secondary** tenses.

1. These classes are sometimes called respectively *principal* and *historical* tenses.

Analyze tenses for time and nature of the action; do not be misled by the mere form of the English.

4. The concords.

I. An adjective, whether attributive or predicate, agrees with its noun in gender, number, and case.

II. A relative pronoun agrees with its antecedent in gender, number, and person; its case depends on its relation to its own clause.

III. A finite verb agrees with its subject in number and person.

5. Word order.

The normal word order of a Latin sentence is (1) the subject and its modifiers; (2) the objects, indirect and direct, with their respective modifiers; (3) modifiers of the verb; (4) the verb. This order is often changed for the sake of clearness or emphasis. The emphatic word is placed usually at the beginning of the sentence, less frequently at the end. Words repeating or summing up or expanding the thought of a preceding sentence come regularly at the beginning of the sentence in which they occur. Any displacement from the normal order tends to emphasize the displaced word.

a. No general rule can be given for the position of adjectives in Latin. They precede the noun oftener than they follow it; and their position often depends on the relative emphasis of noun and adjective, the more emphatic word tending to precedence. Latin adjectives of quantity (such as *all, many,* etc.) and numerals regularly precede the noun. A proper adjective follows the noun.

6.   VOCABULARY

all,[1] **omnis, -e.**

already,[2] **iam.**

and, **et** (*most general word*); **-que,** *encl., added to the second of the words connected* (*connects closely into group*).

and,[3] **atque,** *before vowels and consonants;* **ac,** *before consonants only* (*emphasizes what follows*).

arms,[4] **arma, -ōrum,** *n. pl.*

army, **exercitus, -ūs,** *m.*

assault,[5] **oppugnō, I.**

be, **sum, esse, fuī, futūrus.**

but, **sed.**

camp, **castra, -ōrum,** *n. pl.*

conquer,[6] **superō, I.**

divide, **dīvidō, -ere, -vīsī, -vīsum.**

do, **faciō, -ere, fēcī, factum.**

forces,[7] **cōpiae, -ārum,** *f. pl.;* *sing.,* plenty, supply.

give,[8] **dō, dare, dedī, datum.**

great,[9] **magnus, -a, -um.**

journey,[10] **iter, itineris,** *n.*

land,[11] **ager, agrī,** *m.* (*special ref. to property*).

legion,[12] **legiō, -ōnis,** *f.*

make, **faciō**.

man,[13] **homō, -inis,** *m.*

much, *pl.* many, **multus, -a, -um.**

not, **nōn.**

not yet, **nōndum.**

now, **nunc** (*refers to point of time*).

now at last, **iam** (*after what has taken place*).

part,[14] **pars, partis,** *f.*

see, **videō, -ēre, vīdī, vīsum.**

start,[15] **proficīscor, -ī, -fectus.**

take,[16] **capiō, -ere, cēpī, captum.**

three, **trēs, tria.**

to-day, **hodiē.**

to-morrow, **crās.**

town, **oppidum, -ī,** *n.*

two, **duo, -ae, -o.**

yesterday, **herī.**

Idiom

to march, iter facere

Synonyms. 1. every; *in pl. without a noun,* every one, everything. 2. by this (that) time. 3. and also. 4. weapons. 5. attack (*places only*), besiege. 6. beat, crush, defeat, overcome, vanquish, win. 7. troops. 8. grant. 9. big, large. 10. march, road, right of way, route. 11. district, field, territory. 12. regiment. 13. *In pl.*, men, mankind. 14. division, portion. 15. set out. 16. capture, catch.

7. 1. I shall see the men to whom [1] you gave the weapons. 2. The great army starts to-morrow. 3. I have not yet seen two of [2] the three parts into [3] which Gaul is divided.[4] 4. The legions captured the camp and also besieged the town. 5. Many legions will have assaulted the camp and the town. 6. The forces are now starting and will march into Gaul. 7. Yesterday the Romans overcame the great forces of the Gauls. 8. The camp has already been taken. 9. I haven't seen Caesar to-day. 10. You have now crushed the Gauls and will march into the town. 11. We shall conquer their [5] army and divide their lands. 12. Their army has not yet been defeated, but the legions are now attacking its [6] camp. 13. I'll do it [7] to-morrow. 14. Do it now. 15. We tried [8] to do it yesterday. 16. Take the camp, men!

1. quibus. 2. 'of' after a cardinal numeral is expressed by **ex** with abl. 3. Acc. w. **in, quās in partēs.** 4. Completed action in present time. 5. eōrum. 6. eius. 7. id or ea. 8. See **3**, *c.*

LESSON II

PECULIARITIES OF AGREEMENT

8. A verb having two or more subjects is regularly plural; if the subjects are of different persons, the plural verb agrees with the first person in preference to the second and the third, and with the second in preference to the third.

You and I have taken our stand here, **hīc ego et tū cōnstitimus.**

9. In Latin when an adjective describes two or more nouns of different genders,

a. Attributive adjectives regularly agree in gender and number with the nearest noun.

Many pack animals and carts, **multa iūmenta et carrī** or **multī carrī et iūmenta**; *with not the same eagerness and enthusiasm,* **nōn eādem alacritāte ac studiō.**

b. Predicate adjectives, including participles in compound tenses, are very often plural: if the nouns all denote persons, the plural adjectives are masculine; if the nouns all denote things, the plural adjectives are neuter; if the nouns include both persons and things, the adjectives may be masculine or neuter plural, or may agree with the nearest noun. In Caesar, however, under all these conditions, the adjective regularly agrees with the nearest noun.

The work of the winter camp and the fortifications had not been entirely completed, **opus hībernōrum mūnītiōnēsque nōn plēnē erant perfectae**; *so great, said they, was the fame of his army and also the impression (produced by it),* **tantum dīxērunt esse nōmen atque opīniōnem eius exercitūs**; *his daughter and one of his sons were captured,* **fīlia atque ūnus ē fīliīs captus est** (here the emphatic **ūnus** requires a singular verb).

NOTE. In practice it is best to introduce the common adjective early in the sentence, immediately before or after one of the nouns, and to make it agree with that noun.

10. Sometimes in Latin an adjective or a verb will conform to the sense of a noun rather than to its form.

He persuaded the state (i.e., *the citizens*) *to go out*, **cīvitātī persuāsit ut exīrent** (here **cīvitātī** implies **cīvibus**).

11. A noun meaning *man, woman, soldier, property, thing,* etc., modified by an adjective, is usually omitted in Latin, especially if the noun is in the plural; the adjective is then said to be used substantively.

They retreated to their own men, **sē ad suōs recēpērunt**; *our soldiers were ready under arms*, **nostrī parātī in armīs erant**.

a. An adjective thus used for an English adjective and the noun *things* is neuter.

All these things, **haec omnia.**

12. VOCABULARY

ally, **socius, -ī,** *m.*

both . . . and, **et . . . et.**

boundaries,[1] *pl. of* **fīnis, -is,** *m.*

brave,[2] **fortis, -e.**

building, **aedificium, -ī,** *n.*

chief,[3] **prīnceps, -cipis,** *m.*

compel,[4] **cōgō, -ere, coēgī, -āctum,** *w. inf.*

cross,[5] **trānseō, -īre, -īvī (-iī), -itum.**

daughter, **fīlia, -ae,** *f.*

encourage,[6] **cōnfīrmō, I.**

enemy, **hostis, -is,** *m., usually pl.*

flight, **fuga, -ae,** *f.*

from, **ē (ex),** *prep. w. abl.*

go, **eō, īre, īvī (iī), itum.**

go out,[7] **exeō, -īre, -īvī (-iī), -itum**; **ēgredior, ēgredī, ēgressus.**

good, **bonus, -a, -um.**

goods,[8] **bona, -ōrum,** *n., usually omitted when modified by an adj.*

hostage, **obses, obsidis,** *m.*

mind,[9] **animus, -ī,** *m.*

mountain, **mōns, montis,** *m.*

procure,[10] **comparō, I.**

provisions,[11] **rēs frūmentāria,** *f.*

ravage,[12] **vāstō, I.**

resolve,[13] **cōnstituō, -ere, -uī, -ūtum,** *construed, in this sense, with the inf.*

river, **flūmen, -minis,** *n.*

send, **mittō, -ere, mīsī, missum.**

soldier, **mīles, mīlitis,** *m.*

son, **fīlius, fīlī,** *m.*

state,[14] **cīvitās, -tātis,** *f.*

thing,[15] **rēs, reī,** *f.* (See **11,** *a.*)

with, **cum,** *prep. w. abl.*

•

IDIOM

put to flight, in fugam dare

Synonyms. 1. borders, country, territories. 2. courageous, valiant.
3. prince. 4. force. 5. go across. 6. confirm, strengthen. 7. go forth.
8. possessions, property. 9. character, courage, feelings, spirit (*especially
in the plural*). 10. prepare, provide. 11. supplies. 12. lay waste.
13. determine, make up the mind. 14. citizens. 15. Any of the vast
number of ideas for which *thing* can be used in English; **rēs** has been well
defined as " a blank check to be filled out as the context may require."

13. 1. The state resolved to go forth from its[1] borders with all
its[2] troops. 2. The sons and the daughters of the chiefs were
captured. 3. Many hostages and weapons were given to the
Romans. 4. All the weapons and provisions of the Haedui
were sent into the camp of the Romans. 5. Many mountains
and rivers were crossed. 6. The state was compelled to give
hostages to the Romans. 7. Troops and weapons had now been
procured. 8. You[3] and I are going to town to-morrow.
9. You[3] and Caesar are now providing arms for the Romans.
10. Both Caesar and I[3] will encourage the minds of the soldiers and the allies. 11. Caesar with all his soldiers[4] has
put the enemy to flight. 12. The conquered enemy gave all
their possessions[4] to the Roman soldiers. 13. All these[5]
things are good. 14. The many[6] great fields and buildings
of the enemy were ravaged. 15. The brave allies and their[7]
chiefs put the enemy to flight. 16. The army and its[8] weapons are good.

1. **suus.** 2. Omit; do not express a possessive adj. when no mis-
understanding can arise from its omission. 3. Express the pronouns;
the first person precedes the second or the third, and the second precedes the third. 4. See **11.** 5. Use the proper form of **hīc** and
arrange your sentence to avoid hiatus, *i.e.*, so that a final vowel shall
not precede the initial **h** of this pronoun. 6. When **multus** and another adjective modify a noun, they are usually connected by **et**; say
' many and great.' 7. **eōrum.** 8. **eius.**

LESSON III

ENGLISH CONSTRUCTIONS REPRESENTED IN LATIN BY THE INDIRECT OBJECT

14. Many verbs transitive in English are intransitive in Latin and govern a dative of indirect object, on the principle that the action or feeling of these verbs is directed toward the person or thing represented by the dative object rather than exerted directly upon it. Such verbs are those meaning *favor*, *help*, *please*, *trust*, and their contraries; also *believe*, *persuade*, *command*, *obey*, *serve*, *resist*, *pardon*, *spare*, *indulge*, *threaten*, *envy*, and the like.

He persuaded the state, **cīvitātī persuāsit**; *he favors the Helvetians*, **favet Helvētiīs**.

15. Where an English verb is represented in Latin by a verb compounded with **ad, ante, con, in, inter, ob, post, prae, prō, sub, super**, this compound verb frequently governs a dative of indirect object. If the Latin primitive is transitive, the compound may govern both an indirect and a direct object.

Since they surpassed all, **cum omnibus praestārent** (intransitive primitive, **stō**); *he assigned Labienus to command the defenses*, **mūnītiōnī Labiēnum praefēcit** (transitive primitive, **faciō**).

a. Latin verbs which in the active govern a dative are used impersonally in the passive, and retain the dative of the noun.

These could not be persuaded, **hīs persuādērī nōn poterat**; *I cannot be injured by them*, **mihi ab eīs nocērī nōn potest**.

16. A verbal idea contained in a Latin noun, adverb, or adjective will govern the dative if the verb from which the word is derived governs the dative. This construction is found most frequently with adjectives.

Their ships, putting out from port, took their stand against ours, nāvēs eōrum, profectae ex portū, nostrīs adversae cōnstitērunt (adversae is derived from advertō, *turn toward); he had confidence in Diviciacus,* Dīviciācō fidem habēbat (fidem is akin to fīdō, *trust*).

17. Adjectives of *nearness, fitness, likeness, service, inclination,* and the like, usually followed by *to* or *for* phrases in English, govern a dative in Latin, as the object to which their quality is directed.

They are nearest to the Germans, proximī sunt Germānīs; *he chose a place suitable for a camp,* castrīs locum idōneum dēlēgit.

18. The person or thing chiefly concerned in receiving the effect of an action, or liable to benefit or injury from an action, state, or condition, even though not connected syntactically with the verb closely enough to be considered an indirect object, is represented in Latin by a dative, which is called the *Dative of Reference* or *Concern.* Such a relation is usually expressed in English by some idiomatic phrase.

He pardons the past for the sake of his brother, praeterita frātrī condōnat; *he ordered these to bring them back if they wished to be guiltless in his sight,* hīs utī redūcerent, sī sibi pūrgātī esse vellent, imperāvit (here the phrase *in his sight* is rendered by sibi); *unfortunately for Pulio, his shield is pierced,* trānsfīgitur scūtum Puliōnī.

19. VOCABULARY

be able,[1] **possum, posse, potuī, —.**

cavalryman, **eques, equitis,** *m.;* *pl.,* cavalry.

be in command,[2] **praesum, -esse, -fuī, -futūrus,** *w. dat.*

construct,[3] **faciō, -ere, fēcī, factum.**

demand,[4] **imperō, I,** *w. dat. of pers. and acc. of thing demanded;*

postulō, I, *w.* ā (ab) *and abl. of pers. and acc. of thing.*

be eager for,[5] **studeō, -ēre, -uī, —,** *w. dat.*

fortification, **mūnītiō, -ōnis,** *f.*

furnish,[6] **cōnficiō, -ere, -fēcī, -fectum.**

hold, **teneō, -ēre, -uī, -tum.**

like,[7] **similis, -e.**

name, **nōmen, -minis,** *n.*

near, **prope,** *adv. and prep. w. acc.; comparative and superlative when used with noun are adjs. w. dat.*

neighboring,[8] **fīnitimus, -a, -um**; *pl. as subst.,* neighbors.

new, **novus, -a, -um.**

number, **numerus, -ī,** *m.*

permit,[9] **patior, patī, passus,** *w. inf.*

persuade, **persuādeō, -ēre, -suāsī, -suāsum,** *w. dat. of pers. as ind. obj.; a neuter pron. or a clause may stand as dir. obj.; impers. in passive.*

place in command, **praeficiō, -ere, -fēcī, -fectum,** *w. acc. of pers. placed in command and dat. of thing commanded.*

province, **prōvincia, -ae,** *f.*

quickly,[10] **celeriter.**

revolution,[11] **rēs novae,** *f. pl.*

for the sake of (a person), *often expressed by dat. of the pers.*

so, **sīc** (*w. verbs only*); **tam** (*w. adjs. and advs. only*); **ita** (*w. verbs, adjs., or advs.*).

stand,[12] **cōnsistō, -ere, -stitī, -stitum.**

supremacy, **prīncipātus, -ūs,** *m.*

thus, **sīc, ita.**

IDIOM

in my (your, his) own name,
for reasons of my own,   } **meō (tuō, suō) nōmine**

Synonyms. 1. can, have power to. 2. command (*in sense of* having authority, *not in sense of* giving an order). 3. build, make. 4. levy upon, make requisition for. 5. be anxious for, court, desire, pay attention to. 6. contribute. 7. resembling, similar. 8. bordering on (*w. dat.*). 9. allow, suffer. 10. hastily, rapidly, swiftly. 11. change of government, political change. 12. halt, make a stand, stand firm, stop, take position, take one's stand.

20. 1. He demanded of [1] all the provinces the greatest number of cavalry which [2] they were able to furnish. 2. Thus the Helvetii were persuading their neighbors. 3. The cavalry of the Gauls are so quickly persuaded.[3] 4. I court the Helvetii for reasons of my own. 5. The Gauls were eager for revolution. 6. Caesar put Labienus in command of the fortification which [4] he had constructed. 7. Labienus is in command of [1] three legions. 8. Orgetorix, for reasons of his own, was anxious for a political change. 9. I have thus persuaded the Helvetii so quickly. 10. The camp was like a fortification. 11. The troops took their stand nearer the river. 12. The camp of the Romans was nearest the army of the Gauls. 13. I am placing Labienus in command of the camp. 14. For the sake of Diviciacus I shall permit the Haedui to hold the supremacy. 15. Men in [5] Gaul desired [6] revolution. 16. Caesar made a requisition on Gaul for two legions.

1. English prepositions are often to be entirely ignored; translate the *meaning*, not the *form*. 2. **quem.** 3. See **15**, *a.* 4. **quam.** 5. **in** w. abl. 6. Use impf. tense.

LESSON IV

NOUNS AS MODIFIERS OF NOUNS

21. An appositive, whether attributive or predicate, agrees in case with the noun which it explains, often called its subject.

He persuades Casticus, the son of Catamantaloedis, a Sequanian, **persuādet Casticō, Catamantaloedis fīliō, Sēquanō.**

a. A predicate appositive is connected in English with its subject by the verbs *be, become, seem,* or by *make, choose, call, regard, show,* and the like. In Latin a predicate appositive is connected with its subject by verbs of similar meaning.

Now Galba is king, **nunc Galba est rēx;** *a good many seemed responsible parties in this matter,* **plūrēs auctōrēs eius reī vidēbantur;** *he had appointed Commius king there,* **Commium rēgem ibi cōnstituerat;** *Ariovistus had been called king and friend by the senate,* **Ariovistus rēx atque amīcus appellātus erat ā senātū.**

b. In Latin translations of such expressions as *the city of Rome, the province of Gaul,* etc., the proper name is not a genitive, but is a true appositive of *city, province,* etc.

From the town of Alesia, **ex oppidō Alesiā.**

22. A noun limiting or describing another noun, and not meaning the same thing, usually in English stands in the possessive case or in a phrase with *of*. In Latin such modifying nouns stand in the genitive and may express the following ideas:

a. Possession or ownership.

In Caesar's army, **in exercitū Caesaris.**

b. The whole of which a part is taken.

He sent part of the cavalry, **partem equitātūs mīsit.**

> 1. After cardinal numerals ē (**ex**) with the ablative is used instead of a genitive.
>
> > *One of his sons,* **ūnus ē fīliīs.**
>
> 2. The English expressions *enough, as much, so much, how much, more, less, any, what?* (indicating kind or quantity), *no* (as adjective of measured quantity) are represented in Latin by neuter nouns modified by a partitive genitive.
>
> > *Enough protection,* **satis praesidī** ; *what plan,* **quid cōnsilī** ; *no wine,* **nihil vīnī.**
>
> 3. English partitive expressions of position are rendered in Latin by adjectives in agreement with a noun instead of by a noun and a genitive.
>
> > *The top of the mountain,* **summus mōns**; so with **īmus,** *bottom of, foot of;* **medius,** *middle of;* **extrēmus,** *extreme, end of;* **ultimus,** *last* or *farthest part of.*

c. Composition or make-up.

He drew up a line of veteran legions, **aciem īnstruxit legiōnum veterānārum.**

d. Subject or object of a verbal idea. In a word-group containing two nouns, one of which is in the genitive, the genitive often expresses the logical subject or the logical object of a verbal idea contained in the other noun. The genitive is then called *Subjective* or *Objective Genitive*.

By the arrival of Caesar, **adventū Caesaris** (subjective); *by desire for power*, **cupiditāte regnī** (objective).

e. Many other phases of description and limitation less readily classified.

The offense of detaining the knights, **iniūria retentōrum equitum.**

23. Word order.

a. A genitive or other oblique case in Latin regularly follows the word on which it depends; when emphatic, however, it may precede the word on which it depends.

b. When a noun modified by a genitive also has an adjective in agreement with it, the regular order in Latin is *adjective, genitive, noun.*

24.   VOCABULARY

aid,[1] **auxilium, -ī,** *n.*

arrival,[2] **adventus, -ūs,** *m.*

as much . . . as, **quantum, -ī,** *n.*, *w. gen.*

attack,[3] **impetus, -ūs,** *m.*

auxiliaries,[4] **auxilia, -ōrum,** *n. pl.*

battle, **proelium, -ī,** *n.*

battle line, **aciēs, -ēī,** *f.*

bear,[5] **ferō, ferre, tulī, lātum.**

become, **fīō, fierī, factus.**

column (of soldiers), **agmen, agminis,** *n.*

confidence, **fidēs, -eī,** *f.*

contend, **contendō, -ere, -dī, -tum.**

draw up,[6] **īnstruō, -ere, -xī, -ctum.**

enough, **satis,** *adv. and indecl. noun w. gen.*

even, **etiam,** *conj.*

for (*conj.*), **nam** (*stands first in clause*)*;* **enim** (*weaker and postpositive*, i.e. *never first in clause*).

forest, **silva, -ae,** *f.*

friendly, **amīcus, -a, -um,** *w. dat.*; *as subst., w. gen.*, friend.

grain, **frūmentum, -ī,** *n.*; *pl.*, crops.

have, **habeō, -ēre, -uī, -itum.**

how much? **quantum, -ī,** *n.*, *w. gen.*

no, **nihil,** *indecl., w. gen. (used of measure, never of count).*

nothing,[7] nihil.

protection,[8] praesidium, -ī, n.

remaining,[9] reliquus, -a, -um.

seize[10] (a place *or* office), occupō, I.

still (*of time*), etiam nunc (*up to the present*); etiam tum (*up to a definite point in past time*).

top of,[11] summus, -a, -um, *in agreement w. noun.*

wait for,[12] exspectō, I.

zeal,[13] studium, -ī, n.

Idioms

the rear, novissimum agmen

have confidence in, fidem habēre, *w. dat. of person*

Synonyms. 1. assistance, help. 2. coming. 3. assault, charge. 4. irregular troops. 5. bring, carry; endure. 6. form (*as a military idiom*). 7. none (*of measured quantity*). 8. garrison (*when referring to a place*), guard (*a body of men*, not *an individual*). 9. left. 10. occupy, seize upon. 11. summit of. 12. await, expect. 13. enthusiasm.

25. 1. As much of the crops as was still in the fields they laid waste. 2. The Haedui have no grain left for Caesar's army. 3. There[1] is still protection enough for my[2] camp. 4. There[1] is no protection for the rear. 5. Caesar drew up a battle line of two legions. 6. The Romans had no confidence in irregular troops. 7. The auxiliaries quickly brought assistance to Caesar, and even took their stand nearest the enemy's line. 8. The Haedui became friendly to the Romans and brought grain enough for their army. 9. Labienus seized the top of the mountain and waited for the attack of the enemy. 10. The arrival of Caesar brought help to the battle line. 11. The brave Gauls even contended with the Romans' best troops. 12. Three of the Gauls contended with two of the Romans and were overcome. 13. How much grain have we left? None; for we had already given part of it to the cavalry. 14. The enthusiasm of the troops for battle is becoming greater. 15. How much zeal for battle is there[1] in the army? 16. The legions' arrival brought assistance to our[3] men, for they were still fighting[4] with the enemy.

1. Do not express this word. 2. meīs. 3. nostrīs. 4. Use contendō.

LESSON V

PREPOSITIONS

26. Nearly all relations of nouns to other nouns, to many adjectives, and to verbs (except their relation to verbs as subject and object) are expressed in English by prepositions, owing to the lack of inflectional forms. In the highly inflected Latin most of these relations are shown by the case-forms.

27. All prepositions originally expressed concrete, physical ideas of motion or location, and all other ideas now expressed by them are derived from the figurative use of these original meanings. Therefore, when hesitating between the use of a case-form or a preposition in Latin, *search for an idea of motion or location: if you find it, use a preposition; if not, use a case-form.* Above all, never use the mere vocabulary equivalent of the English preposition without carefully considering the meaning and the precise force of the English phrase, and the nature of its relation to its governing word.

a. Latin avoids the use of prepositional phrases as noun modifiers, except where position or motion (including the direction of sentiment or feeling) is expressed after a noun derived from a verb, or where the sense is *about, concerning.* Generally an adjective or participle or a relative clause is substituted.

The war with Cassius, **bellum Cassiānum** (lit., *the Cassian war); a revolt after surrender,* **rebelliō facta post dēditiōnem** (here the participle **facta** prevents the modifying of **rebelliō** by the prepositional phrase); *the angle on the Kent side,* **angulus quī est ad Cantium**; but, *the road through the Alps,* **iter per Alpēs**; *the shortest passage to Britain,* **brevissimus in Britanniam trāiectus**; *zeal for the Roman people,* **in populum Rōmānum studium.**

28. The chief prepositions governing the ablative case are **ā (ab), cum, dē, ē (ex), prae, prō, sine.**

When **in** and **sub** indicate position, they govern the ablative; when they indicate motion, they govern the accusative.

Most other prepositions govern the accusative only.

29. Word order.

When a preposition governs a noun modified by an adjective, the order is usually *adjective, preposition, noun*. This order is especially common with monosyllabic prepositions.

In great danger, **magnō in perīculō.**

30.   VOCABULARY

accordingly,[1] **itaque** (*indicates reason for an action*).

arrive,[2] **perveniō, -īre, -vēnī, -ventum,** *w.* **ad** *or* **in** *and acc., or w. acc. of limit.*

bravely,[3] **fortiter.**

climb,[4] **ascendō, -ere, -scendī, -scēnsum.**

danger,[5] **perīculum, -ī, n.**

day, **diēs, diēī, m., *sometimes f.***

death, **mors, mortis, f.**

fear, **timor, -ōris, m.**

fiercely,[6] **ācriter.**

fight, **pugnō, I ; *pers. w. whom one fights is expressed by* cum *w. abl. or by* contrā *w. acc.***

high, **altus, -a, -um** (*cf.* deep, **75**).

hope, **spēs, speī, f.** (*use sing. always*).

javelin,[7] **tēlum, -ī, n.**

kill,[8] **interficiō, -ere, -fēcī, -fectum.**

leader, **dux, ducis, m.**

night, **nox, noctis, f.**

place,[9] **pōnō, -ere, posuī, positum.**

reply,[10] **respondeō, -ēre, -spondī, -spōnsum.**

setting, **occāsus, -ūs, m.**

small,[11] **parvus, -a, -um.**

speak, **loquor, -quī, locūtus.**

speech, **ōrātiō, -ōnis, f.**

sun, **sōl, sōlis, m.**

throw,[12] **coniciō, -ere, -iēcī, -iectum.**

time, **tempus, -oris, n.**

try,[13] **cōnor, -ārī, -ātus.**

victory, **victōria, -ae, f.**

wall (for defense), **vāllum, -ī, n.**

IDIOMS

pitch camp, **castra pōnere**
deliver a speech, **ōrātiōnem habēre**
sunset, **sōlis occāsus** (lit., *the setting of the sun*)

Synonyms. 1. and so, therefore. 2. come to, reach. 3. courageously, valiantly. 4. ascend, scale. 5. peril, risk. 6. sharply. 7. dart; *pl. often* weapons. 8. execute, put to death, slay. 9. put, set. 10. answer, make answer, make reply. 11. little. 12. cast, fling, hurl. 13. attempt.

31. REFERENCE TABLE OF THE ENGLISH IDEAS EXPRESSED BY THE COMMON LATIN PREPOSITIONS

I. PREPOSITIONS WITH THE ABLATIVE

FROM (in sense of *away from*, in expressions of motion, distance, separation, time, source of action, demand);

ON, ON THE SIDE OF (in expressions of place);

AWAY, DISTANT, OFF (as Eng. adv., but governs numerals in expressions of distance exc. w. verb *to be*);

BY (in expressions of agency w. pass. voice)..................**ā, ab**

WITH (in all Eng. uses of *with* exc. instrument,[1] obj. of emotion, and expressions involving personal influence,[2] estimate, or presence)..........................**cum**

FROM (in sense of *down from;* also in sense of *out from, away from,* if the verb in Lat. is a compound of **dē**; also w. force of diminishing or subtracting);

ABOUT, CONCERNING (also *of,*[3] *for,*[3] in sense of *about*);

IN, ABOUT, DURING (of the time within which action occurs);

FOR (in cause-phrases w. **causā** expressed; as in **quā dē causā**, *for this reason*)....................................**dē**

FROM (in sense of *out from, out of;* lit. and fig., of motion, separation, time, cause, source, and of part after numerals)...**ē, ex**

IN FRONT OF (motion);

FOR, ON ACCOUNT OF, BY REASON OF (a preventing obstacle);

IN COMPARISON WITH......................................**prae**

BEFORE, IN FRONT OF (position);

FOR (in behalf of, in defense of; instead of; in proportion to; in return for; on account of);

AS, IN THE CHARACTER OF;

IN ACCORDANCE WITH, IN CONSIDERATION OF.................**prō**

WITHOUT...**sine**

II. PREPOSITIONS WITH THE ACCUSATIVE

TO, TOWARD, IN THE DIRECTION OF (persons or places);

AT, NEAR, IN THE VICINITY OF (persons or places);

AGAINST (of motion or action);

ABOUT (in numerical approximations);

TO, IN REPLY TO (used in replying to a question or argument; replying to a person requires the person to be expressed as a dat. of ind. obj.);

UP TO, UNTIL (of time limit, emphasizing the duration of the action);

FOR (in expressions of preparation, provision, opportunity, difficulty, purpose of action or fitness for action);

TO (in expressions of addition);

AT, TO, UP TO (w. verbs of arrival);

AT, TO, ACCORDING TO (in expression of adaptation and w. nouns of judgment and command)......................**ad**

BEFORE (of place or time)....................................**ante**

AMONG, BEFORE, IN PRESENCE OF (persons);

WITH (in expressions of personal influence, estimate, or presence)..**apud**

AROUND, ABOUT (in physical sense).......................**circum**

AGAINST (of motion and opposition);

CONTRARY TO, IN SPITE OF;

OPPOSITE, FACING;

IN REPLY TO...**contrā**

OUTSIDE OF...**extrā**

AMONG, BETWEEN...**inter**

INSIDE, WITHIN (of position or motion)......................**intrā**

ON ACCOUNT OF (use limited to phrases with **causa** and **rēs**)......**ob**

THROUGH (of time, place, cause, agency, means, hence, also *by, on account of*);

OVER (of mountains);

DURING, THROUGHOUT, FOR (of extent of time)................**per**

AFTER, BEHIND, BACK OF (of time or place)..................**post**

PAST, BY (of motion);

BUT, EXCEPT (after negatives);

BESIDES, IN ADDITION TO;
CONTRARY TO..praeter
BECAUSE OF, ON ACCOUNT OF (chiefly of the motive for
      action or ground of opinion)........................propter
ALONG, BESIDE......................................secundum
ABOVE (lit. and fig.)......................................suprā
ACROSS (of motion or position)............................trāns
BEYOND (of motion or position).............................ultrā

III. PREPOSITIONS WITH EITHER THE ABLATIVE OR THE ACCUSATIVE

INTO, IN; ON, UPON (of motion or direction, lit. or fig.);
OVER (of throwing);
TO, UNTIL, FOR (of time limit, emphasizing the time to
      which action is deferred or through which it is to con-
      tinue);
AGAINST (of act or inclination);
TO, TOWARD (of feeling or disposition) ....**in**, *w. acc.*
IN, ON, UPON (of position and situation, lit. or fig.);
OVER (of bridges *over* rivers)............................**in,** *w. abl.*
UNDER, TOWARDS, NEAR (of motion or elapsing time).....**sub,** *w. acc.*
UNDER (of position, lit. or fig.);
AT BASE OF, AT FOOT OF;
AT, IN, NEAR (of point of time)........................**sub,** *w. abl.*

   1. Expressed by abl. alone.   2. See **apud.**   3. As in: *he told me of this,
they fought for power.*

   REMARK. The use of prepositions in English is very extensive and
correspondingly idiomatic. Their possibilities and the variety of
their uses may be seen from the following brief consideration of the
prepositions *by* and *for.*

   a. **By.** *He was slain by Brutus*, agency w. pass. voice, expressed
by ā w. abl.; *he was killed by a stone*, instrument, expressed by abl.
alone; *he informed Caesar by messenger*, person as means, expressed
by **per** w. acc.; *he informed Caesar by letter*, thing as means, expressed by abl. alone; *he sat by the river*, nearness, expressed by **ad**
w. acc.; *he rode by the city*, motion past, expressed by **praeter** w. acc.

b. **For.**   *He sent for Cassius,* — ' send for ' is a simple verb idea, hence expressed by verb *summon* w. dir. obj.; *he sent a messenger for Cassius,* — change idiom entirely and express by *he sent a messenger to bring C.; he died for love* — here cause is indicated, expressed by causal abl. or by **propter** w. acc.; *he died for Rome,* that is, in behalf of Rome, expressed by **prō** w. abl.; *he could not speak for weeping,* a preventing obstacle, expressed by **prae** w. abl.; *for that reason,* a cause, expressed by causal abl., by **propter** or **ob** w. acc., or by **dē** w. abl.; *their boundaries were too narrow for their numbers,* proportion, expressed by **prō** w. abl.; *his crime was too great for pardon,* a relative idiom, expressed thus: *his crime was greater than* (*which*) *could be pardoned; to ask for,* — as in the first example, use *request, demand.*

32. 1. With great danger Caesar arrived at a river.   Across this [1] river all the Helvetii were waiting for him [1] in arms at the foot of a high mountain.   2. Accordingly, on account of the time of day, for it was now near sunset, he pitched camp for the night.   3. The army of Caesar was small in comparison to the great number of the enemy.   4. During the night the enemy crossed the river and fiercely attacked his camp with all their forces.   5. They threw many javelins over the wall and tried to climb it. [1]   6. But the soldiers of Caesar without fear hurled javelins at them and killed many.   7. They drove [2] them into the forest and even captured their [1] leader.   8. In Caesar's presence the captured leader delivered a speech.   9. "In pro-portion to the number of your [1] troops you have fought most valiantly against us.   10. All my men have been slain around your camp or [3] have been put to flight.   11. I went out from my camp in great hopes, but I am now in greater fear.   12. With [4] me were two of my [1] sons.   13. They marched in front of my army and were killed before your camp.   14. Instead of victory, I see death before night."   15. He spoke thus, and his conquered army marched past Caesar and gave their [1] arms to the Roman soldiers.   16. To these things Caesar made no reply,[5] but

Diviciacus, who was in Caesar's camp, spoke in the leader's behalf.

1. An elementary knowledge of the simple pronouns on the part of the student will henceforth be assumed. 2. Say 'put to flight.' 3. aut. 4. **cum** is enclitic with personal and relative pronouns; that is, it is appended to them. 5. Say 'replied nothing.'

LESSON VI

NOUNS AND NOUN PHRASES AS MODIFIERS OF VERBS

33. In English, verbs are frequently modified by prepositional phrases expressing *agency, accompaniment, cause, manner, means, instrument,* and the *circumstances attending an action.* All these ideas are closely related and shade into one another naturally. Thus agent and instrument are distinguished only by the fact that the agent possesses life and the will to act; the means and the instrument are distinguished by the fact that the instrument possesses tangibility. All of them may be used to answer the question, *How? He was killed by his enemy* (agent); *he was killed by a sword* (instrument); *he was killed by grief* (means or cause); *he died with great suffering* (manner, accompaniment, or attendant circumstance). Again, all these sentences form an answer to the question, "*How did he die?*"

34. In Latin all these kindred ideas are expressed by one case, the ablative, with or without a preposition, as follows:

a. The person by whom an act is performed (that is, the agent with the passive voice) is expressed by the ablative with **ā (ab)**.

The Haedui have been reduced to slavery by Caesar, **Haeduī ā Caesare in servitūtem redāctī sunt**.

1. Agency with the active voice is expressed by **per** with the accusative.

He informs Caesar by messengers, **Caesarem per nūntiōs facit certiōrem.**

b. Accompaniment is expressed by the ablative with **cum**; but in military expressions, especially those employing **cōpiae**, the ablative may be used alone if modified by an adjective.

Crassus leaves with the courier, **exit cum nūntiō Crassus**; *they hastened to the camp with all their troops,* **ad castra omnibus cōpiīs contendērunt.**

c. A noun regarded as the cause of an action, state, or feeling stands in the ablative, either alone or with **ab, dē, ex,** irrespective of the form of the English expression.

For this reason, **quā dē causā** or **quā ex parte**; *who desired a change of government because of the fickleness and changeableness of their character,* **quī mōbilitāte et levitāte animī novīs imperiīs studēbant;** *they boasted of their victory,* **victōriā suā glōriābantur.**

1. The expression of cause by the ablative without a preposition is to be restricted chiefly to expressions involving verbs of emotion, or to the ablative of nouns like **gaudium, laetitia,** which themselves express emotion.

The Gauls take special pleasure in imported draft horses, **iūmentīs importātīs maximē Gallī dēlectantur;** so with **studēbant** and **glōriābantur** above.

2. Akin to a causal modifier is the principle in accordance with which a thing is done, which is expressed by the ablative without a preposition.

I take tribute in accordance with the law of war, **stīpendium iūre bellī capiō** (*i.e.* because such is the law of war).

d. A noun expressing the manner of an action stands in the ablative with **cum**: but if an adjective or adjective modifier limits the noun, **cum** may be omitted.

He came with haste, **cum celeritāte vēnit**; *it flows with incredible smoothness,* **incrēdibilī lēnitāte fluit;** *embracing Caesar with many tears,* **multīs cum lacrimīs Caesarem complexus.**

e. A noun expressing the means or instrument of an action stands in the ablative without a preposition.

They drove them away with spears, eōs tēlīs reppulērunt.

f. A noun, or a noun with an adjective, indicating the circumstances attendant upon an action, stands in the ablative without a preposition.

Under the rule of the Roman people he despairs of power, imperiō populī Rōmānī dē rēgnō dēspērat; *he follows the enemy at the usual distance,* quō cōnsuērat intervāllō hostēs sequitur.

REMARK. It is often difficult, and indeed unnecessary, to classify such modifying phrases with perfect accuracy and certainty. The main thing is to recognize any given phrase as being among those represented in Latin by the ablative, and to know whether or not a preposition is required.

35. VOCABULARY

always, semper.

ambush (*fig.*, plot), īnsidiae, -ārum, *f. pl.*

attack (persons), aggredior, -ī, -gressus.

baggage, impedīmenta, -ōrum, *n. pl.*; *in sing.,* hindrance.

boast, glōrior, I, *dep., w. abl. of thing boasted of.*

bravery,[1] virtūs, -tūtis, *f.*

cavalry, equitātus, -ūs, *m.* (*sing. coll.*); *also* equitēs, -um, *m., pl. of* eques.

chieftain, prīnceps, -cipis, *m.*

custom,[2] mōs, mōris, *m.*

despair, dēspērō, I, *w.* dē *and abl.*

especially, maximē, *always limits a verb, adj., or adv.; does not introduce a clause.*

follow, sequor, -ī, secūtus.

fortify, mūniō, -īre, -īvī (-iī), -ītum.

frighten,[3] perterreō, -ēre, -uī, -itum.

greatly, magnopere.

harass,[4] lacessō, -ere, -īvī (-iī), -ītum, *of military operations;* vexō, I, *of oppression in general.*

hinder,[5] impediō, -īre, -īvī (-iī), -ītum.

interval,[6] intervāllum, -ī, *n.*

leave,[7] relinquō, -ere, -līquī, -lictum.

liberty,[8] lībertās, -tātis, *f.*

next day, postrīdiē, *adv.*

not even, nē . . . quidem, *w. emphatic word between.*

not only . . . but also, nōn sōlum . . . sed etiam.

pursue,[9] **cōnsequor, -ī, -cūtus.**

reason,[10] **causa, -ae,** *f.*

repulse,[11] **repellō, -ere, reppulī, repulsum.**

rest of, **reliquus, -a, -um,** *agrees w. noun modified.*

right,[12] **iūs, iūris,** *n.*

rule, **imperium, -ī,** *n.*

shout,[13] **vōx, vōcis,** *f.* (*of articulate shouting; cf.* **clāmor,** 87).

sword, **gladius, -ī,** *m.*

war, **bellum, -ī,** *n.*

Synonyms. 1. courage, valor.   2. habit, manner.   3. scare, terrify.
4. annoy.   5. encumber, impede.   6. distance (*of one thing from another*).   7. abandon.   8. freedom, independence.   9. chase, follow up.
10. cause.   11. drive back, drive off, repel.   12. law (*a natural law or right: a mere statute is* **lēx**).   13. cry; *in pl.,* remarks, talk; voice.

36. 1. The enemy had now gone with all their troops into the great forests of Gaul.   2. Caesar therefore left his fortified camp the next day and pursued them at a short [1] interval with all the cavalry.   3. The rest of the army was following with the baggage.   4. The soldiers were greatly hindered on the march by Dumnorix, a chieftain of the Gauls, who was in command of the enemy's rear.   5. Dumnorix with the greatest valor attacked them often with javelins and even with swords.
6. For these reasons the Romans were frightened, for because of [2] their courage and number of men the Gauls fought fiercely.
7. Not only did [3] they make attacks on us from ambush, but they also harassed our column with cavalry.   8. They desire liberty especially, and under our rule they despair of it.[4]   9. We, with the greatest bravery, would [5] often [6] drive them back with spears.   10. But with loud [7] cries they attacked us even more fiercely.   11. Those whom we captured spoke without fear : " We do the things which we do by right of war and because of our enthusiasm [8] for liberty."   12. We are contending with the Gauls according to our custom.   13. We are fighting for liberty, and we shall fight to the death with all courage.   14. Not even with your [9] great army can you overcome the Romans.
15. Thus they were always boasting of their courage.   16. But

they were overcome by Caesar in the war, and were driven back into their [10] territories,

1. 'small.' 2. 'because of ' = **propter** w. acc. 3. Only an auxiliary; express it by the tense: ' did make ' = ' have made.' 4. **eā.** 5. 'would . . . drive back' expresses repeated action: what tense? 6. **saepe.** 7. 'great.' 8. Causal abl.; no prep. required. Why? 9. Use proper case of **tuus** or **vester** with sing. or pl. verb respectively. 10. **suus**, in proper case.

LESSON VII

PRONOUNS

37. Personal pronouns as subjects of verbs, being usually sufficiently indicated by the personal endings of the verbs themselves, are commonly not expressed in Latin. They are expressed, however, to secure emphasis or special clearness, or to bring out a contrast.

The next day they move camp, **posterō diē castra movent**; *as we have previously stated,* **ut ante dēmōnstrāvimus** : but, to secure emphasis, *I, at least, shall have done* MY *duty,* **ego certē meum officium praestiterō.**

a. When personal pronouns of different persons occur in a sentence in the same case relation, the first person precedes in Latin.

You and I, **ego et tū.**

b. There is in Latin no third personal pronoun except the reflexive. When a third personal pronoun is needed, its place is supplied by forms of **is**, or, less frequently, by forms of one of the other demonstratives.

Considius dashes up to him, **Cōnsidius ad eum accurrit**; *he accuses them,* **eōs accūsat.**

38. Possessive pronouns in Latin are pronominal adjectives which agree in gender, number, and case with the thing possessed. They are usually expressed only to secure clearness, contrast, or emphasis. When they are expressed, they regularly follow their nouns, but they may secure additional emphasis by preceding the noun.

Drawing their swords, **gladiīs dēstrictīs**; *the march of our column was hindered*, **iter agminis nostrī impediēbātur** ; *in which* OUR *soldiers easily proved superior*, **quā nostrī mīlitēs facile superābant**.

a. There is in Latin no possessive pronoun of the third person, except the reflexive. When such a pronoun is needed, its place is supplied by the genitive of **is**, less frequently by the genitive of one of the other demonstratives.

He pitches camp three miles from their camp, **mīlia passuum tria ab eōrum castrīs castra pōnit**.

39. In Latin a separate pronoun, **suī**, and a pronominal adjective, **suus**, exist for all reflexive uses of the personal and possessive pronouns in the third person, irrespective of gender or number.

Caesar betook himself to his own men, **Caesar sē ad suōs recēpit** ; *they betake themselves to Caesar*, **sē ad Caesarem recipiunt**; *he said that his integrity was clearly seen*, **dīxit suam innocentiam esse perspectam** ; *they thought their flight might be unnoticed*, **suam fugam occultārī posse exīstimābant**.

a. The reflexives **suī** and **suus** in a principal clause refer to the subject of the verb of the clause.

The others took themselves off to the mountain, **alterī sē in montem recēpērunt**; *Caesar led out his troops*, **Caesar suās cōpiās prōdūxit**.

b. In dependent clauses **suī** and **suus** may refer to the subject of the clause in which they stand or to the subject of the principal clause. They are then called, respectively, direct and indirect reflexives.

He advised the officers that the legions should join themselves together,
tribūnōs monuit ut sēsē legiōnēs coniungerent (direct reflexive);
he ordered these to seek them out if they wished to be blameless before him,
hīs utī conquīrerent, sī sibi pūrgātī esse vellent, imperāvit (indirect
reflexive).

REMARK. This double use of the reflexive is especially frequent
in indirect discourse, indirect questions, and purpose clauses: see **198**.

c. No separate forms exist in Latin for the reflexive uses of
the first and second personal and possessive pronouns.

40. In Latin, demonstrative pronouns in addition to their
regular uses as demonstratives supply the lack of a third personal pronoun (**37**, *b*) and of a third person possessive pronominal
adjective (**38**, *a*).

By noting carefully the distinctions between the Latin demonstratives, all the ambiguity which so frequently arises in the
use of English pronouns is avoided.

a. For the ordinary unemphatic *this, that,* for the unemphatic third personal pronoun *he, she, it,* when needed, and as
an unemphatic antecedent to a relative, **is** is employed.

b. For the emphatic *this, this man, he,* denoting the person
or thing nearer the speaker in place, time, or thought, and for
the latter (*i.e.* the nearer) of two things previously mentioned,
use **hīc.**

c. For the emphatic *that, that man,* denoting the person or
thing farther from the speaker in place, time, or thought, and
for *the former* of two things previously mentioned, use **ille.**
Ille is also used in the sense of *the following,* and after a proper
name in the sense of *the famous, the well-known.*

d. Referring to the person addressed, *that* (= *that of yours*) is
expressed by **iste,** which may also be used to strengthen a possessive pronoun, as in *that plan of yours,* **istud tuum cōnsilium.**
Iste is also used in a depreciative sense, as in *that is weak-
mindedness,* **animī est ista mollitia.**

e. Self, the emphatic demonstrative of emphasis and contrast, is represented in Latin by **ipse**. Many English idioms must be expressed in Latin by this pronoun : *it is Dumnorix himself* or *D. is the very man*, **ipse est Dumnorix**; *on the very day*, **eō ipsō diē**; *they throw the ranks into confusion by the mere panic caused by the horses*, **ipsō terrōre equōrum ōrdinēs perturbant**; *they fall of themselves* (*i.e.* by their own weight, of their own motion), **ipsae concidunt**; *he began the battle in person*, **ipse proelium commīsit**. From these examples we see that **ipse** may strengthen a noun or another demonstrative, or may stand alone. **Ipse** may also strengthen a personal pronoun in any person. In the genitive case it may strengthen a possessive pronoun in any case or a possessive idea with the sense of *own*.

You yourself, **tū ipse**; *with my own army*, **meō ipsīus exercitū**; *who in their own tongue are called Celts, in ours Gauls*, **quī ipsōrum linguā Celtae, nostrā Gallī appellantur**, where contrast also is expressed by **ipsōrum** as compared with **nostrā**.

A reflexive pronoun may also be strengthened by **ipse**, which may agree in case with it, but usually agrees in case with the subject of the verb.

Orgetorix brought death upon himself, **Orgetorix ipse sibi mortem cōnscīvit**.

f. The same is expressed by **īdem**.

41. *a.* **Agreement.** When a demonstrative pronoun agrees with two or more nouns of different genders it follows the principles of agreement stated for predicate adjectives (**9**, *b*).

He demanded hostages, arms, and slaves. While these are being sought, . . . **obsidēs, arma, servōs poposcit. Dum ea conquīruntur.** . .

b. **Word order.** Demonstrative pronouns in Latin, except **ille** in the sense of *the famous, the well-known*, regularly precede the noun.

42. VOCABULARY

adopt, **capiō, -ere, cēpī, captum.**

burn [1] (*by setting fire to*), **incendō, -ere, -cendī, -cēnsum.**

certainly,[2] **certē.**

city, **urbs, urbis,** *f.*

dwell in,[3] **incolō, -ere, -uī, —.**

famous,[4] *often rendered by* **ille, -a, -ud,** *following its noun.*

general,[5] **imperātor, -ōris,** *m.*

he (she, it), **is, ea, id.**

himself (herself, itself, themselves), **suī,** *reflex.*

his (her, hers, its), **eius,** *never reflex.*

his (her, hers, its), **suus, -a, -um,** *reflex.*

I, **ego, meī**; *pl.* **nōs.**

my (mine), **meus, -a, -um.**

our (ours), **noster, -tra, -trum.**

own, *strengthening a possessive, often gen. of* **ipse.**

plan,[6] **cōnsilium, -ī,** *n.*

receive,[7] **recipiō, -ere, -cēpī, -ceptum.**

retain,[8] **retineō, -ēre, -uī, -tentum.**

same, **īdem, eadem, idem.**

self, **ipse, -a, -um,** *intensive.*

show,[9] **praestō, -āre, -stitī, -stitum.**

that (*emphatic*), **ille, -a, -ud.**

that (of yours), **iste, -a, -ud.**

that, this (*unemphatic*), **is, ea, id.**

their (theirs), **eōrum, eārum,** *never reflexive.*

their (theirs), **suus, -a, -um,** *reflex.*

this (*emphatic*), **hīc, haec, hoc.**

very, *as intensive pron.,* **ipse, -a, -um.**

village, **vīcus, -ī,** *m.*

you, **tū, tuī**; *pl.* **vōs.**

your (yours), **tuus, -a, -um,** *indicates one possessor;* **vester, -tra, -trum,** *indicates more than one possessor.*

IDIOMS

adopt a plan, **cōnsilium capere**

retire, retreat, withdraw, **sē recipere** (lit., *betake one's self*)

Synonyms. 1. set fire to, *w. dir. obj.* 2. at least, surely. 3. inhabit, live in. 4. well-known. 5. commander. 6. arrangement, design, intention, plot. 7. *With* **sē**, retire, retreat, withdraw. 8. detain, hold back, hold off, keep, restrain. 9. perform, prove.

43. 1. *I*, at least, have shown my own courage. 2. We soldiers shall, by ourselves,[1] prove our courage against the enemy, and we shall put them to flight. 3. That plan of yours will certainly give us the victory without great danger to our soldiers.[2]   4. The Helvetii set fire to all their villages, towns, cities, and buildings. They retreated into the territories of their neighbors and began [3] to lay waste their lands.   5. The famous Julius Caesar was in command of this army.   6. I shall start for [4] Gaul to-morrow with my best legion, but you will retire to my fortified camp with the rest of my troops.   7. I will send you my own cavalry, auxiliaries, and arms. They will conquer the province for you.   8. The Haedui and the Helvetii dwelt in Gaul : the former were always friends of the Romans ; the latter were their enemies.   9. The Gauls attack their neighbors from ambush, but they will not be able to defeat our troops thus.   10. In these men I have the greatest confidence ; those men will attack even their friends from ambush.   11. Caesar will not send his troops into the forest, for in this forest the enemy are holding their troops in ambush.   12. Caesar sent his friend, Labienus, to this province, but kept his [5] son in camp.   13. You will at least wait for Caesar, for your troops cannot win without him. I shall not wait for him, but shall withdraw into the province.   14. I have myself seen Caesar, the famous general. 15. That plan will not defeat the enemy for us.   16. The very fortifications of the camp terrified the enemy.

1. Cf. **40**, *e*.   2. No prep.; use obj. gen.   3. Cf. **3**, *c*.   4. **ad.** 5. Note the ambiguity in English : you cannot tell whether it means Caesar's son or Labienus'. Show the greater accuracy of the Latin by writing the sentence both ways.

LESSON VIII

PRONOUNS (Continued)

44. The relative pronoun in Latin agrees with its antecedent in gender, number, and person ; its case depends upon its relation to the verb or to some other word of its own clause.

Cursing Ambiorix, who had been the author of this plan, dētestātus Ambiorīgem, quī eius cōnsilī auctor fuerat ; *he persuades Casticus, whose father had held the kingdom*, persuādet Casticō, cuius pater rēgnum obtinuerat; *he talks with him through a friend in whom he had the utmost confidence*, per familiārem, cuī summam fidem habēbat, cum eō colloquitur.

a. Relative pronouns in Latin, when agreeing with two or more antecedents of different genders, follow the principles of agreement stated for predicate adjectives (**9**, *b*).

The mob of boys and women began to scatter in every direction, in pursuit of whom (them) he sent the cavalry, multitūdō puerōrum mulierumque passim fugere coepit, ad quōs cōnsectandōs equitātum mīsit.

b. A relative pronoun may have a sentence or clause for its antecedent, and is then of course neuter.

He knew their hostages were in the possession of Ariovistus, which he deemed a great disgrace, eōrum obsidēs esse apud Ariovistum intellegēbat, quod turpissimum esse arbitrābātur.

45. Peculiarities of relative idiom in Latin.

a. A subject pronoun is regularly attracted into agreement in gender and number with a predicate noun.

All the Belgians, who, I have said, are the third division of Gaul, are conspiring, omnēs Belgae, quam tertiam esse Galliae partem dīximus, coniūrant.

b. The antecedent is often repeated in the relative clause.

There were only two routes by which they could leave home, erant omnīnō itinera duo, quibus itineribus domō exīre possent.

c. The antecedent is often incorporated in the relative clause and is represented by a demonstrative in the principal clause, which then follows the relative clause in the order of the sentence.

That part which had caused the disaster first paid the penalty, **quae pars calamitātem intulerat, ea prīnceps poenās persolvit** (lit., *which part had caused the disaster, that first paid the penalty*).

d. The antecedent is sometimes omitted, especially if it is a pronoun and if the relative is in the same case with it.

Those inhabit the third part who are called Celts, **tertiam incolunt partem quī Celtae appellantur.**

1. A similar idiom occurs frequently in English, when the relative *what* (= *that which*) is employed. In translating such sentences into Latin, the antecedent may or may not be expressed when it is in the same case as the relative.

He tells what he had previously concealed, **quod anteā tacuerat, prōpōnit**; *hither they bring what they had prepared*, **hūc ea, quae parāverant, cōnferunt.**

2. If, however, in rendering such English idioms the Latin requires the relative and its antecedent to be of different cases, the antecedent should be expressed.

If they stood by what had been agreed to, **sī in eō manērent, quod convēnisset.**

e. The relative itself is never omitted in Latin, though often wanting in English.

These men are keeping the populace from giving the grain (which) they owe, **hī multitūdinem dēterrent nē frūmentum cōnferant quod debent.**

f. Where a sentence in English begins with a demonstrative, or even with a demonstrative preceded by a coördinating conjunction, referring to some previous noun or statement, the Latin regularly uses a relative alone.

These things have not happened through the fault of the Roman people. For if they had been conscious of wrong doing, etc., **eae rēs meritō populī Rōmānī nōn accidērunt. Quī sī iniūriae sibi cōnscius fuisset**, etc.

g. When the antecedent of a relative is a sentence or clause, it is often represented and summed up in Latin by an appositive **id** or **rēs**, which then stands as the technical antecedent. (Cf. **44,** *b.*)

There he placed his camp. This measure protected one flank, **ibi castra posuit. Quae rēs ūnum latus mūniēbat** (for **quae rēs, id quod** could have been used); *great anxiety was aroused throughout the entire army, which was natural,* **magna tōtīus exercitūs perturbātiō facta est, id quod necesse erat accidere.**

h. To the real antecedent of a relative in English is sometimes added an explanatory appositive which becomes the technical antecedent. In Latin this appositive is either wholly lacking or is incorporated in the relative clause in case-agreement with the relative.

Labienus arrived, a man in whom he had the greatest confidence, **Labiēnus advēnit, cuī** (or **cuī virō) summam fidem habēbat.**

i. *That* or *as* following *the same* is expressed in Latin by the relative pronoun.

By the same route that the enemy had gone, **eōdem itinere, quō hostēs ierant.**

46. VOCABULARY

alarm,[1] **commoveō, -ēre, -mōvī, -mōtum.**

announce,[2] **nūntiō, I.**

bank (of a stream), **rīpa, -ae,** *f.*

carry on,[3] **gerō, -ere, gessī, gestum.**

certain [4] (*adj.*), **certus, -a, -um.**

dawn,[5] **prīma lūx** (*lit.*, first light).

enough [6] (*adv.*), **satis.**

fear, **timeō, -ēre, timuī, —— .**

first, **prīmus, -a, -um.**

here, **hīc.**

injury,[7] **iniūria, -ae,** *f.*

just, just now (*adv. of time*), **modo.**

letter, **littera, -ae,** *f.*; *sing.,* a letter of the alphabet; *pl.,* epistle, communication.

light, **lūx, lūcis,** *f.*

meanwhile,[8] **interim, intereā.**

messenger, **nūntius, -ī,** *m.*

move, **moveō, -ēre, mōvī, mōtum.**

place,[9] **locus, -ī,** *m.*; *n. in pl.*

please, **placet, -ēre, -uit, -itum,** *impers., w. dat. of person.*

propose (*in sense of* suggest),
 prōpōnō, -ere, -posuī, -positum.
scout, explōrātor, -ōris, *m.*
seem, **videor**, -ērī, **vīsus**, *w. inf.*
surrender, dēditiō, -ōnis, *f.*
take by storm,[10] **expugnō**, I.
then (at that time), **tum.**

then (next), **inde, deinde.**
there (*of position*), **ibi.**
use,[11] **ūsus, -ūs**, *m.*
where (*of position*), **ubi**, *rel. and interrog.*
winter quarters, **hīberna, -ōrum**, *n. pl.* (*properly an adj., with* **castra** *understood*).

Idioms

advantageous,[12] **ex ūsū**, *absolute or w. gen. of person* (cf. Eng. *of use*)
break camp, **castra movēre**
inform, **certiōrem facere**, *w. acc. of person and* **dē** *w. abl. of thing* (lit., *to make one more certain about*)
be informed, **certior fierī** (lit., *to be made more certain. In both these idioms the adj. agrees with the word representing the person or persons informed*)
make an attack on,[13] **impetum facere in**, *w. acc.*

Synonyms. 1. excite, influence, move. 2. tell. 3. accomplish, achieve, do, wage (*of war*); *in pass.*, go on, occur. 4. sure, undoubted. 5. daybreak. 6. sufficiently. 7. damage, harm. 8. in the meantime, meantime. 9. location, site, situation. 10. carry (by assault), storm. 11. advantage; experience. 12. to the advantage of. 13. charge, make a charge on.

47. 1. Caesar gave three legions to Labienus, a man whose[1] name the Gauls feared. 2. I, certainly, shall prove *my* courage to my commander. *You* do[2] what you please. 3. Caesar was informed by scouts of what went on in the enemy's camp. 4. I am going to the mountains myself, and there[3] I shall see many friends. 5. All the plans of the enemy were announced to the Roman general. Alarmed by this information,[4] he quickly informed Caesar by[5] messengers. 6. I have often crossed the Rhine, which is a very large river. 7. Those[6] who attacked Caesar there were Germans. They made a charge on his fortified camp, which cannot be done without great risk.

8. Inform us of what those scouts tell you about the enemy's march.   9. We shall start to-morrow by the same route [7] Caesar went yesterday.   10. Meanwhile we shall adopt this plan, which seems to be the best of all that have been proposed here. 11. General,[8] break camp before dawn; this will be greatly to the advantage of the army, for we can capture that town more quickly.   12. I haven't yet received the letter you sent me about that plan of yours.   13. I have just been informed of the surrender of the camp, which was a strongly-fortified place. 14. This is the very army that so bravely stormed the town and fortifications which the enemy's troops occupied.   15. The Gauls were besieging Caesar's winter quarters and fortifications, which he had himself placed on the bank of the river.   16. The camp I fortified here has been seized by the Gauls; these I shall attack and put to flight.

1. ' of whom.'   2. Imperative strengthened by personal pronoun. 3. See **45**, *f*.   4. ' by which things '; cf. **12**, *Syn.* 15.   5. **per** w. acc. 6. **45**, *d*.   7. **45**, *e* and *i*.   8. A vocative case seldom begins a clause.

LESSON IX

PRONOUNS (Continued)

48. The interrogative words *who? which? what?* are used both as true pronouns and as pronominal adjectives.

Who could have permitted this to be taken from them? **id iīs ēripī quis patī posset** ? *what result will Cotta's plan have?* **Cottae quidem cōnsilium quem habēbit exitum?**

49. Indefinite pronouns, *some, any, certain, each*, etc., exist in great variety in Latin.

a. The most general word for *some, any*, denoting some person or thing whose identity is entirely unknown, is **aliquis**; but following the words **sī, nisi, nē, num**, the indefinite is usually **quis**.

They demand that he select some place for an interview, **postulant ut aliquem locum colloquiō dēligat**; *he replied that if they wanted anything, they should come back,* **respondit, sī quid vellent, reverterentur**; *that they may suffer no loss,* **nē quid incommodī accipiant**.

b. If a negative idea is expressed or implied in a sentence or clause, *any* (which then means *any at all, a single one*) is expressed by **quisquam**, which is regularly a true pronoun. **Quisquam** is *all-exclusive* and combines with the negative idea in the sentence as a whole to mean *no one*.

Not even then did any one leave his post, **nē eō quidem tempore quisquam locō cessit**; *neither does any one but traders go there, nor is anything but the coast known even to them,* **neque praeter mercātōrēs illō adit quisquam, neque iīs ipsīs quicquam praeter ōram nōtum est**.

c. In an affirmative sentence *any*, in the sense of *any at all* (which then means *every one, all*), is expressed by **quīvīs** or **quīlibet**. These words are the opposites of **quisquam** : they are *all-inclusive* in affirmative sentences.

Their ships are built of oak, for enduring any violence whatever, **nāvēs factae ex rōbore ad quamvīs vim perferendam**.

1. These two composite indefinites consist of a pronoun element compounded with **vīs**, second singular, present indicative of **volō**, and with **libet**, an impersonal, thus literally signifying *any you please, every one you please*.

d. Certain, a certain is expressed by **quīdam**. This is the least indefinite of the entire group of indefinite pronouns or pronominal adjectives, and refers to a particular person or thing of whose identity the speaker or writer is aware, but about which he is unwilling to speak unreservedly.

He chose a certain Gaul, **Gallum quendam dēlēgit**.

1. In such idioms as *a man from Spain*, where the noun itself is indefinite, **quīdam** is regularly used; thus, **ex Hispāniā quīdam.**

2. A partitive following **quīdam** must be expressed by **ē (ex).**

Certain of the Gauls, **quīdam ex Gallīs.**

e. The English distributive indefinite *each, every*, applying to the individual what is stated of the group of which he is a part, is expressed by **quisque.**

To whatever place each came, **quam quisque in partem dēvēnit.**

1. The English *all* with a plural superlative, when used distributively, is expressed in Latin by **quisque**, postpositive, and the singular superlative.

The children of all the noblest men, **nōbilissimī cuiusque līberōs** (lit., *of each noblest man*).

f. The English relative indefinite *whoever, whatever* is generally expressed by **quīcumque.**

Whatever part of the camp seemed exposed, **quaecumque pars castrō-rum nūdāta vidēbātur.**

1. A partitive following **quīcumque** must be expressed by **ē (ex).**

g. *Every, every one, everything*, in the distributive sense, used as antecedent to a relative, is equivalent to *whoever, whatever*, and is expressed by **quīcumque.**

They ordered the proclamation that everything that the Romans left was reserved for them, **prōnūntiārī iussērunt illīs reservārī quae-cumque Rōmānī relīquissent.**

h. The English reciprocals *each other, one another* are always expressed by **inter nōs, inter vōs, inter sē**, for the first, second, and third persons respectively.

They give hostages to each other, **inter sē obsidēs dant.**

50.   VOCABULARY

and not,[1] **nec; neque** (*no distinc-tion in use*).

avoid,[2] **vītō,** I.

be here,[3] **adsum, -esse, adfuī, -futūrus.**

bear back,[4] **referō, -ferre, rettulī, relātum.**

centurion,[5] **centuriō, -ōnis,** *m.*

cohort,[6] **cohors, cohortis,** *f.*

come, **veniō, -īre, vēnī, ventum.**

duty, **officium, -ī,** *n.*

envoy,[7] **lēgātus, -ī,** *m.*

exposed,[8] **apertus, -a, -um.**

foot, **pēs, pedis,** *m.*

gather around,[9] **circumsistō, -ere, -stitī, ——** (*of standing around;* lit., *set one's self around*).

here [10] (*place to which*), **hūc.**

if, **sī.**

infantryman, **pedes, -itis.** *m.*; *pl.,* infantry.

lieutenant, **lēgātus, -ī,** *m.*

lose, **āmittō, -ere, āmīsī, āmis-sum.**

open, **aperiō, -īre, -uī, apertum.**

rank (*of troops*), **ōrdō, -dinis,** *m.* (*also* rank *in sense of* grade).

recognize, **cōgnōscō, -ere, -gnōvī, -gnitum.**

report, **renūntiō,** I.

return,[11] **revertor, -ī, reversus,** *dep. except in perf. system;* **redeō, -īre, -īvī (-iī), -itum.**

shield, **scūtum, -ī,** *n.*

side,[12] **latus, -eris,** *n.*

very many,[13] **complūrēs, -a** *or* **-ia,** *pl.*

wish,[14] **volō, velle, voluī, ——,** *in Caesar always governs inf.*

withstand,[15] **sustineō, -ēre, -uī, -tentum.**

IDIOMS

fall back, retreat, **pedem referre**

on the right flank, **ab apertō latere** (lit., *on the exposed flank. The soldiers held their shields with the left arm: hence the exposed or unprotected side was the right*)

Synonyms. 1. nor.   2. escape (*tr.*), evade, shun.   3. be present. 4. bring back, carry back.   5. captain.   6. company.   7. ambassador, commissioner.   The literal meaning of **lēgātus** is ' commissioned,' ' deputed ': if the commission is civil or diplomatic, we have an ' envoy '; if military, a ' lieutenant,' which is the traditional translation of the word in military sense, though the rank of this officer corresponded more nearly to that of a colonel or brigadier general in modern armies.   8. open, unprotected.   9. stand

around, surround.   10. hither.   11. come back, go back.   12. flank.
13. a good many, quite a number, several.   14. desire, want, be
willing.   15. hold out (*i.e.*, against attack; *used in this sense without
a noun*), sustain.

51. 1. Who's here? Quite a number. Certain of them are
Caesar's soldiers, but the rest I do not recognize. 2. The Sequani and the Helvetii gave hostages to each other. 3. We
have lost the shields we gave each other. 4. Not even then did
any one fall back and evade the danger. 5. Every one who
was anxious for a political change took his stand in the ranks
of the enemy. 6. Some one came here from Caesar and reported
his victory over [1] the Gauls. 7. If any one loses his shield in
battle, he is in great danger. 8. If you men want any grain,
come back to-morrow and some one will give it to you. 9. Certain of the irregular troops of the Gauls attacked our men on the
right flank. 10. The commander sent against the battle line
of the enemy all the bravest captains with their companies.
11. Each captain stood firm and did [2] not [3] fall back, but bravely
withstood the attack of the enemy. 12. If anything here in
camp does [2] not please you, return to the city. 13. All the
bravest soldiers gathered around their general and bore him
back to a certain village out of danger. 14. What danger [4] is
there? What war [4] do we fear? 15. Send to me whoever
comes here from Caesar. 16. You shall have whatever you
wish.

1. See **27**, *a* : say, ' his Gallic victory,' or preferably, ' the Gauls
conquered by him.' 2. When ' do ' and ' did ' are mere auxiliaries,
never try to express them in Latin by separate words : use the proper
tense of the verb. 3. For ' and . . . not ' use **nec** or **neque** rather
than the conjunction ' and ' with **nōn**. 4. See **22**, *b*, 2 and **48**. How
do these paragraphs apply here ? These two brief questions should
be joined into one sentence by connecting them by means of **aut**, *or*.

LESSON X

QUESTIONS AND ANSWERS

52. Questions in Latin, as in English, may be word-questions or sentence-questions; that is, they may or may not contain an interrogative word. *Why are you going?* contains the interrogative word *why?* On the other hand, *are you going?* is an interrogative sentence but contains no interrogative word.

a. Word-questions are perfectly simple and require no comment.

b. Sentence-questions are asked in English by placing the subject after the verb. In Latin they must be asked by using the interrogative particles. These are -**ne**, enclitic, and usually appended to the emphatic word which itself stands first in the sentence; **nōnne**; **num**. These words may be called question marks in the form of words. The enclitic -**ne** is employed to ask a question without indicating whether the answer 'yes' or 'no' is expected: **nōnne** indicates that the questioner expects the answer 'yes': **num** indicates that the questioner expects the answer 'no.' *Do you ask?* **rogāsne**? *do you not ask this?* **nōnne hoc rogās**? *do you ask this?* (implying that you do not) **num hoc rogās**? This last idea can be indicated in English only by the tone of the voice or by a roundabout form of expression, such as *you don't ask this, do you?*

53. Double questions in English employ no particle to introduce the first member, and introduce the second member by the particle *or*. Double questions in Latin introduce both members by particles, the first of which is untranslatable, the second means *or*. These particles are **utrum . . . an**, or -**ne . . . an**.

Does honor or fear weigh most with you? **utrum apud vōs pudor an timor valet**? *is it better to charge the enemy or to defend the camp?* **cōpiāsne adversus hostem dūcere an castra dēfendere praestat**?

a. Occasionally the particle of the first member is omitted.

Do you vote for burning or defense? **incendī tibi placet an dēfendī** ?

b. Or not, as the second member of a direct double question, is expressed by **an nōn** or less often by **necne.** If the question is indirect, **necne** is common. (**An nōn** does not occur in Caesar.)

The old women used to tell by divination whether it was worth while joining battle or not, **mātrēs familiae vāticinātiōnibus dēclārābant utrum proelium committī ex ūsū esset necne.**

c. Double questions such as the above ask for a choice between two subjects, two objects, two verbs, etc. Thus, as a choice between two subjects, *was it your father or your mother that said this?* between two objects, *was it his father or his mother that you saw?* between two verbs, *did they win or did they fail?* between two adverbs, *did they speak well or ill?*

d. The Latin idiom frequently requires a multiple question where the English asks in quick sequence a number of brief questions expressing separate ideas either wholly independent of one another structurally or connected by *and.* Such questions are usually connected in Latin by **aut,** *or,* which may, however, be absent, as in Ariovistus' sharp questions to Caesar:

What do you want? why do you come into my domain? **quid tibi vīs ? cūr in meās possessiōnēs venīs ?**

e. Where the second question merely amplifies or complements the first, no connective is needed.

What do you come to me for? to spy ? **quid ad mē venītis ? an speculandī causā ?** The **an** here indicates another possible alternative purpose of the visit, which is considered too improbable to mention.

54. Answers.

a. In Latin an affirmative answer, *Yes,* is expressed by **ita, certē, etiam, vērō, maximē,** indicating various degrees of

54   THE WRITING OF NARRATIVE LATIN

emphasis and idioms of assent, such as *yes, certainly, even so, surely, by all means;* or the verb of the question may simply be repeated, as in *does he go? he goes.*

b. In Latin a negative answer, *No,* is expressed by **nōn, minimē, minimē vērō,** *no, by no means, certainly not,* or by repeating the verb of the question with **nōn.**

55.   VOCABULARY

cavalry (*adj.*), **equester, -tris, -tre.**

dare, **audeō, -ēre, ausus,** *semi-dep.*

defend, **dēfendō, -ere, -fendī, -fēnsum.**

depart,[1] **discēdō, -ere, -cessī, -cessum.**

desert,[2] **dēserō, -ere, -seruī, -sertum.**

ever, **umquam** (*in neg. expressions*).

hill, **collis, -is,** *m.*

hold,[3] **contineō, -ēre, -uī, -tentum.**

immediately,[4] **statim.**

intrust,[5] **committō, -ere, -mīsī, -missum.**

join [6] (*of fighting*), **committō.**

lead,[7] **dūcō, -ere, dūxī, ductum.**

more (*adv. of quantity*), **plūs.**

never, **numquam.**

nevertheless,[8] **tamen.**

people (*in national sense*), **populus, -ī,** *m., sing. only.*

prefer,[9] **mālō, mālle, māluī, —.**

prevail,[10] **valeō, -ēre, -uī, -itum.**

public, **pūblicus, -a, -um.**

real,[11] **vērus, -a, -um.**

really, **vērō.**

remain,[12] **remaneō, -ēre, -mānsī, -mānsum.**

republic, **rēs pūblica, reī pūblicae,** *f.*

safety, **salūs, -ūtis,** *f.*

seek, **petō, -ere, -īvī (-iī), -ītum.**

successful,[13] **secundus, -a, -um.**

than, **quam.**

there [14] (*place to which*), **eō.**

unsuccessful,[15] **adversus, -a, -um.**

why, **cūr** (*from what motive*); **quārē** *or* **quā rē, quam ob rem** (*from what external cause*).

IDIOMS

fail in duty, **ab officiō discēdere** (lit., *to depart from duty*)

hold to duty,[16] **in officiō continēre**

join battle, begin battle, **proelium committere**

Synonyms. 1. leave (*intr.*), withdraw (*intr.*). 2. abandon. 3. bound (*geographically*), contain, hold in, keep in. 4. at once, without delay.

5. commit, consign.   6. begin.   7. take (*in sense of* lead with).   8. still, yet.   9. wish rather.   10. be strong, be well.   11. true.   12. stay. 13. favorable (*in result or outcome*).   14. thither.   15. adverse, unfavorable (*in result or outcome*).   16. hold to allegiance, keep in order.

56.   1. Is fear or duty the stronger [1] with you?   2. Will you fail in your duty to the Roman people?   3. Who are you? and why have you come to me?   What do you seek [2]?   4. Why did you join battle with the enemy on the top of the hill? 5. Can't you hold this people to their allegiance?   6. Are you starting for Gaul or Germany?   7. Do you dare to intrust your safety to the cavalry soldiers of the Gauls?   No, indeed! 8. Will you begin a cavalry battle with the enemy at once?   I will.   9. Would you rather defend your camp with great danger or seek safety in flight?   10. Will you ever desert the republic? Truly, I never will.   11. Won't you persuade him of [3] this for me?   By no means.   He is already persuaded [4] of it, and yet he will do nothing for you.   12. Why can't you take me with you to Gaul?   13. Shall we set fire to the camp at the foot of the hill, or remain and defend it?   14. Are you going there to-morrow?   Yes.   Are you coming back or shall you stay there? 15. Was that cavalry battle yesterday successful or unsuccessful?   16. Are you doing anything there, Captain?   Yes; I'm waiting for Caesar.   Will he come to-day?   Certainly.

1. Say ' does . . . prevail more.'   2. **53**, *d*.   3. 'persuade this to him '; **19**.   4. **15**, *a*.

LESSON XI

RELATIONS OF PLACE AND TIME

57. Place relations may be considered as involving the ideas of place where, place whence, place whither.

I. Place where with a verb of rest is expressed in Latin by the ablative with **in**; but if the word of place is the name of a

town or of a small island, or the word *home* (**domus**) or *country*
(**rūs**; i.e., *country* as contrasted with *town* or *city*), the locative
case is used.

In the forests, **in silvīs**; *in Rome* or *at Rome*, **Rōmae**; *at home*, **domī**.

a. If the noun of place is general, such as *place* (**locus**), *part*
(**pars**), etc., or if an adjective meaning *all*, *whole*, *entire* (**omnis,
tōtus, cūnctus**) agrees with it, the preposition may be omitted
in Latin.

In an unfavorable place, **aliēnō locō** or **aliēnō in locō**; *in all Gaul*,
tōtā Galliā.

b. Frequently where the English uses an expression of the
place where, the Latin treats the idea differently, often as
involving means, and so employs no preposition.

He held his army in camp, **exercitum castrīs continuit.** Here the
camp is regarded as the means by which the army is held.

II. Place whence with a verb of motion is expressed in Latin
by the ablative with **ab, dē, ex**; but if the word of place is the
name of a town or of a small island, or the word *home* or *country*, the preposition is omitted.

From camp, **ē castrīs**; *from Rome*, **Rōmā**; *from home*, **domō**.

III. Place whither with a verb of motion is expressed in
Latin by the accusative with **ad** or **in**; but if the word of place is
the name of a town or of a small island, or the word *home* or
country, the preposition is omitted.

To Gaul, **in Galliam**; *toward Gaul*, **ad Galliam**; *to Rome*, **Rōmam**
(*toward Rome*, *in the direction of Rome*, retains the preposition, **ad
Rōmam**); *they returned home*, **domum revertērunt**.

a. An apparent "place where" construction may frequently
really involve the idea of "place whither."

They send letters to the senate at Rome, **litterās Rōmam ad senātum
mittunt**, for the letters were sent to Rome as well as to the senate.

58. Extent of space (space throughout which) is expressed in Latin by the accusative.

That day he advances twenty miles, **eō diē mīlia passuum XX prōcēdit.**

59. Time relations may be considered as involving the ideas of time when (= at which), time within which, time in the future for which arrangement is made, time how long (time throughout which = duration of time).

I. The time when (= at which) an event occurs is expressed in Latin by the ablative.

At that time, **eō tempore;** (*on*) *that day*, **eō diē.**

II. The time within which an event occurs or does not occur is expressed in Latin by the ablative.

All the work being finished in ten days, **diēbus decem omnī opere effectō.**

REMARK. It is also possible to express time within which by **in** with ablative or by **intrā** with accusative.

III. The time in the future for which arrangement is made is expressed in Latin by the accusative with **in**.

They fix their departure for the third year, **in tertium annum profectiōnem cōnfirmant.**

IV. Time how long (= duration of time) is expressed in Latin by the accusative.

He kept himself many months in camp, **multōs mēnsēs castrīs sē tenuit.**

a. Care is sometimes required to distinguish time within which from duration of time, especially in negative sentences. The sentence *I have not seen him for three years* does not express duration of time, but means that *at no time within three years* have I seen him. Hence the Latin for such a sentence would be **tribus annīs eum nōn vīdī.**

REMARK.   Duration of time may also be expressed by **per** with accusative.

60.   VOCABULARY

about (*adv.*), **circiter**.

advance, **prōgredior, -ī, -gressus**.

arrange,[1] **cōnfirmō, I.**

as (*adv. of comp.*), **ut**, *w. indic.*

conquer,[2] **vincō, -ere, vīcī, victum.**

continuous,[3] **continuus, -a, -um.**

departure, **profectiō, -ōnis,** *f.*

die, **morior, morī, mortuus;** *fut.
ptc.* **moritūrus.**

disaster, **calamitās, -tātis,** *f.*

drive, **agō, -ere, ēgī, āctum.**

drive out,[4] **pellō, -ere, pepulī,
pulsum.**

either . . . or, **aut . . . aut** (*of
opposite and mutually exclusive
alternatives*); **vel . . . vel** (*where
it is indifferent to the writer
or speaker which alternative is
selected*).

following (*adj.*), **posterus, -a, -um.**

generally, **plērumque.**

halt,[5] **cōnsīdō, -ere, -sēdī, -sessum.**

hour, **hōra, -ae,** *f.*

house,[6] **domus, -ūs,** *f.*; *loc.*, **-ī;**
abl., **-ō.**

level,[7] **aequus, -a, -um.**

make ready, **comparō, I** (— — for,
ad *w. acc.*).

middle of, **medius, -a, -um.**

mile, **mīlle passūs** (*lit.*, a thousand paces).

miles, **mīlia passuum.**

month, **mēnsis, -is,** *m.*

nearest,[8] **proximus, -a, -um** (*of
time it may indicate the next
following or last preceding,
according to tense of verb*).

or, **aut; vel** (*see* either *above*).

pace, **passus, -ūs,** *m.*

rest, **quiēs, -ētis,** *f.*

speed,[9] **celeritās, -tātis,** *f.*

spend the winter,[10] **hiemō, I.**

supplies, **commeātus, -ūs,** *m.*

swamp, **palūs, -ūdis,** *f.*

unfavorable (*in nature*), **aliēnus,
-a, -um; inīquus, -a, -um.**

wagon, **carrus, -ī,** *m.*

watch,[11] **vigilia, -ae,** *f.* (*one of
the four periods into which the
night was divided for guard
duty*).

year, **annus, -ī,** *m.*

IDIOM

they fought, the battle raged, the fight lasted, there was a fight, *etc.*,
     pass. of **pugnō** *used impersonally.*

Synonyms.   1. determine upon, fix.   2. beat, defeat, subdue, vanquish,
whip.   3. in succession, successive.   4. expel.   5. encamp, settle (**cōnsīdō** *emphasizes the duration of the halt;* **cōnsistō,** *the act of stopping*).

6. home.   7. fair, just (*these are similar ideas; cf. the Eng.* on the level).
8. next.   9. haste, swiftness.   10. winter (*as verb*).   11. *Also in personal application*, guard, sentry, watchman.

61.   1. I returned to Rome the following day, for I had now been in Gaul several months.   2. For five continuous hours the battle raged on the river bank.   3. Advance against the enemy's works [1] either in the second or in the third watch, as you please, Colonel.   4. There is not an enemy left in all these provinces.   5. They had fixed their departure for the next night.   6. For eight years Caesar waged war in Gaul, for he had resolved either to conquer the Gauls or die.   7. Certain of Caesar's soldiers had not been in Rome for eight years, but generally spent the winter either at Vesontio or at Ocelum.   8. Labienus sent messengers to Caesar at Geneva concerning the disaster.   9. They reached Geneva about three o'clock in the afternoon [2] and reported everything.   10. With the utmost [3] haste Caesar made ready his troops for the march and left [4] Geneva before six o'clock.   11. That very night the army advanced sixteen miles [5] and pitched camp for three hours in an unfavorable place in the forest.   12. Make ready your troops, for the enemy will attack you at dawn.   13. The enemy had halted in a swamp and were there awaiting the attack of our men.   14. Within three hours our men had driven [6] them from the swamp and five miles into the forest.   15. The Haedui brought Caesar supplies in wagons which he compelled to stop in a level place outside the fortifications.   16. The colonel is not fair; for he compels his regiment to march until midnight, but he with his guard halts for [7] rest.

1. 'fortifications.'   2. The Roman day began at sunrise and ended at sunset.   The varying length of days made the hours also vary in length.   A rough average of the time of sunrise for the year is 6 A.M.; hence 3 P.M. is the 9th hour.   The day only was divided into hours; the night, which began at sunset, was divided into watches.
3. 'greatest.'   4. 'went out from.'   5. **mïlle**, *one thousand*, is a car-

dinal numeral adjective and agrees with its noun: mīlia, *thousands*, is a numeral noun and always governs a partitive genitive. The Roman mile was *one thousand paces*, mīlle passūs, but *two miles* must be written *two thousands of paces*, duo mīlia passuum. Numeral nouns in English also govern a partitive; cf. *a pair of gloves, a dozen of eggs.* 6. Note the double idea in ' drive ' here; hence two Latin verbs must be used, one for ' driving out of the swamp,' the other for ' pressing the enemy back into the forest.' 7. causā, w. gen.

LESSON XII

PRONOMINAL ADJECTIVES

62. Certain words are at times adjectives, and at other times partake of the nature of pronouns in their signification, and in Latin in their form also. These words, called pronominal adjectives, and their Latin equivalents are as follows:

another, other (of any number), **alius, -a, -ud.**

the other (of two only), **alter, -era, -erum**; in plural, *the other, the others* (of two groups).

any (with neg. implication; the adj. corresponding to **quisquam, 49,** *b*), **ūllus, -a, -um.**

no, none (of counted quantity; for measured quantity, **22,** *b*, 2), **nūllus, -a, -um.**

alone, only, **sōlus, -a, -um.**

all, entire, the whole of, **tōtus, -a, -um.**

one, only, **ūnus, -a, -um.**

either, which (of two only), **uter, utra, utrum,** interrogative and indefinite.

neither (of two only), **neuter, -tra, -trum.**

a. Each (of two only) is expressed by **uterque, utraque, utrum-que,** which also expresses *both* where the application is distributive. Where the application is collective, *both* is expressed by **ambō.**

Ariovistus demanded that each (or *both*) *should come with cavalry,* Ariovistus postulāvit . . . uterque cum equitātū venīret; *both* (together) *retire safely,* ambō incolumēs sē recipiunt.

b. Observe that *which* (interrogative, indefinite), *each, other,* referring to any number, are expressed respectively by quis, quisque, alius; but when they refer to two only, they are expressed by uter, uterque, alter.

c. One (of two), *second,* and *opposite* may often be rendered by alter.

The soldiers captured two battleships, in one of which was Cassius, mīlitēs quīnquerēmēs duās, in quārum alterā erat Cassius, cēpērunt; *the second class is composed of knights,* alterum genus est equitum; *the chief of the opposite faction he considers a public enemy,* alterīus prīncipem factiōnis hostem iūdicat.

63. Idiomatic uses of the word *other*.

a. One . . . another (plural, *some . . . others*) is expressed by alius . . . alius (or, of two only, by alter . . . alter).

Avarice influences some, rashness others, impellit aliōs avāritia, aliōs temeritās.

b. Where the members of a group are represented as acting differently or being in different relations, the Latin idiom condenses to a repetition of alius (or alter) in the same clause in a different case.

One man from one ship, one from another, alius aliā ex nāvī (lit., *another man from another ship*); *some rushed in one direction, some in another,* aliī aliam in partem ferēbantur (lit., *others rushed in another direction*).

c. These idioms may be analyzed as follows: Of two persons or things, A and B, if the attention be fixed on A, B is *the other;* if on B, A is *the other;* hence both may be called *the other.* Thus the condensed idiom is just half of the full expression. The same principle readily extends to series of pairs of persons and things or actions: each person is thus *another;* each thing or act, *another,* and the meaning of the condensed idiom is apparent.

64.   VOCABULARY

at all[1] (*adv.*), **omnīnō** (*emphasizing a neg. clause or word*).

barbarous, **barbarus,** -a, -um; *as noun,* barbarian, savage.

condition,[2] **condiciō,** -**ōnis,** *f.*

control,[3] **imperium,** -ī, *n.*

custom, **cōnsuētūdō, -dinis,** *f.* (*founded on habit, while* **mōs** *is founded on belief and morals: the pl.* **mōrēs** *regularly denotes the* character *of persons*).

direction, **pars, partis,** *f.*

disturb,[4] **perturbō,** I.

friendship, **amīcitia, -ae,** *f.*

import, **importō,** I.

much (*adv.*), **multum.**

multitude,[5] **multitūdō, -dinis,** *f.*

neither . . . nor, **nec . . . nec; neque . . . neque.**

obtain,[6] **obtineō, -ēre,** -uī, -tentum.

order (arrangement), **ōrdō, -dinis,** *m.*

pack animal, **iūmentum,** -ī, *n.*

peace, **pāx, pācis,** *f.*

scarcity, **inopia, -ae,** *f.*

senate, **senātus, -ūs,** *m.*

suddenly, **subitō.**

tell, **dīcō, -ere, dīxī, dictum.**

trust,[7] **cōnfīdō, -ere, -fīsus,** *semidep., w. dat. of person; the thing trusted in is expressed by the abl.*

well (*adv.*), **bene.**

wine, **vīnum,** -ī, *n.*

IDIOM

a forced march, **magnum iter**

Synonyms. 1. only (*as adv.*). 2. terms. 3. government, rule, sovereignty. 4. throw into confusion, break up. 5. great number, swarm (*fig.*). 6. secure. 7. confide in, have confidence in, trust in.

65. 1. Suddenly the ranks were thrown into confusion and the enemy were put to flight, some in one direction, others in another. 2. One of Caesar's lieutenants commanded the infantry, the other the cavalry: both performed well their duty to their commander and to the state. 3. The Romans have not much confidence in either of the two leaders of the Gallic auxiliaries. 4. Five companies in no fixed[1] order, some from one regiment, some from another, charged the enemy on the right flank. 5. The one division [2] retired quickly to the mountain; the other fiercely charged our right flank. 6. Two daughters of the chief and the little son of one of his sons were captured [3] and held as hostages. 7. To Caesar alone of all the Roman commanders the senate intrusted the entire province of Gaul. 8. If you have no grain left, you can arrive at Caesar's camp to-morrow by a forced march without any danger. 9. Neither captain performed well his duty either to his commander or to the state. 10. Some of the messengers tell one story,[4] some another. 11. Those barbarians wish to obtain control of the whole province. 12. They allow no wine and no pack animals at all to be imported into their territories. 13. I shall place neither of you in command of an entire regiment, for I have not much confidence in you. 14. No friendship can exist between us [5]; for you are remaining in Gaul with your army, nor will even scarcity of provisions drive you into your own territories. 15. With a swarm of darts the men of the tenth legion alone drive out the enemy from both camps to the opposite bank of the river. 16. It is not the custom of the Roman people to grant any conditions of peace to an enemy. I shall therefore allow you neither to remain here nor to settle in Gaul at all.

1. ' certain.' 2. Express by the plural of **alter** without a noun. 3. Watch the agreement here. 4. ' tell other things '; use no noun. 5. ' No friendship can be to me with you.'

LESSON XIII

THE CONSTRUCTION OF RESPECT PHRASES

66. Certain phrases in English express the respect in which an assertion is made or in which an estimate is taken. These phrases are introduced chiefly by *in respect to, in the way of, in,* *by.* The noun used in these phrases is put in the ablative in Latin, and the construction is known as the *Ablative of Respect* or *Ablative of Specification.*

These all differ in language, institutions, and laws, **hī omnēs linguā, īnstitūtīs, lēgibus inter sē differunt** ; *a Nervian, Vertico by name,* **Nervius, nōmine Verticō.**

a. A good practical expedient to determine whether or not to employ this construction in Latin is to insert in the English sentence the phrase *in respect to,* if it is not already expressed. If the result gives *intelligible* English (though not necessarily good English), use in Latin the ablative of specification. Thus in the above examples, *differ in respect to language* and *Vertico in respect to his name* are intelligible expressions.

67.   VOCABULARY

almost,[1] **paene, prope** (*approaching a limit*); **ferē** (*in loose approximations*).

amount to,[2] **possum, posse, potuī, —; valeō, -ēre, -uī, -itum** (*of power; never of number*).

appearance,[3] **speciēs, -ēī,** *f.*

be born, **nāscor, -ī, nātus.**

compare, **cōnferō, -ferre, contulī, collātum** (— with, **cum** *w. abl.*).

differ, **differō, -ferre, distulī, dīlātum** (— from, **ā** *w. abl.*).

different, **alius, -a, -ud.**

differently,[4] **aliter.**

differently from,[5] **aliter ac (atque).**

exhaust, **exanimō,** I.

far [6] (*of degree*), **longē.**

feed,[7] **alō, -ere, -uī, -tum** *or* **-itum.**

find (*by chance*), **inveniō, -īre, -vēnī, -ventum.**

flee, **fugiō, -ere, fūgī, fugitum.**

from [8] (*after adj. or adv. of difference*), **ac (atque).**

horse, **equus, -ī,** *m.*

inferior, **īnferior, -ius.**

institution,[9] **īnstitūtum, -ī,** *n.*

kind,[10] **genus, -eris,** *n.*

knowledge, **scientia, -ae,** *f.*

at last,[11] **ad extrēmum.**

a little, **paulum** (*except in expressions of comparison*).

long, **longus, -a, -um.**

long (*adv.*), **diū.**

military, **mīlitāris, -e.**

nature, **nātūra, -ae,** *f.*

savage, **ferus, -a, -um** (*of disposition*); *as noun, often* **barbarus, -ī,** *m.*

scarcely,[12] **vix.**

on (*or* from) all sides, **undique.**

size, **magnitūdō**, -dinis, *f.*

surpass,[13] **antecēdō**, -ere, -cessī, -cessum, *w. acc. or used absolutely.*

tree, **arbor**, -oris, *f.*

very much (*adv.*), **plūrimum.**

wound, **vulnus**, oris, *n.*

IDIOMS

achievements, **rēs gestae** (lit., *things accomplished*)

be very powerful,[14] **plūrimum posse** *or* **plūrimum valēre**

the art of war, **rēs mīlitāris** (lit., *military affairs*)

Synonyms. 1. about, nearly. 2. be worth. 3. look, show. 4. otherwise. 5. otherwise than. 6. by far. 7. raise, support. 8. than. 9. *In pl.*, institutions, political institutions. 10. race, sort, stock. 11. finally. 12. barely, hardly. 13. exceed, excel. 14. be influential, have great influence.

68. 1. The Americans do not differ much from the British in character or even in political institutions. 2. The Romans and the Gauls differ greatly from one another in courage. 3. The forests of Gaul are far different from the German forests in the sorts of trees which are found in each. 4. The little horses of the Gauls, born and raised among them, are very different in size and nature and appearance from the large pack animals we took into their country.[1] 5. The Roman army advanced ten miles to a certain river, the Arar [2] by name. 6. The army of the Gauls was very strong in number, but amounted to little or nothing in the way of courage. 7. An attack was made on this town, Ocelum by name, from all sides at once.[3] 8. I can scarcely compare the Romans with the Gauls in respect to achievements. 9. The Gauls are savage in their nature, barbarous in their habits. 10. Long and fiercely the battle raged; but at last, almost exhausted by wounds and inferior in number, the Gauls fled. 11. As was seen in this long war, the Romans far surpassed their enemies in knowledge and experience of the art of war. 12. About all the Gallic cities are very different from Rome in size and appearance. 13. The Gauls and Romans differ greatly from each other in their knowledge of military affairs.   14. Caesar surpassed all men in achievement.   15. You and I differ from each other in looks and size.   16. You raise horses differently from the Gauls, and yours exceed theirs [4] in size.

1. 'boundaries.'   2. Acc. in -im.   3. Note how different in meaning from 'at once' in the sense of *immediately*: seek the real meaning and translate accordingly.   4. As 'theirs' is not reflexive and as there is no 3d pers. possessive pronoun, it will be translated by eōrum.   But there will then be no direct object of 'exceed': hence 'horses' must be supplied, or eōrum must be omitted and the verb used absolutely.

LESSON XIV

COMPARISON AND ITS IDIOMS.   DEGREE OF DIFFER-ENCE.   DISTANCE

69. The comparative and superlative degrees, in addition to their regular meanings, may express in Latin certain idioms, as follows :

a. Rather, somewhat, too, as adverbs, are expressed by the comparative of the adjective or adverb which they modify.

When too many were present, **plūribus praesentibus**.

b. The adverb *very* is expressed by the superlative degree.

A very deep river, **flūmen altissimum**.

c. The *greatest possible* degree of a quality is expressed by the superlative strengthened by the adverb **quam**.

To buy the greatest possible number of carts, **carrōrum quam maximum numerum coëmere**.

70. *a. Than* after a comparative is regularly expressed in Latin by the comparative conjunction **quam**.

b. When the comparison is between nouns, the second noun in a comparison with **quam** stands in Latin in the same case construction as the first, or in the nominative with a form of **sum**, according to the evident sense of the passage.

More economical of human life than of money, **continentior in vītā hominum quam in pecūniā;** *they made these timbers higher than the walls were,* **hās trabēs ēminentiōrēs, quam parietēs erant, effēcērunt.**

c. When the comparison is between phrases consisting of the same noun with different modifiers, the noun is generally omitted from the second member of the comparison in Latin, though in English it is either expressed or more often represented by the pronoun *that.*

The fate of the Sequani was harder than that (or *than the fate*) *of the rest,* **fuit gravior fortūna Sēquanōrum quam reliquōrum.**

d. In comparisons between nouns, when the first of the two nouns stands in Latin in the nominative or accusative, **quam** may be omitted and the second noun then stands in the ablative.

One horn stands out, higher than the horns which are known to us, **ūnum cornū exsistit, excelsius hīs quae nōbis nōta sunt cornibus.**

1. The ablative may be used in certain phrases even with the comparative of an adverb.

More quickly than any one believed possible (lit., *more quickly than the belief of all*), **celerius omnium opīniōne.**

2. The ablative construed with the comparative degree is akin to the ablative of specification. Thus, if *A is greater than B,* then *in respect to B, A is the greater.*

3. The ablative with comparatives is especially common in negative sentences, though by no means confined to them.

71. The amount by which one thing exceeds or falls short of another is expressed in Latin by the ablative.

Ireland, smaller by half than Britain, **Hibernia, dīmidiō minor quam Britannia.**

a. This construction is called the *ablative of degree of difference*, or *measure of difference*, and is especially common with **multō,** *much;* **paulō,** *a little;* **aliquantō,** *somewhat,* and like adverbial expressions.

A much easier road, **iter multō facilius;** *a little too far,* **paulō longius;** *somewhat flatter hulls,* **carīnae aliquantō plāniōrēs.**

72. The distance between two places may be regarded either as the extent of space between them, or as the degree of difference between their respective positions. Hence in Latin, in such cases, we may use either the accusative or the ablative.

At the foot of a mountain eight miles from his own camp, **sub monte octō mīlia passuum ā suīs castrīs;** *the troops of Ariovistus are 24 miles distant from ours,* **Ariovistī cōpiae ā nostrīs mīlibus passuum XXIV absunt.**

a. English phrases of distance, involving *away, distant, off,* in which the place from which the distance is measured is not mentioned, are expressed in Latin by **ā (ab)** governing the noun of measure.

They pitched camp two miles away, **ā mīlibus passuum duōbus castra posuērunt.**

73. *More, above, farther, over,* and *less, under,* with expressions of number or extent, are usually rendered in Latin by **plūs, amplius, longius, minus.** The omission of **quam** with these comparatives is without effect on the case of the following noun, though this noun may stand in the ablative.

More than 800 ships had been seen, **amplius octingentae erant vīsae nāvēs;** *he was not more than 18 miles from Bibracte,* **ā Bibracte nōn amplius mīlibus passuum XVIII aberat.**

74. *a.* Adverbial phrases expressing time *before* or *after* are rendered in Latin by the adverbs **ante** or **post** in connection with an ablative of degree of difference.

A few days before, **paucīs ante diēbus**; *a few days after,* **paucīs post diēbus** (note word order).

b. Prepositional phrases expressing time *before* or *after* an event indicated by a noun are rendered in Latin by the prepositions **ante** or **post** governing the accusative of the noun in connection with an ablative of degree of difference.

A few days before the arrival of Caesar, **paucīs diēbus ante Caesaris adventum.**

c. *Ago* is expressed by **abhinc** followed by the accusative or the ablative.

A few days ago, **abhinc paucōs diēs** or **abhinc paucīs diēbus** (note word order).

75.   VOCABULARY

approach, **accēdō, -ere, -cessī, -cessum,** *w.* **ad** *and acc.;* **appropinquō, I,** *w. dat.*

bridge, **pōns, pontis,** *m.*

common, **commūnis, -e.**

deep, **altus, -a, -um** (*cf.* high, **30**; **altus** *expresses vertical extent either up or down*).

be distant,[1] **absum, -esse, āfuī, āfutūrus.**

dwelling place,[2] **sēdēs, -is,** *f.* (*usually pl.*).

few, **paucī, -ae, -a.**

gate (*of city*), **porta, -ae,** *f.*

hesitate, **dubitō, I,** *w. inf.*

higher,[3] **superior, -ius.**

highest [4] (*fig.*), **summus, -a, -um.**

however, **autem** (*postpositive*).

labor,[5] **labor, -ōris,** *m.*

lead back, **redūcō, -ere, -dūxī, -ductum.**

lead out, **ēdūcō, -ere, ēdūxī, ēductum.**

likewise,[6] **item.**

locate [7] (*tr.*), **collocō, I,** *of stationing troops;* **pōnō, -ere, posuī, positum,** *of locating a town or camp.*

more (*adv. of degree*), **magis.**

much (*adv. in comp. expressions*), **multō** (*an abl. of degree of difference used adverbially*).

next [8] (*adv. of time*), **deinde, inde.**

opinion,[9] **opīniō, -ōnis,** *f.* (*a more or less unsupported belief*).

opposite (*adj.*), **adversus, -a, -um.**

remain (be left), *pass. of* **relinquō,** leave (*cf.* **35**).

for the sake of (a thing), **causā** (*governs gen. and stands next after it*).

severe,[10] **gravis, -e.**

suitable,[11] **idōneus, -a, -um,** *w. dat. in noun constructions.*

thence,[12] **inde** (*cf.* **46**).

way, **via, -ae,** *f.* (*never in sense of* plan *or* manner).

where [13] (*place to which*), **quō** (*rel. and interrog.*).

wide,[14] **lātus, -a, -um.**

Idioms

a commanding position (*military phrase*), **superior locus**
build a bridge over a river, **pontem in flūmine facere**
more quickly than one would suppose possible, **celerius opīniōne**
up stream, **adversō flūmine**
down stream, **secundō flūmine**

Synonyms. 1. be absent, be away. 2. abode, home. 3. former. 4. greatest, loftiest (*never of physical height, which is* altissimus); *also* summit of, top of (*cf.* **24**). 5. hardship. 6. also, in the same way. 7. place, station. 8. then (*in sense of* next). 9. belief. 10. hard, heavy, serious. 11. fit. 12. from that place, from there. 13. whither. 14. broad.

76. 1. I shall place in command of the army a braver man than you. 2. I have never hesitated to build bridges over wider rivers than the Rhine. 3. This place is more suitable [1] for a camp than for a dwelling place. 4. My army is larger than Caesar's by three thousand men. 5. From that place Caesar marched up stream and reached the enemy's camp five miles from Vesontio more quickly than all supposed possible. 6. The enemy's camp was less than two miles away. Caesar accordingly led his troops out from the fortifications and approached the gates of this camp. 7. I shall march to-day less than ten miles. Then I shall halt and locate my forces in a commanding position no farther than three miles from the enemy. 8. The Helvetii are in arms: the Sequani likewise with the highest courage took arms three days ago for the sake of the common safety. 9. One way remained through the Sequani, by which the Helvetii had led their troops back home a few years before. 10. Where are you going? I am going to Vesontio; it is less than ten miles away, and there I shall be no more than a mile from the enemy. 11. I shall not attack them to-day, but I shall give my soldiers a rest from [2] their labors; to-morrow, however, I shall advance much more quickly than the enemy think possible. 12. The enemy's troops had arrived three days before at a very wide and deep river which was less than two miles from us, and over this river was a bridge. 13. This labor is somewhat too severe for my troops, General; for they fought a battle only two days before your arrival. 14. He arrived at our camp three days ago with all his troops, a little more quickly than one would suppose possible. 15. The famous [3] Caesar used [4] to build the best possible bridges. I have never seen a better bridge than the one [5] he built over the Rhine. 16. These mountains are much higher than those which we see in our country.

1. idōneus is compared by means of **magis** and **maximē**. 2. 'from' after 'a rest' is expressed by the use of a genitive, 'a rest of labors.' 3. **40**, *c*. 4. Customary action in past time: what tense? 5. Express by the proper case of **ille**.

LESSON XV

THE EXPRESSION OF PURPOSE

77. Purpose expressed by a noun.

a. A noun may indicate the end or purpose which something serves or for which it is designed. The English form of expression in these cases is a phrase with *for* or *as*, or sometimes a mere predicate noun after the verb *to be* when that verb is equivalent to *serves as*. Nouns expressing purpose are put in the dative in Latin, and the noun representing the person or thing to which

the purpose or service is directed or for which it is intended
stands in the dative of reference (**18**).

The friendship of the Roman people ought to be (i.e., *serve as*) *an ornament and a protection to me, not an injury*, **amīcitiam populī Rōmānī
mihi ōrnāmentō et praesidiō, nōn dētrīmentō esse oportet.**

b. A noun in the dative may also indicate in Latin the purpose of an action expressed by a transitive verb and its object,
if the verb be active, or by a transitive verb and its subject,
if the verb be passive.

They selected a place for a residence, **locum domiciliō dēlēgērunt;**
the Haedui had sent cavalry for assistance to Caesar (or *as an aid to
C.*, or *to C.'s assistance*), **equitātum auxiliō Caesarī Haeduī mīserant.**

78. Purpose expressed by a verb in English.

The English form for expressions of purpose involving a verb
may be (1) an infinitive, as in *I came to see you* (this is the most
common English form) ; (2) *in order to* governing an infinitive,
as in *I came in order to see you;* (3) *that, so that, in order that*,
with a dependent clause, as in *I came* (*in order*) *that I might see
you;* (4) the verbal in *-ing*, introduced by *for, for the purpose of,
for the sake of, with a view to, with the design of*, etc., as in *I came
for the purpose of seeing you.*

79. Purpose expressed by a verb in Latin.

I. The infinitive in prose Latin never expresses purpose.

II. Expressions with finite verb forms.

a. Purpose may be expressed in Latin by a clause having its
verb in the subjunctive introduced by **ut**, if the purpose is
positive, by **nē** if the purpose is negative.

*Labienus waited for our troops, in order that an attack might be made
on the enemy*, **Labiēnus, ut in hostēs impetus fieret, nostrōs exspectābat;** *he orders Crassus to start, that aid may not be sent into Gaul*,
Crassum proficīscī iubet, nē auxilia in Galliam mittantur.

b. If the purpose clause contains the comparative of an adjective or adverb, **quō** is substituted for **ut.**

That he might the more easily hold the state to its allegiance, **quō facilius cīvitātem in officiō continēret.**

1. A comparative naturally occurs only in affirmative clauses.

c. Purpose may be expressed in Latin by a clause having its verb in the subjunctive introduced by a relative pronoun or a relative adverb.

They sent envoys to say, **lēgātōs mīsērunt quī dīcerent.**

80. Tenses in subordinate clauses.

The tense of a verb in a subordinate clause is determined by the **Law of Sequence of Tenses.** This law is as follows:

Primary tenses in principal clauses are associated with primary tenses in subordinate clauses: secondary tenses in principal clauses are associated with secondary tenses in subordinate clauses.

a. TABLE OF TENSES

Indicative

Primary	*Secondary*
Present	Imperfect
Future	Perfect historical
Perfect definite	Pluperfect
Future perfect	

Subjunctive

Present	Imperfect
Perfect	Pluperfect

1. The historical present may be regarded either as primary or secondary. It is usually, however, treated as secondary.

REMARK. The above Law of Sequence of Tenses is given as a mechanical rule of procedure for the beginner in writing Latin. In the Latin language there are many exceptions to its necessary application, especially in clauses of result, in dependent questions and in relative clauses not final, to say nothing of individual instances where the Latin author has deliberately violated the law in order to bring out some special meaning or emphasis. With all these the beginner has no concern, unless they are specially indicated to him: otherwise he will plunge into inextricable confusion.

81. Only the tenses formed on the present stem (the stem of continued action) can be used in purpose clauses; for a purpose can never lie in the sphere of completed action.

82. No negative word other than **nē** is ever regularly used in a purpose clause, for in such clauses it is the action (verb) alone that is negatived. Where the English purpose clause contains a negative such as *no one, nothing, never, nowhere,* etc., the Latin clause has **nē** with the word for the indefinite *any one, anything, ever, anywhere* (**nē quis** or more rarely **nē quisquam, nē quid, nē umquam, nē usquam**).

They agreed on oath that no one should tell, **cōnstituērunt iūre iūrandō nē quis ēnūntiāret.**

REMARK. Purpose clauses are often called *Final Clauses* (*final* is derived from **fīnis,** *end;* for *end* even in English is often used as a synonym of *purpose*).

83.   VOCABULARY

aid [1] (*military*), **subsidium, -ī, n.**; *pl.,* reënforcements.

call in, **arcessō, -ere, -īvī (-iī), -ītum.**

call together,[2] **convocō, I.**

captive (*adj.*), **captīvus, -a, -um;** *as subst.,* **-us, -ī, m.**

choose,[3] **dēligō, -ere, -lēgī, -lēctum.**

council,[4] **concilium, -ī, n.**

dismiss, **dīmittō, -ere, -mīsī, -missum.**

earthworks, **agger, -eris, m.**

easily, **facile.**

establish, **cōnfīrmō, I.**

faith,[5] **fidēs, -eī, f.**

find (*by search*), **reperiō, -īre, repperī, repertum.**

hear,[6] **audiō, -īre, -īvī (-iī), -ītum.**

lead across, **trādūcō, -ere, -dūxī,**

-ductum; *takes two accusatives, one denoting a person, dir. obj. of verb element of compound, the other a place, dependent on the prep. element.*

let pass,[7] **intermittō**, -ere, -mīsī, -missum.

at night (*adv.*), **noctū**.

preserve,[8] **servō**, I.

rescue,[9] **ēripiō**, -ere, -uī, -reptum; *takes dir. obj. and a dat. of the pers. from whom as ind. obj., or* ē *w. abl. of thing from which.*

send ahead,[10] **praemittō**, -ere, -mīsī, -missum.

struggle, **labōrō**, I, *w.* ā *or* ē *and abl.*

tribe,[11] **gēns, gentis**, *f.*; **nātiō**, -ōnis, *f.*

IDIOMS

in (for) the future, **in reliquum tempus**
keep faith, **fidem servāre**

Synonyms. 1. reserves. 2. call, summon. 3. select. 4. assembly. 5. confidence. 6. hear of. 7. let slip. 8. keep. 9. seize from, take from. 10. send forward. 11. nation.

84. 1. Colonel, leave what seems sufficient for the protection of both camps, and send the rest forward to drive the enemy out of the woods. 2. The friendship of the Roman people is a protection to any man. 3. The army which Caesar has in Gaul is a protection to the allies of the Romans. 4. He sent the cavalry ahead to select a site for the camp. 5. Captain, lead out four companies immediately as reënforcements for our men. 6. In accordance with [1] their custom they summoned a council of all Gaul to establish peace with the Romans. 7. I led my troops across the bridge three days ago, so that I could seize the town more easily. 8. Men, send supplies into the town that the garrison may not struggle with scarcity. 9. I shall send envoys to the Gauls to establish peace. 10. He quickly dismissed the council, but detained Diviciacus, that he might be informed of the Gauls' plans. 11. I shall advance within two hours and try to find an open place for a camp, so as not to be attacked at night by the enemy. 12. I shall send the captives into camp that they may not be rescued by the barbarians whom we are now approaching. 13. This victory will be of use to our army

for [2] the war, that these tribes who have been called in for help
by the Gauls may keep faith in the future.   14. The general
started immediately so as not to let any time slip; and [3] he
did not send any scouts ahead that the enemy might not hear
of his arrival in their country.   15. He sent two legions to storm
the enemy's earthworks.   16. He summoned all the cavalry to
him, so as to follow the enemy more quickly.

    1. Abl. of accordance, **34**, *c*, 2.   2. **ad**.   3. 'nor did he send,' **50**.

LESSON XVI

THE EXPRESSION OF PURPOSE (Continued)

85. **Purpose expressed by a verb in Latin** (*continued*).

III. Expressions with non-finite verb forms.

a. Purpose may be expressed in Latin by the accusative of
the gerund or gerundive governed by **ad**.

   To carry out these plans, Orgetorix is chosen, **ad eās rēs cōnficiendās
Orgetorīx dēligitur.**

   1. When the principal verb is **cūrō** or **dō**, the gerundive
is used agreeing with the object of the verb, without a
preposition.

   He has a bridge built, **pontem faciendum cūrat**; *he gave one legion
to Fabius to lead* (*to be led*) *among the Morini*, **ūnam legiōnem in
Morinōs dūcendam Fabiō dedit.**

b. The genitive of the gerund or gerundive governed by
causā may be employed.

   He is sent to have an interview, **mittitur colloquendī causā**.

   1. The gerundive with **causā** in a purpose construction involving a personal pronoun admits no distinction of gender or
number.

   We have come to excuse ourselves, **nostrī purgandī causā vēnimus.**

2. **Causā** in these constructions always immediately follows the verb form.

c. The supine in **-um** may be used after a verb of motion to express purpose.

They flocked to Caesar to congratulate him, **ad Caesarem grātulātum convēnērunt.**

86. Use of the several forms of purpose constructions.

In Latin, as in English, the form of expression to employ in a given instance is largely a matter of personal choice, so that no definite rule of selection can be given. The following general principles, however, may be observed.

I. When the purpose clause in English is brief, affirmative, and without adverbial modifiers, give preference in Latin to a non-finite form of expression.

II. When the emphasis of thought rests on the action of the verb of the purpose clause, use **ut** (**nē**) with the subjunctive.

III. When the emphasis of thought rests on a noun in the principal clause, use a relative clause with this noun as its antecedent.

IV. When the emphasis of thought rests on a noun in the purpose clause, use a gerundive expression involving this noun.

87. VOCABULARY

accomplish,[1] cōnficiō, -ere, -fēcī, -fectum; efficiō.

bring upon, īnferō, -ferre, intulī, illātum.

care for,[2] cūrō, I.

collect,[3] colligō, -ere, -lēgī, -lēctum; cōnferō, cōnferre, contulī, collātum.

complain, queror, -ī, questus;

in noun constructions w. **dē** *and abl.; in verb constructions w. causal clause or w. acc. and inf.*

fill up, compleō, -ēre, -plēvī, -plētum.

finish,[4] perficiō, -ere, -fēcī, -fectum.

fort,[5] castellum, -ī, *n.*

march out, ēgredior, -ī, -gressus.

moat,[6] **fossa, -ae,** *f.*

raise,[7] **tollō, -ere, sustulī, sublā-tum.**

rather (*adv. of comp.*), **potius.**

shouting [8] (*inarticulate*), **clāmor, -ōris,** *m.*

sign,[9] **sīgnum, -ī,** *n.*

work, **opera, -ae,** *f.* (*the effort put forth, not the result of that effort*).

Idioms

do one's best,[10] **operam dare,** *w. clause of purpose ;* **agere,** *w. clause of purpose*

have (a task) done, **cūrāre;** *the thing to be done expressed by accusative and gerundive in agreement*

make war on, **bellum īnferre,** *w. dat. of person*

Synonyms. 1. finish; exhaust. 2. arrange for, cause to be done, take care. 3. assemble (*tr.*), bring together, gather. 4. accomplish. 5. castle, fortress. 6. ditch, trench. 7. elate, elevate, lift up. 8. clamor, noise. 9. signal; *pl., often w. adj.* **mīlitāria,** standards. 10. take pains.

88. 1. Certain of the *soldiers* [1] were *selected* to build the *bridge* over the Rhine. 2. These soldiers did their best to finish the bridge in ten days. 3. I have come to you to complain of the Gauls. 4. You have done all this, not for the purpose of defending yourselves, but of attacking our allies. 5. I shall have a bridge built over the Rhine; and, to accomplish this, envoys are being sent to Caesar. 6. Captain, I am giving you this company to take back to camp. 7. They were collecting small *trees* [2] with which to fill up the *moat* before the Romans' camp. 8. There were very many great *trees* [2] in the forest near the river bank to build the *bridge* with. 9. I have come to see you for the purpose of defending myself against the plots of Galba. 10. I have had the army sent over [3] the mountains in order to terrorize the Gauls who have assembled [4] their forces to invade [5] our province. 11. I have certainly not come to make war on you, but on the Allobroges. 12. I select large *trees* [2] rather than small ones [6] to build *bridges* with. 13. There is no

tribe [7] left in Gaul for me to make war on.   14. Why are all the
soldiers raising a shout in the camp?   They have just received
the standards with which they are to march out against the
enemy.   15. They had just finished a fort in the place they had
selected to defend themselves in.   16. A legion was given [8] to
Labienus to lead into winter quarters among the Remi.

1. Write this sentence three times, assuming that each italicized
word in turn contains the emphatic idea.   2. Write twice, on principle of note 1.   3. **per.**   4. ' assemble ' is here transitive; use
' bring together,' ' call together,' ' collect.'   5. Translate the idea,
' cross over into.'   6. Make no attempt to express this word.   7. Cf.
86, III.   8. Cf. **85**, III, *a*, 1.   This construction may occur with **dō**
in the passive : the pupil will readily note the change in case thus
rendered necessary.

LESSON XVII

THE EXPRESSION OF PURPOSE (CONTINUED)

**89. English constructions regarded in Latin as purpose
clauses.**

Clauses depending on verbs signifying *advise, demand, forbid,
order, permit, persuade, request, resolve, urge, warn, will, wish*, etc.,
or, in general, *any verb which puts another verb into action*, are
regarded as purpose clauses in Latin and are to be rendered
by **ut** (**nē**) with the subjunctive.

He persuaded the citizens to go out, **cīvitātī persuāsit ut exīrent;**
he had been ordered not to begin battle, **erat eī praeceptum nē proelium
committeret;** *he permitted him to quarter his legion in these places*,
huic permīsit utī in hīs locīs legiōnem collocāret.

90.   Certain verbs, kindred in sense to those above mentioned,
govern an accusative of the person with the infinitive.   Such
are **iubeō**, *command;* **vetō**, *forbid;* **cōgō**, *compel;* **patior**, *permit.*
Imperō, *command*, is regular in construction (**89**) and governs

a dative of the person and a clause with **ut** (**nē**) and the subjunctive.

He ordered the Helvetii to return, and commanded the Allobroges to furnish them a supply of grain, **Helvētiōs revertī iussit, et Allobrogibus imperāvit ut iīs frūmentī cōpiam facerent.**

a. If the verb depending on a verb of command is passive or deponent, use **iubeō**. Caesar, it is true, uses **imperō** with a passive or deponent infinitive three times, **cōgō** with **ut** and the subjunctive once, and **patior** with **ut** and the subjunctive twice in negative sentences, but these rare exceptions to normal Latin constructions should never be employed.

REMARK. Grammarians variously interpret the nature of these clauses and their relation to the principal verb. Some (Allen and Greenough, Bennett, Harkness) regard them as true substantive clauses, as being the object of the principal verb (or its subject if it be passive) or in apposition with a noun or especially with a pronoun object or subject. Others (Gildersleeve-Lodge, Lane) regard them as mere complements, serving to complete the sense of the principal verb.

91. In English most of the verbs above named govern the infinitive. Some govern an infinitive or a clause indifferently; as, *he resolved to go* and *he resolved that he would go; I wish you to do this* and *I wish (that) you would do this.* A similar variation in construction occurs in Latin. Thus **cōnstituō**, **dēcernō**, *decide, determine, resolve,* and **volō**, *wish,* regularly govern the infinitive when the subject of the verb depending on them is also their own subject: they usually govern a subjunctive with **ut** (**nē**) when the subject of the dependent verb is not their own subject, though rarely they may even then govern an accusative with the infinitive (so **volō** always in Caesar).

He had resolved to keep this fellow with him, **hunc sēcum habēre cōnstituerat;** *the Gauls resolve that noncombatants shall leave the town,* **Gallī cōnstituunt ut iī, quī inūtilēs sint bellō, oppidō excēdant;**

he wished to visit these tribes, **eās nātiōnēs adīre volēbat**; *he wished them to fear*, **eōs timēre voluit**.

92. VOCABULARY

advise,[1] **moneō, -ēre, -uī, -itum,** *w. acc. of pers. and clause.*

ask,[2] **rogō,** I, *w. acc. of pers. and clause;* **petō, -ere, -īvī (-iī), -ītum,** *w. ā and abl. of pers. and clause.*

assemble[3] (*intr.*), **conveniō, -īre, vēnī, -ventum.**

command,[4] **iubeō, -ēre, iussī, iussum,** *w. acc. and inf.;* **imperō,** I, *w. dat. of person and clause, impers. in pass. except w. neuter pron.*

demand, **postulō,** I, *w. ā and abl. of pers. and dir. obj. or a clause.*

direct,[5] **praecipiō, -ere, -cēpī, -ceptum,** *w. dat. of pers. and clause; impers. in pass.*

exhort,[6] **hortor, cohortor,** I, *dep., w. acc. of pers. and clause.*

forbid, **vetō, -āre, -uī, -itum,** *w. acc. and inf.*

lead to[7] (*lit. and fig.*), **addūcō, -ere, -dūxī, -ductum,** *in fig. sense w. acc. of person and clause.*

persuade, **persuādeō, -ēre, -suāsī, -suāsum,** *w. dat. of person and clause; used impersonally in passive.*

resist, **resistō, -ere, -stitī, -stitum,** *w. dat.*

sortie,[8] **ēruptiō, -ōnis,** *f.*

supply,[9] **cōpia, -ae,** *f.*

suspicion, **suspiciō, -ōnis,** *f.*

yoke,[10] **iugum, -ī,** *n.*

IDIOMS

move forward,[11] **sīgna īnferre** (lit., *bear on the standards*)

send under the yoke, **sub iugum mittere**

Synonyms. 1. warn. 2. beg, request, seek. 3. come together, meet (*in intr. sense*). 4. order. 5. instruct, enjoin. 6. encourage, urge. 7. induce. 8. rush. 9. plenty. 10. ridge (of a mountain). 11. advance to the attack.

93. 1. I have now warned you to avoid all suspicions for the future. 2. Caesar ordered[1] his captives to return home and commanded[2] their neighbors to give them a supply of grain. 3. As Labienus[3] had been directed to hold the mountain, he bravely resisted the enemy there. 4. The commander exhorted

his men to stand firm and to sustain the enemy's charge.
5. We request you, General, to do your best not to allow us to
be sent over the mountains.   6. The soldiers suddenly assembled
and raised a shout, demanding of Caesar that they be allowed [4]
to march out of camp and return home.   7. Induced by scarcity
of provisions and by the vast number of the enemy around the
camp, Caesar had forbidden a sortie to be made, with this
design,[5] that he might persuade the enemy to attack him inside
the walls.   8. I have just now issued orders [6] to the troops to
move forward.   9. Directions had been given [6] not to compel
the auxiliaries to make war upon their own neighbors.   10. I
am not yet induced to send out scouts to seek grain.   11. I am
not yet persuaded to send the captured army under the yoke.
12. I am at last persuaded to this,[7] not to allow the soldiers to
return home.   13. Caesar exhorted his men to resist the enemy
bravely, and himself quickly led an attack on their line.
14. General, urge your men to do [8] their duty to the state.
15. I do not urge you to retire, but I advise you.   16. I beg of
you to order your soldiers to come to me as quickly as possible.

1. **iubeō**.   2. **imperō**: write this sentence again, using **imperō** with
the first clause and **iubeō** with the second.   3. Make ' Labienus '
the subject of the principal clause and represent the name in the dependent clause by a pronoun.   4. Since the only verb thus far given
for *allow* is deponent, it is obvious that the clause must be shifted
to the active form.   5. Abl. of attendant circumstance, **34**, *f*.
6. Translate ' issued orders ' and ' directions had been given ' each
by a single verb.   7. Make ' this ' the subject of the principal clause.
8. **praestō**.

LESSON XVIII

THE EXPRESSION OF RESULT

94. Result clauses express the result of an action in a formal
way, with the aid of certain special conjunctive phrases.   In

English they are introduced by *so . . . that, so that, such that,* and like phrases. Never confuse a formal result clause with a mere statement of the consequences of an act. In the sentences, " *The soldier was badly wounded and died,*" " *The soldier was badly wounded. He died,*" " *The soldier was so badly wounded that he died,*" death is indicated in every sentence as the result of the wound, but only the last sentence contains a formal result clause.

95. Result clauses in Latin are introduced by **ut** (negative, **ut . . . nōn**) and have the verb in the subjunctive. The principal clause frequently contains some demonstrative word (pronoun, adjective, or adverb), such as **ita, sīc, tam,** *so;* **tantus,** *so great;* **tālis,** *such, of such a kind;* **tot,** *so many;* **tantopere,** *so greatly.* Such clauses have no relation to their principal verb except to express its result, and are called pure result clauses.

They so place the chariots that they have an easy retreat, **ita currūs collocant ut expedītum receptum habeant;** *so suddenly did the enemy charge, that time was not given to throw the javelins,* **ita hostēs repente prōcurrērunt, ut spatium pīla coniciendī nōn darētur.**

a. Sometimes a result may be expressed by a subjunctive clause introduced by a relative pronoun or relative adverb.

One road (so) narrow that wagons were with difficulty hauled there, **ūnum iter angustum, vix quā carrī dūcerentur** (lit., *where wagons,* etc.).

b. **Ita ut,** *so that,* may introduce a clause expressing the result of a principal statement not itself containing a demonstrative word. Such clauses are frequent in English.

It (the river) *flows in with incredible slowness, so that it cannot be detected by the eye,* **īnfluit incrēdibilī lēnitāte, ita ut oculīs . . . iūdicārī nōn possit.** The more usual form would be *flows in with such incredible slowness that,* etc.

c. Sometimes neither clause contains a demonstrative word, result being indicated by the evident sense of the passage.

The engagement took place under the eye of Caesar, so that no exploit could escape his notice, **in cōnspectū Caesaris rēs gerēbātur, ut nūllum factum latēre posset.**

d. Any negative word may be used in connection with **ut** in a result clause (cf. **82**).

96. English constructions regarded in Latin as result clauses.

Clauses which in English follow such verbs and expressions as *bring about, cause, chance, happen, enable, make,* etc., are regarded in Latin as the result of the action of their principal verb, and take the regular construction of result clauses.

(*This fact*) *enabled supplies to be brought,* (**quae rēs**) **ut commeātūs portārī possent, efficiēbat;** *it chanced that it was full moon the same night,* **eādem nocte accidit ut esset lūna plēna.**

a. For the relation of such clauses to their principal verb, see **90**, REMARK.

97. Tense sequence in result clauses.

Although result clauses generally conform to the requirements of the Law of Sequence of Tenses (**80**), the following exceptions may occur, due chiefly to the fact that the necessity of expressing certain shades of thought by the meaning of the tense itself overrides considerations of form only.

a. When the result is to be indicated as a fact, fully realized in the past, the perfect subjunctive may be used after a secondary principal tense. This use is exactly parallel to the use and signification of the historical perfect in principal clauses.

Such was the shortness of the time, that there was no time to put on their helmets, **temporis tanta fuit exiguitās ut ad galeās induendās tempus dēfuerit;** *it had such weight with the savages, that scarcely a single state was not under suspicion,* **tantum apud barbarōs valuit ut nūlla ferē cīvitās fuerit nōn suspecta.**

b. When the result clause must convey the force of the perfect definite (*i.e.*, the auxiliary *have*), the perfect subjunctive may be used after a secondary principal tense.

Caesar so thoroughly subdued the Remi that they have never revolted, **Caesar ita Rēmōs subēgit ut numquam dēfēcerint.**

c. When the result is to be indicated as continuing into present time (*i.e.*, present with reference to the writer or speaker), the present subjunctive is used after a secondary principal tense.

Caesar so won over the Haedui that this tribe still furnishes us with cavalry, **Caesar ita Haeduōs conciliāvit ut illa nātiō equitēs nōbīs etiam nunc praebeat.**

98.   VOCABULARY

be accustomed, *perf. system of* **cōnsuēscō, -ere, -suēvī, -suētum** (*the pres. system means* grow accustomed).

band (*of men*), **manus, -ūs,** *f.*

began, **coepī, coepisse, coeptus,** *preteritive; borrows the voice of the inf. it governs.*

bring about,[1] **efficiō, -ere, -fēcī, -fectum,** *w. clause.*

bring in, **īnferō, -ferre, intulī, illātum;** *of actual motion, w. dir. obj. and* in *w. acc. of place.*

delay[2] (*tr. and intr.*), **moror, I,** *dep.*

fact,[3] **rēs, reī,** *f.*

give over,[4] **trādō, -ere, -didī, -ditum.**

hand, **manus, -ūs,** *f.*

happen,[5] **accidō, -ere, -cidī, —;** *noun constructions, w. dat. of pers.; verb constructions, impers. w. clause of result.*

no one, **nēmō,** *dat.* **nēminī;** *no gen. or abl., which are supplied from* **nūllus;** *no pl.*

often, **saepe.**

perceive, **perspiciō, -ere, -spēxī, -spectum.**

regard,[6] **habeō, -ēre, -uī, -itum.**

ship,[7] **nāvis, -is,** *f.*

situation[8] (*fig.*), *often pl. of* **rēs;** (*lit.*) **locus.**

some (*of count,* not *measure*), **nōnnūllus, -a, -um.**

be unwilling, **nōlō, nōlle, nōluī, —.**

Synonyms. 1. cause, enable, make (one do something), render. 2. check, detain; stay, wait. 3. circumstance. 4. hand over. 5. befall, happen to, occur. 6. consider, hold (*mentally*). 7. boat. 8. Note again that **rēs** has a great number of uses, as has its English equivalent, *thing*. Cf. **12**, *Syn.* 15.

99. 1. So great fear had seized the minds of the Gauls in the towns[1] that they dared not resist the bands of the Germans. 2. There was then only one legion in camp, so that some soldiers from the garrison, despairing of the situation, fled to the enemy and handed over their arms. 3. The Belgae were so fiercely attacking our men that they could scarcely hold out till night. 4. It happened that these men were unable[2] to obtain the supremacy of Gaul. 5. This fact enabled grain to be brought into camp without any danger. 6. They were all carrying weapons in their hands, so that we were unwilling to permit them to come into camp. 7. The band of the enemy was so small that it could scarcely lay waste the lands of our allies or attack their towns. 8. The wounds of the soldiers in that battle were so severe that Caesar has already delayed three days in camp. 9. The Germans had begun to come across the Rhine so often that they were now accustomed to regard Gaul as their province. 10. I will enable you to obtain ships in which to cross to Britain. 11. The town began to be besieged so fiercely that the garrison could obtain no provisions. 12. I shall delay so long in camp that the enemy will not perceive my plans. 13. We have so subdued Gaul that no one at all resists us there. 14. I have not yet perceived your plans, which[3] has so delayed me that I have not been able to finish the fortification of the camp. 15. The result will certainly be[4] that you will be defeated. 16. Caesar so thoroughly[5] defeated the Belgae that they are to-day allies of the Roman people.

1. Say 'who live in the towns.' A Latin noun should not be modified by a prepositional phrase, unless the noun is derived from a verb of motion or feeling (e.g., *love, hate*). Render such English expressions by a genitive, or by an adjective or participle, or by a relative clause. 2. 'unable' = 'not able.' 3. Cf. **44**, *b* and **45**, *g*. 4. Say, 'it will certainly happen': when a phrase with noun and verb in English represents the action of a single verb, this equivalent verb must be used in Latin. 5. Say, 'so defeated,' **ita**, etc.

LESSON XIX

IDIOMS OF CASE CONSTRUCTION

100. Secondary object.

Verbs signifying *ask, conceal, demand, teach* govern two objects, one of the person, the other of the thing. In Latin both these objects stand in the accusative case, and are called the direct and the secondary object. When the construction is changed to the passive, the person becomes the subject nominative; the thing remains accusative.

Caesar demanded grain of (or *from*) *the Haedui* (or *C. asked the H. for grain*), **Caesar Haeduōs frūmentum flāgitābat;** *they asked Caesar* (*for*) *his opinion,* **Caesarem sententiam rogāvērunt;** *Caesar was asked* (*for*) *his opinion,* **Caesar sententiam rogātus est.**

REMARK. The accusative of the thing remaining with the passive voice may also be called the *retained object.*

a. After **petō,** *seek,* and **postulō,** *demand,* the person stands in the ablative with **ab;** after **quaerō,** *inquire,* in the ablative with **ab, dē,** or **ex;** after **imperō,** in the dative (cf. **90**).

When he was asking this of Caesar, **haec cum ā Caesare peteret;** *this is what I demand of you,* **haec sunt quae ā tē postulō;** *wondering what the reason was, he asked them,* **quae causa esset mīrātus, ex ipsīs quaesiit;** *I shall demand this of the Ubii,* **hoc ego Ubiīs imperābō.**

101. The Latin verbs **ūtor,** *use;* **fruor,** *enjoy;* **fungor,** *finish, perform;* **potior,** *gain possession of;* **vēscor,** *eat, live on,* govern an apparent direct object in the ablative.

They do not use imported animals, **iūmentīs importātīs nōn ūtuntur;** *our men gained possession of their baggage and camp,* **impedīmentīs castrīsque nostrī potītī sunt.**

102. Separation. That of which one is deprived, or that from which one is excluded, freed, or separated stands in Latin in the ablative. This construction is called the *Ablative of Separation*.

They bar them out from their lands, **suīs fīnibus eōs prohibent**; *to free Italy from fear*, **Ītaliam metū līberāre**; *to cut Caesar off from grain and supplies*, **utī frūmentō commeātūque Caesarem interclūderet**.

a. Do not confuse this construction with the construction of the place whence, which requires a preposition (**57**, II); nor with that of the person from whom a thing is forcibly seized, which requires (see REMARK below) an ablative with **ā** or **ab**, or a dative of the person as a true indirect object (**83**, **ēripiō**).

He seized a shield from a soldier, **scūtum mīlitī dētrāxit**.

REMARK. Separation may also be indicated by the preposition **ā** (**ab**), which is, indeed, occasionally found with verbs of seizing from.

103.   VOCABULARY

ask,[1] **rogō**, I.

at length, **tandem**.

body, **corpus, -oris**, *n.*

keep away,[2] **prohibeō, -ēre, -uī, -itum**; *in noun constructions w. acc. dir. obj. and abl. w. or without* **ab**.

left (side), **sinister, -tra, -trum**; *f. as subst.*, the left hand.

liberate,[3] **līberō**, I.

opinion, **sententia, -ae**, *f.* (*a deliberate opinion, formed after due consideration*).

right (side), **dexter, -tra, -trum**; *f. as subst.*, the right hand.

say,[4] **dīcō, -ere, dīxī, dictum**.

severely,[5] **graviter**.

siege,[6] **oppugnātiō, -ōnis**, *f.*

summer, **aestās, -tātis**, *f.*

take possession of,[7] **potior, -īrī, -ītus**, *dep.*, *w. abl.*, *except in phrase* **rērum potīrī**, to gain (*political*) mastery.

teach, **doceō, -ēre, -uī, doctum**, *with two accusatives.*

undertake, **suscipiō, -ere, -cēpī, -ceptum**.

use, **ūtor, ūtī, ūsus**, *dep.*, *with abl.*

winter, **hiems, hiemis**, *f.*

IDIOMS

day after day, **diem ex diē**

take the field against one, **contrā aliquem castra habēre**

the front (*in military sense*), **prīmum agmen** *or* **prīma aciēs** (*referring respectively to the front of a marching column and the foremost battle line*)

the men in front, **prīmī** *or* **priōrēs** *as substantive*

Synonyms. 1. ask for, request. 2. keep from, keep off, keep out. 3. free, set free. 4. tell. 5. gravely, seriously. 6. assault, attack (*of places only*), blockade. 7. gain possession, get possession, get control, take.

104. 1. Day after day he kept asking[1] the Haedui for grain, which they would[2] not give him, for Dumnorix had persuaded them to give nothing[3] to the Romans. 2. Long and fiercely they fought, but at length our men gained possession of Ariovistus' camp and baggage. 3. Caesar taught the Romans the art of war. 4. Caesar was asked by Diviciacus his opinion of the cavalry battle in which Dumnorix and his horsemen had fled. 5. All winter the brave troops of the Belgae kept the Germans out of their boundaries. 6. The enemy were severely defeated by Caesar in the battle at Ocelum[4]; and by this battle the province was freed from all danger. 7. We shall take the field against the Gauls and shall liberate the towns of our allies from blockade and themselves from fear. 8. All summer our army uses grain from the fields of its enemies, but in winter we are compelled to use pack animals to bring it to us from the province. 9. He seized a shield from a soldier in the third line[5] to use[6] against a certain one of the enemy who had attacked him. 10. He inquired of the Sequani the cause of the war. " We have undertaken the war," they replied, " for the purpose of keeping ourselves from danger and our lands from our enemies." 11. There was a fierce fight at the river. The men in front tried to cross, but were killed or severely wounded in the river itself. The rest, nevertheless, most bravely crossed over[7] the bodies of these. 12. Soldiers use the shield in the left

hand and the sword in the right.   13. I advise you not to use
infantry for [8] this march, so that you may return more quickly
after the battle and may not be compelled to delay.   14. He
suddenly asked a soldier for a javelin, and took from him his
sword also.[9]   15. Use both infantry and cavalry in order to gain
possession of this camp the more quickly.   16. I will both keep
the enemy away from your towns and set you free from all fear.

1. 'kept asking'; what tense?   2. This English form here expresses the attitude of continuous opposition and refusal; hence the
imperfect.   3. **82.**   4. **99**, n. 1.   5. Here, of course, 'battle line';
see also n. 4.   6. **86**, III.   7. **per.**   8. **ad.**   9. **quōque.**

LESSON XX

IDIOMS OF CASE CONSTRUCTION (CONTINUED)

105. Idioms of possession.

a. The fact of possession, involving the verbs *have, possess,
own,* is regularly expressed in Latin by the dative of the possessor with **sum.**

Traders have no access to them, **nūllus aditus est ad eōs mercā-
tōribus.**

1. This is a variety of the dative of reference (**18**) ; for the
bare fact of possession simply means that something exists or
does not exist with reference to a particular person.

b. The idea *belong to,* whether literal or figurative, is expressed
by a possessive genitive in the predicate after **sum.**   In its
figurative sense the idea is extended to include such expressions
as *duty of, characteristic of, mark of,* etc.

The decision belongs to the commander (or *is the prerogative of the
commander*), **iūdicium imperātōris est;** *for this is characteristic of
Gallic custom,* **est enim hoc Gallicae cōnsuētūdinis.**

1. When the possessor is in the first or second person or in the third person reflexive, the possessive pronoun is employed instead of a genitive.

My duty is to attack the enemy, **meum est hostēs aggredī.**

106. Descriptive noun phrases.

A prepositional phrase with *of*, involving a noun and an adjective, may describe another noun. Such phrases are translated into Latin by either the genitive or the ablative, and may be attributive or predicate.

They are men of great valor, **sunt hominēs magnae virtūtis;** *these they render (capable) of the hardest labor*, **haec summī ut sint labōris efficiunt;** *men of hostile disposition*, **hominēs inimīcō animō.**

a. If the phrase expresses dimension or measure, the genitive, not the ablative, is used.

A sixteen-foot moat, **pedum sēdecim fossa.**

b. The adjective or an adjective modifier is necessary to this construction in Latin : in a phrase like *a man of valor*, common enough in English, *of valor* must be expressed in Latin by a simple adjective, *brave;* thus, *a man of valor*, **fortis vir.**

107.   VOCABULARY

approach,[1] **aditus, -ūs,** *m.* (— to, **ad** *w. acc.*).

at first, **prīmō.**

decision,[2] **iūdicium, -ī,** *n.*

depth, **altitūdō, -dinis,** *f.* (*cf.* **30** and **75**).

everything, **omnia, -ium,** *as n. subst.*

from where,[3] **unde,** *rel. and interrog.*

height, **altitūdō** (*cf.* depth).

merchant,[4] **mercātor, -ōris,** *m.*

region, **regiō, -ōnis,** *f.*

reputation,[5] **auctōritās, -tātis,** *f.*

surround, **circumdō, -dare, -dedī, -datum,** *w. an acc. dir. obj. and an abl. of means* (*used only of placing or constructing around, never of standing or coming around*).

three days, **trīduum, -ī,** *n.*

wall, **mūrus, -ī,** *m.*

Idioms

as far as possible, **quantum potest (poterat)**
for this (following) reason, **eā dē causā**
for this (preceding) reason, **quā dē causā**

Synonyms. 1. access. 2. judgment. 3. from which (place), whence.
4. trader. 5. authority.

108. 1. The men stand around the traders in the towns,
which [1] is characteristic of the Gallic custom, and compel them
to tell everything about the regions they come from. [2]   2. There
was a hill of no [3] great height at the edge [4] of the forest, which
men of less courage than ours never dared climb.   3. It is my
duty to keep my men from death in war, as far as possible;
still I will never desert my post [5] nor fail in my duty [6] to my
commander and to the republic.   4. The entire decision about
the war belongs to Caesar, and I dare not join battle without
him.   5. He is a soldier of great reputation, and has ordered
me to await his arrival here.   6. Does Gaul belong to Ariovistus
or to the Roman people?   7. Why do you ask this?   Gaul
belongs by right to the Gauls themselves; but they are not
men of valor in war and cannot defend their own country.
8. The Germans are of very great size of body, so that our soldiers at first were greatly alarmed.   9. The traders have access
to the Germans for this reason, that they may have some one [7]
to tell them about affairs [8] in Gaul.   10. Caesar surrounded his
entire camp with a ten-foot wall to keep the enemy out.   11. This
army belongs to me.   By what right do you come here to
take it from me?   12. I have five companies of soldiers which
I have now had with me for three years.   13. Caesar with the
utmost [9] haste accomplished a twenty-mile march in five hours,
to defend the town of Ocelum with heavier [10] reënforcements.
14. Labienus with three thousand [11] men of the greatest courage
marched rapidly to the assistance of Caesar.   15. The Roman
commanders led their men rapidly over hills and mountains

without any rest in camp for many days in succession; and this rendered them capable of the greatest labors. 16. Three thousand horses belong to these savages, with which they have made a three days' march [12] in a little more than two days.

1. **45**, *g.* 2. 'from which they come'; **45**, *e.* 3. 'not of great height.' 4. Use **extrēmus** in the proper construction. 5. What is the real meaning of this word here? 6. Express this noun here; the expression evidently does not fall under **105**, *b.* 7. Omit this word, and use the plural of the proper indefinite pronoun; or say 'that they may have who may tell,' the antecedent of 'who' being the unexpr ssed object of 'have.' 8. 'things.' 9. 'greatest.' 10. 'greater.' 11. See **61**, n. 5. 12. 'a march of three days': **trīduum** and similarly formed words are compounded of a numeral adjective and **diēs**. The adjective necessary to the construction of **106** is therefore *present in the word itself*, and the apparently unmodified genitive may consequently be used.

LESSON XXI

IDIOMS OF CASE CONSTRUCTION (Continued)

109. Dimension and extent.

The dimensions of an object may be expressed in Latin either by the genitive of measure or by the accusative of extent of space. The direction of extent, *in height*, *in width*, etc., is expressed in Latin by **in** with the accusative.

He constructed a wall nineteen miles (long), sixteen feet in height, **mīlia passuum XIX mūrum in altitūdinem pedum sēdecim perdūcit.**

a. When the dimensions are expressed in Latin by the accusative instead of by the genitive, the adjectives *high*, *wide*, etc., may be used in agreement with the noun, as well as the phrases *in height*, etc.

Trenches were constructed, each five feet deep, **fossae quīnōs pedēs altae dūcēbantur.**

110. When an adjective requires a noun to complete its meaning, this noun stands in the genitive in Latin. Such adjectives are those of *desire, fullness, guilt, knowledge, memory, power, sharing, skill*, etc., and their contraries. To these add, in the Latin, present participles used with objective genitive (**22**, *d*).

Fond of political change, **cupidus novārum rērum**; *most skilled in the science of war*, **perītissimus reī mīlitāris.**

111. Price and value.

A noun stating or meaning definite price or value with verbs of *buying, selling, estimating*, and *valuing* stands in Latin in the ablative.

They procure pack animals at a high price, **iūmenta impēnsō parant pretiō.**

a. Expressions of indefinite value, not employing a noun, are translated into Latin by the genitive of certain adjectives. These are: **tantī**, *for so much, of such value;* **quantī**, *for how much? of what value?* **magnī**, *of great value;* **parvī**, *of small value;* **plūris**, *for more, of greater value;* **minōris**, *for less, of less value;* **maximī, plūrimī**, *of very great value;* **minimī**, *of very little value.*

He tells him that his goodwill is so valuable to him that he pardons the injury, **tantī eius apud sē grātiam esse ostendit, utī iniūriam condōnet.**

112. Memory and forgetfulness.

In expressions of memory and forgetfulness, the thing remembered or forgotten stands in Latin in the genitive, unless it is expressed by a neuter pronoun, which is regularly in the accusative.

Recall the old disaster, **reminīscere veteris incommodī**; *can I forget the fresh insult?* **num recentis contumēliae oblīvīscī possum?** *I remember this*, **haec meminī.**

113. **Certain emotions.**

The emotions of mental distress or anxiety, *disgust, pity, repentance, shame, weariness,* are expressed in Latin by the impersonal verbs **piget, miseret, paenitet, pudet, taedet,** respectively. The person experiencing the emotion stands in Latin in the accusative, and the person or thing exciting the emotion stands in the genitive.

They repent of their plans, **eōs cōnsiliōrum paenitet;** *I am ashamed of my brother and disgusted with him,* **frātris mē pudet pigetque.**

114. **Concern and interest.**

In expressions of concern or interest, the *verb idea* is expressed in Latin by the impersonal verbs **rēfert** and **interest**: *the person or thing concerned* is expressed by the genitive, except that instead of the genitive of the personal pronouns, the ablative singular feminine of the possessive pronouns is employed unless the adjective *all* agrees with the pronoun: *that about which one is concerned* is expressed (1) by a neuter pronoun as subject, for many verbs otherwise impersonal admit such a subject, (2) by an infinitive (**186**), or (3) by an indirect question (**201**): *the degree of concern* is expressed (1) by a genitive of indefinite value, (2) by an adverb, or (3) by a neuter adjective used adverbially.

It is not more for our interest than for yours, **nōn nostrā magis quam vestrā rēfert**; *this concerns me,* **hoc meā interest**; *this is of importance to us all,* **hoc nostrum omnium interest**; *it is highly important to the common safety that the bands of the enemy be kept apart,* **magnō opere commūnis salūtis interest manūs hostium distinērī.**

REMARK. **Rēfert = rē fert**; hence **meā rē fert** is readily intelligible. The use of the feminine pronouns with **interest** is by analogy to this.

115.   VOCABULARY

ancestors, **maiōrēs, -um,** *m.*
breadth,[1] **lātitūdō, -dinis,** *f.*
brother, **frāter, -tris,** *m.*
buy, **emō, -ere, ēmī, ēmptum.**

it concerns,[2] **interest, -esse, -fuit, -futūrum.**
conscious,[3] **cōnscius, -a, -um,** *w. gen. (often accompanied by a re-*

flexive pronoun in the dat. of refer-ence).

construct, **perdūcō**, -ere, -dūxī, -ductum (*w. special ref. to military works*).

cost, **stō**, -āre, stetī, statum, *w. dat. of pers. and abl. of price.*

eager for,[4] **cupidus**, -a, -um, *w. gen.*

forget, **oblīvīscor**, -ī, oblītus, *w. gen. of noun object.*

full, **plēnus**, -a, -um, *w. gen.*

how,[5] **quō modō.**

indeed,[6] **quidem.**

manner,[7] **modus**, -ī, *m.*

pity,[8] **miseret**, -ēre, -uit.

popularity,[9] **grātia**, -ae, *f.*

price, **pretium**, -ī, *n.*

remember,[10] **meminī**, -isse (*in general*); **reminīscor**, -ī (*of an effort of memory*), *w. gen. of noun object.*

repent, **paenitet**, -ēre, -uit, —.

revolt, **dēficiō**, -ere, -fēcī, -fectum (— from, ā *w. abl.*).

sell, **vēndō**, -ere, -didī, -ditum.

skilled in, **perītus**, -a, -um, *w. gen. of that in which the person is skilled.*

IDIOMS

of such a kind, **eius modī** or **eiusmodī** (cf. **106**)
rush out, **sē ēicere** (lit., *cast one's self forth*)

Synonyms.   1. width.   2. it is to the interest of, it is of importance to, it makes a difference.   3. aware.   4. desirous of, fond of.   5. *Lit.*, in what manner.   6. at least, in truth.   7. method, mode, way.   8. be sorry for. 9. favor, influence.   10. recall, recollect.

116.   1. The camp was surrounded by a wall sixteen feet in height, which was defended by men of the greatest bravery and most skilled in the art of war.   2. Dumnorix was the brother of Diviciacus and was a man of the highest[1] popularity with his tribe as well as[2] so eager for political change that he revolted from the Romans.   3. The river on the bank of which the camp had been pitched was about ten feet in depth and two hundred paces in width, and bounded on one side the territories of the Belgians.   4. The merchants have no access to these barbarous tribes, whose lands are full of good crops which they can sell at a high[1] price; and of this,[3] indeed, they are aware.   5. Merchants always prefer to sell their goods for much more than they buy them.   6. This victory cost the Romans many men and much baggage. 7. He constructed a wall ten feet in height and two miles long, for the camp had no other protection. 8. What is he after now [4]? He has no supplies left,[5] and wishes to buy grain for the army at much too high a price. 9. The forest is full of men to rush [6] out against the enemy encumbered in the river. 10. The battle which was begun was at last successful, but it cost the commander many men; for it is the duty of brave soldiers to fight to the death. 11. The Helvetii always remembered the valor of their ancestors, so that they were always willing to fight with any nation whatsoever.[7] 12. Caesar had advised Labienus always to send his cavalry to attack the rear of the enemy and never to divide his army. This, however, Labienus on that day forgot.

———

13. The general is so ashamed of his unsuccessful battle that he has retired to Rome, and I feel extremely sorry for him. 14. These savages always are compelled [8] to repent of the plans which they have hastily adopted. 15. I pity the Haedui, for the enemies of the Roman people, who are also their enemies, have persuaded them to revolt. 16. This concerns me deeply [1]; but how does it concern the republic?

1. Here figurative: what is the proper word? 2. 'as well as' = 'and also.' 3. Express the word *thing*. 4. Find the real meaning: the English idiom is untranslatable literally. 5. 'He has nothing of remaining supplies.' 6. Not infinitive. 7. 'any . . . whatsoever': see **49**. 8. Say 'necessarily (**necessariō**) repent.'

LESSON XXII

APPOSITIVE CLAUSES

117. In English, clauses frequently stand in apposition to nouns and pronouns, and explain them. Such clauses are introduced by *that*, *the fact that*, *because*, and may express the cause, purpose, or result summed up in the noun or pronoun which they explain; or they may consist of a simple statement with or without some such introduction as *namely*, *that is*, etc.; or they may even stand in the infinitive. Such clauses are represented in Latin by:

a. Clauses introduced by **quod** and having the verb in the indicative.

Many things urged the Gauls to this: the scarcity of food, and (*the fact*) *that men gladly believe what they desire*, **multae rēs ad hoc Gallōs hortābantur: inopia cibāriōrum, et quod libenter hominēs id quod volunt crēdunt.**

1. When in English the appositive clause is causal in its nature and explains a reason, the **quod** clause is to be employed in the Latin. In such clauses, whatever may be the word or phrase introducing the English clause, if we substitute *because* for it, we shall have an intelligible sentence.

b. Clauses introduced by **ut** and having the verb in the subjunctive. The negative in such clauses is **nōn** in statements of fact; but if the dependent clause contains a further idea of purpose or fear, **nē** must be used.

He had done in one day what they with the utmost difficulty had accomplished in twenty — crossed the river, **id quod ipsī diēbus XX aegerrimē cōnfēcerant, ut flūmen trānsīrent, ille ūnō diē fēcerat;** *one thing they beg and implore, that he will not deprive them of their arms*, **ūnum petunt ac dēprecantur, nē sē armīs dēspoliet.**

1. Sometimes an explanatory prepositional phrase in English is best rendered in Latin by an appositive clause, especially when the noun of the phrase is verbal and of passive implication. Thus *the risk of defeat* (i.e., *the risk of being defeated*) should be rendered as *this risk, that one be defeated*, **hoc perīculum, ut vincātur** (or **vincerētur,** if the main verb is secondary).

118. VOCABULARY

chance,[1] **cāsus, -ūs,** *m.*

first (*adv.*), **prīmum.**

gradually, **paulātim.**

only [2] (*adv.*), **tantum** (*limiting a positive assertion*); **omnīnō** (*in sense of* in all; *w. neg.,* at all).

penalty,[3] **poena, -ae,** *f.*

prepared,[4] **parātus, -a, -um** (— for, **ad** *w. acc.;* — to, *w. inf.*).

press on,[5] **īnstō, -āre, īnstitī, īnstātum** (*with special reference to attacking*).

pursue, **subsequor, -sequī, -secūtus** (*with special reference to close pursuit*).

surround, **circumveniō, -īre, -vēnī, -ventum** (*of gathering around*).

Synonyms. 1. emergency. 2. merely. 3. punishment. 4. ready. 5. come on.

119. 1. The penalty was that he should be executed. 2. Several causes urged Caesar to attack the town: the flight of the greater part of the enemy's army, and the fact that there was in his own camp a scarcity of provisions. 3. Caesar's plan was that Labienus should merely hold the mountain and not attack the enemy at all. 4. The cause of this flight was that a horde [1] of Germans suddenly attacked the Gallic cavalry. 5. The horsemen of Ariovistus were gradually gathering around our men with this design, that they should suddenly charge on them with swords. 6. I have at least accomplished this, that they cannot cross the Rhine. 7. I have been hindered by many things: first, that I have very little confidence in the auxiliaries that the Gauls have sent me.[2] 8. Caesar accomplished what no Roman commander had ever done before him: namely, that the Gauls did not try to keep him and his army out of their towns and that they always gave him grain. 9. I have done what you can never do — climb [3] that mountain. 10. This I beg of you earnestly,[4] that you do not send me ahead with the cavalry. 11. This I imperatively [4] enjoin upon you, to press on boldly and not to hesitate to attack the enemy. 12. The cause of this unsuccessful cavalry battle was this, that the leader of the cavalry had pursued the enemy too rapidly and had joined battle with them in an unfavorable place.   13. I enjoined this strongly [4] upon the soldiers, that they should be ready for every emergency.   14. I have very little confidence in the Gauls for this reason, that they never seem to be ready for any emergency. 15. This emergency suddenly confronted [5] us, that we were compelled to fight at the same time with a band of the enemy on each flank.   16. The penalty of execution [6] is most severe.

1. Find an English synonym which will guide you to the Latin word.   2. Note carefully the relation of this word to the action before you try to express it.   3. To determine the person of this verb, consult the first example under **117**, *b*.   4. Employ a superlative adverb which will merely intensify the verb: the one you should use is very common.   Often English adverbs of special meaning, and limited in application to the idea they modify, are to be rendered into Latin by the most general adverbs of degree, applicable to almost any verb.   5. Simply translate the *meaning:* there are several ways of rendering this sentence.   6. Cf. **117**, *a*, 2.

LESSON XXIII

CLAUSES OF HINDRANCE AND PREVENTION, REFUSAL, DOUBT, FEAR

120. Hindrance, prevention, refusal.

Verbs of hindrance and prevention, which in English take after them *from* and the verbal in *-ing*, are regularly construed in Latin with a subjunctive purpose clause introduced by **nē**, **quōminus** or **quīn**.   If the principal clause is affirmative, **nē** or **quōminus** is used with the dependent clause; but if the principal clause is negative, **quīn** generally introduces the dependent clause.   Only the present and imperfect tenses of the subjunctive may be employed in this construction (cf. **81**).

They prevent the populace from giving grain, **multitūdinem dēterrent nē frūmentum cōnferant**; *the ships were prevented from reaching* *port,* nāvēs tenēbantur quōminus in portum venīre possent; *it had not been possible to restrain the Germans from hurling spears,* Germānī retinērī nōn potuerant quīn tēla cōnicerent.

a. The same construction is usually employed with recūsō, *refuse,* which in English governs an infinitive (cf. **123**).

Nor will they refuse to be under their sway, neque recūsābunt quōminus sub illōrum imperiō sint.

121. Doubt.

Negative verbs and expressions of *doubt* are construed in Latin with quīn and a subjunctive clause.

We do not doubt that he will inflict punishment on all the hostages, nōn dubitāmus quīn dē omnibus obsidibus supplicium sūmat; *there is no doubt that the Helvetii are the strongest,* nōn est dubium quīn plūrimum Helvētiī possint.

a. For affirmative expressions of doubt, see **204**.

122. Fear.

a. A fear that something will happen is expressed in Latin by nē, *that, lest, for fear that,* with a subjunctive clause.

He feared that he would hurt the feelings of Diviciacus, verēbātur nē Dīviciācī animum offenderet.

b. A fear that something will not happen is expressed in Latin by ut, *that . . . not, for fear that . . . not,* with a subjunctive clause. Nē . . . nōn sometimes occurs instead of ut.

They feared that it could not be supplied, verēbantur ut supportārī posset.

1. A noun may govern a clause of fear.

By the fear that they would be punished, timōre nē suppliciō afficerentur.

2. Sometimes neither a verb nor a noun of fear is expressed, the evident relation of the dependent clause to the principal clause being sufficient to indicate the emotion of fear.

This thing caused Caesar great perplexity, for fear that all Gaul would revolt, **magnam haec rēs Caesarī difficultātem afferēbat, nē cūncta Gallia dēficeret.**

c. A fear *to do* or a fear *to be* is expressed, as in English, by the infinitive.

Whom he was afraid to kill in the sight of Gaul, **quōs in cōnspectū Galliae interficere verēbātur.**

Remark. In such cases the verb of fear is a strengthened **nōlō,** with its construction.

123.   VOCABULARY

booty,[1] **praeda, -ae,** *f.*

but still,[2] **at.**

command,[3] **imperium, -ī,** *n.*

doubt, **dubium, -ī,** *n.*

doubt, **dubitō,** I, *when neg., construed with clause w.* **quīn.**

fear,[4] **timeō, -ēre, -uī, —; vereor, -ērī, -itus** { *w. dir. obj.; dat. of the obj. of solicitude; a clause w.* **nē (ut).**

press,[5] **premō, -ere, pressī, pressum.**

prevent,[6] **dēterreō, -ēre, -uī, -itum,** *w.* **nē, quōminus,** *or, if neg.,* **quīn,** *and a clause;* **prohibeō, -ēre, -uī, -itum,** *in Caesar always w. acc. and inf., elsewhere w.* **nē, quōminus, quīn.**

refuse, **recūsō,** I, *w. dir. obj.; also w.* **quōminus** *and clause; if neg., w.* **quōminus** *or* **quīn** *and clause, or w. inf.*

restrain, **retineō, -ēre, -uī, -tentum,** *w. dir. obj. and clause; if neg., w.* **quīn.**

Synonyms. 1. plunder. 2. at least, but, still, yet (*a stronger adversative than* **sed**). 3. order. 4. be afraid. 5. press hard (*military term of severe attack*). 6. check, hinder, keep from, stop (**prohibeō** *refers to preventing by active interference;* **dēterreō,** *to preventing by fear*).

124. 1. I shall always refuse to be under your command. 2. I do not doubt that our forces bravely tried to keep the enemy from crossing the river, but still they kept [1] pressing on. 3. I shall prevent you from attempting to deliver any [2] speech to-day. 4. The enemy could not be restrained from hurling javelins at [3] our men. 5. There is no doubt, my friends and

allies, that you have never refused to give grain to my army.
6. I fear that the enemy will press our line hard.   7. I am afraid
you will not be able to capture the town.   8. Caesar was not
afraid that he would not conquer the enemy.   9. The Gauls
feared they would be surrounded by our men, who were even
then attacking them on the right flank.   10. Fear that he
would be defeated by bands of the enemy kept [4] the commander in his fortified camp.   11. Fear that there would not be
sufficient supplies kept the Gauls from advancing farther.
12. First, I am afraid that the enemy's army is greater than ours;
next, that we shall not be able to hold the commanding positions.   13. Do you fear that you are not ready for battle?
Certainly not; but that I shall be prevented from pursuing the
enemy and obtaining great booty.   14. I am afraid to lead my
army into these forests for fear that the enemy may rush out
from some ambush and attack us.   15. The Gallic leaders were
afraid to try to restrain their men from hurling javelins at the
envoy.   16. There is no doubt that my men have not done [5]
their best to cross [5] the river; and they were prevented from
doing it by this fear, that the enemy would attack them in the
stream. [6]

1. Sufficiently indicated by the tense to be used.   2. In choosing
the word for ' any ' here, do not overlook the really negative character of the sentence.   3. in w. acc.   4. ' kept . . . in ' = ' held in.'
5. Watch the tenses carefully.   6. Find the proper Latin word by
seeking English synonyms of 'stream.'

LESSON XXIV

CLAUSES OF TIME

125. We may look at an act by itself, without reference to
the time of any other act.   Here our time-idea is *absolute*.   On
the other hand, we may look at an act in its relation to some

time of which we are thinking.   Here our time-idea is *relative*. Clauses of time express the *time relation* of the subordinate clause to the principal clause.   They are introduced in English by *before, until, when, while, after, since, as soon as, as long as, whenever*, etc.

126.   *Before* is translated into Latin by **antequam** or the more frequent **priusquam**.   These words are often separated into their component parts, so that **ante** or **prius** stands in the principal clause, and **quam** introduces the dependent clause.

a.   When the reference in the ' before ' clause is to an actual fact, **antequam** and **priusquam** are used with the indicative. The present and future perfect tenses are used for present or future time; for past time, the perfect tense is used, especially with a negative principal clause.

I shall fight before more troops are concentrated there, **prius quam erunt maiōrēs eō coāctae cōpiae dīmicābō**; *and they did not stop running before they came to the river,* **neque prius fugere dēstitērunt quam ad flūmen pervēnērunt.**

b.   When any idea of anticipation, apprehension, expectancy, purpose, etc., enters into the subordinate clause, **antequam** and **priusquam** are used with the present subjunctive in present or future statements.   In past statements, if the action denoted by the ' before ' clause did not take place, **antequam** and **priusquam** are used with the imperfect subjunctive.   The perfect and pluperfect subjunctive are very rare, but may be used if required by the necessities of the tense relation.

He forms his plan before the fortifications are (i.e., *before they can be*) *completed,* **priusquam mūnītiōnēs perficiantur, cōnsilium capit**; *before he should take any action, he ordered Diviciacus to be summoned,* **priusquam quicquam cōnārētur, Dīviciācum ad sē vocārī iubet**; *for the use of the rare perfect, they do not let the leaders go before they have consented,* **nōn prius ducēs dīmittunt quam ab hīs sit concessum.**

c. When the principal clause is negative, *until* is frequently used in English instead of *before;* do not be misled by it, but in such clauses use **antequam** or **priusquam**.   (Cf. **126**, *a*, Ex. 2 and *b*, Ex. 3; in both examples *until* may replace *before*.)

127. *Until,* signifying *up to the time that,* following both affirmative and negative principal clauses, is translated into Latin by **dum**, less frequently by **quoad**. These words are used with the indicative to denote an actual event; but when the clause implies expectancy or purpose, the subjunctive is used. With the indicative the main verb usually lies in past time and the dependent verb in the perfect tense: with the subjunctive, the present and imperfect tenses are used according to the time of the main verb.

Our men savagely pressed them back until the cavalry drove the enemy headlong, **nostrī ācriter eōs reppulērunt quoad equitēs praecipitēs hostēs ēgērunt;** *he waited until the rest of his ships should arrive there,* **dum reliquae nāvēs eō convenīrent exspectāvit.**

a. When an actual event is denoted by an *until* clause, **quoad** is preferred to **dum**: with the subjunctive, however, **dum** is the more frequent.

128. *While* in English may evidently be used in two senses, *in the time that* and *all the time that.* Thus, in the sentence *while he is talking, time flies, while* has clearly not the same force as in *wait while he writes the letter.*

a. While (= *in the time that*) is expressed in Latin by **dum** with the present indicative.

While these things were going on, a report reached Caesar, **dum haec geruntur, Caesarī nūntiātum est.**

b. While (= *all the time that,* or, as frequently occurs, *as long as*) is expressed by **dum, quoad,** or **quamdiū** with the indicative in the same tense as that of the main verb.

He resisted while he could (i.e., *as long as he could*), **quoad potuit,
restitit;** *I have kept silent as long as I can,* **quamdiū potuī, tacuī.**

REMARK. These two varieties of *while* clauses are readily seen to
correspond to two case constructions of time. Thus *a : b ::* ablative
of time within which : accusative of extent of time.

129. *After* is translated into Latin by **postquam** or **posteāquam** with the perfect indicative.

After Caesar came there he demanded hostages, **eō postquam Caesar
pervēnit, obsidēs poposcit.**

REMARK. Always distinguish carefully between the conjunction
after and the adverb *afterward*. The conjunction *after* is **postquam**
or **posteāquam,** but the adverb *afterward* is **post** or **posteā.**

130. a. As soon as, referring to a single past event, is translated into Latin by **simul ac (atque), cum prīmum, ubi prīmum,**
with the perfect indicative.

As soon as word came of Caesar's arrival, he came to him, **simul
atque dē Caesaris adventū cōgnitum est, ad eum vēnit;** *the enemy
attacked as soon as they saw our cavalry,* **hostēs, ubi prīmum nostrōs
equitēs cōnspēxērunt, impetum fēcērunt.**

b. As soon as, not referring to a single past event, is expressed
by **cum prīmum** with the indicative to denote present or future
time, with the subjunctive to denote past time.

Set out among the Veneti as soon as you can, **cum prīmum poteris
in Venetōs proficīscere;** *as soon as there began to be plenty of forage,
he came to the army,* **cum prīmum pābulī cōpia esse inciperet, ad
exercitum vēnit.**

131.   VOCABULARY

daily, **cotīdiē.**

interview,[1] **colloquium, -ī, *n.***

prepare,[2] **parō,** I (— to, *w. inf.;* —
    something for, **ad** *w. acc.*)*; perf.
    ptc. as adj.,* prepared, ready.

receive,[3] **accipiō, -ere, -cēpī, -cep-
    tum.**

reconnoiter,[4] **explōrō,** I.

speak with,[5] **colloquor, -ī, -locū-
    tus,** *w.* **cum** *and abl. of person.*

IDIOM

have a conference with, **in colloquium venīre cum** *or* **colloquor cum**

Synonyms. 1. conference. 2. get ready, make ready, prepare for. 3. accept; suffer (a loss *or* disaster). 4. explore, investigate. 5. confer.

132. 1. While Caesar was marching toward Labienus, he daily sent scouts ahead [1] to reconnoiter the route. 2. After he had prepared reserves for every emergency, he took his stand in a commanding position and waited for the enemy's attack. 3. The enemy resisted our army as long as they could; but at length they began to retire, gradually at first, then with all speed. 4. Many things will happen before I see you again. 5. I want to attack their army before it can by any chance reach [2] its fortified camp. 6. Caesar did not attack the enemy until they were only twenty paces distant from his line. 7. Caesar waited for the troops of his two lieutenants until the enemy crossed the river and approached the very gates of his camp. 8. I, at least, shall not delay in the province until the enemy arrive in the territories of our allies. 9. Caesar waited until the enemy crossed the river and could not easily flee with so great an army. Then he attacked them fiercely. 10. While Caesar was speaking with Ariovistus, the Germans began to hurl javelins at the men [3] of the tenth legion. 11. While Caesar remained in Gaul he often conferred with the Gallic chieftains about public business.[4] 12. I was compelled to wait until I had a conference with Caesar before I could inform you about his plans. 13. After he had been informed of the plans of the Gauls, he prepared for the war so well that Gaul has been set free.

---

14. As soon as Caesar came to Labienus' camp, they began to prepare for the campaign. 15. As soon as the messenger arrived, the lieutenant broke camp for fear he should suffer some disaster. 16. As soon as I am informed about

the interview with [5] Ariovistus, I shall send a portion of my army to occupy his lands.

1. ' sent . . . ahead '; verb phrases represented in Latin by a single verb are often separated in this way in English. 2. ' arrive at.' 3. ' soldiers.' 4. Here is an opportunity to fill in the linguistic " blank check." Cf. **12**. 5. Do not use **cum**: never permit a prepositional phrase in Latin to modify a noun; write ' Ariovistus ' in the gen. here; see **99**, n. 1.

LESSON XXV

CLAUSES OF TIME (Continued)

133. *When*, referring to a single past occurrence, is translated by **ubi**, or less frequently by **ut** with the perfect indicative.

When the Helvetii were informed, they sent envoys, **ubi Helvētiī certiōrēs factī sunt, lēgātōs mittunt.**

134. *When*, referring to present, future, or past time, is translated by **cum**, the most frequent and the most important of the time particles.

a. **Cum**, *when*, referring to present or future time, is joined with the indicative.

Most of them, when they are overwhelmed by debt, attach themselves to the nobles in serfdom, **plērīque, cum aere aliēnō premuntur, sēsē in servitūtem dicant nōbilibus;** *when I have any hope, I shall inform you*, **cum in spem vēnerō, vōs certiōrēs faciam.**

b. **Cum**, *when*, referring to past time, is joined with the indicative to indicate the **point of time** at which the event narrated or described by the main clause occurred; with the subjunctive to emphasize the **circumstances accompanying** this event. These two kinds of **cum** clauses may be called, respectively, *determinative* **cum** *clauses* and *descriptive* **cum** *clauses of situation.*

When Caesar came into Gaul, the Haedui were the leaders, **cum
Caesar in Galliam vēnit, prīncipēs erant Haeduī;** *when Ariovistus
had seen them in camp, he shouted,* **quōs cum in castrīs Ariovistus cōn-
spēxisset, conclāmāvit.**

1. In past time it is often optional with the writer whether
he shall emphasize point of time or accompanying circumstances. The Latin author often takes the attendant circumstance idea where the English appears to think only of time.

2. In clauses emphasizing the point of time of the action of
the main verb, *when* is accurately defined by the old English
expression *what time* (as in, *what time I am afraid, I will trust
in thee*). In Latin also **cum** may be replaced by **quō tempore,**
the exact equivalent of the more ancient English form.

REMARK. **Cum** + past indicative : **cum** + past subjunctive : :
ablative of time : ablative of attendant circumstance (cf. **128,**
REMARK: see also **59,** I and **34,** *f*).

135. Occasionally, both in English and in Latin, the leading
idea is incorporated in the time clause, while the logically subordinate idea is expressed in the principal clause. **Cum** is here
joined with the perfect or historical present indicative, and the
construction is known as **cum inversum.** This is a mere trick
of style to secure vividness of description. Thus, *when the
rear of the column was scarcely clear of the defenses, the Gauls
deliver their attack* becomes, *scarcely was the rear of the column
clear of the defenses, when the Gauls deliver their attack,* **vix agmen
novissimum extrā mūnītiōnēs prōcesserat, cum Gallī com-
mittunt proelium.**

136. Whenever, or *when* in the sense of *whenever, as often as,
every time that,* referring to repeated recurrence of an act, is
translated into Latin by **cum, ut, ubi,** or **simul atque (ac)**
joined with the indicative. The tense to be employed stands in
fixed relation to the tense of the principal clause: thus, present

indicative in principal clause, perfect indicative in dependent clause; imperfect indicative in principal clause, pluperfect indicative in dependent clause; future indicative in principal clause, future perfect indicative in dependent clause.

Whenever our cavalry came out into open country, he would send his charioteers out from the woods, **cum equitātus noster sē in agrōs ēiēcerat, essedāriōs ex silvīs ēmittēbat.**

137. Since, as a temporal particle referring to a definite past event, is usually to be translated by **ex eō tempore quō**, often condensed to **ex quō tempore**, with the perfect indicative: sometimes **postquam** is used.

Since the bridge began to be constructed, they had gone away, **ex eō tempore quō pōns īnstituī coeptus est, excesserant.**

138.   VOCABULARY

again, **rūrsus** (*emphasizes the repetition of the act*); **iterum** (*a second time*).

beginning, **initium, -ī,** *n.*

continue,[1] **permaneō,** -ēre, -mānsī, -mānsum.

memory, **memoria, -ae,** *f.*

overtake, **cōnsequor, -ī, -secū-tus.**

resolve,[2] **īnstituō, -ere, -uī, -ūtum.**

sea, **mare, maris,** *n.*

terror, **terror, -ōris,** *m.*

Synonyms. 1. remain, stay.   2. determine.

139. 1. When Caesar was compelled to start into Italy, he feared that the beginning of a new war would be made by the chiefs of the Gauls before he could again reach his army. 2. When he heard everything, he resolved to return at once; and he also sent messengers ahead to Labienus to instruct him to do his best not to lose the hostages. 3. Labienus, meanwhile, when he had persuaded the state of the Haedui to continue in their allegiance, waited until Caesar returned. 4. When I first saw the sea, I wanted to cross it. 5. The Roman army happened[1] to come into Gaul at the very time when the Hel-

vetii were getting ready to go forth from home.   6. Not within
the memory [2] of men has it happened that the Haedui did not
give grain to a Roman army when the commander demanded it.
7. When he saw me before [3] him in the camp, he immediately
said to me: " Why have you come here? "   8. When the
Roman army had arrived at the Rhine, the soldiers feared to
cross into Germany; for the Germans were of such great size
of body that our men shunned them with the utmost dread.[4]

---

9. Scarcely had he crossed the mountains, when the messengers that Labienus had sent to find him overtook him.
10. He feared the enemy would attack his column from
ambush; for since the messengers had reached him he had not
seen a single [5] Gaul.   11. This is the battle-custom [6] of all the
tribes of Gaul.   Whenever the enemy approach their ambush
they at once send out [7] their cavalry to throw the ranks into
confusion.   12. Many things have happened since I saw you.
13. Whenever Caesar takes the field against a Gallic tribe he
demands of his allies that they furnish him with grain.
14. Since Caesar has been in command of the army in Gaul
no attack has been made upon the allies of the Roman people.
15. No sooner [8] had the army crossed the river than [8] the
enemy charged them fiercely.   16. As often as Caesar sees me
he asks me to come to him in [9] camp; but I am afraid he will
detain me as a hostage.

1. **96**: translate, ' it happened that the R. army,' etc.   2. ' within the memory '; express by a case construction.   3. **apud**.   4. What
is ' dread '?   Rely on an English synonym to help you.   5. **49**, b.
6. When in English a noun (in this instance ' battle ') modifies
another noun adjectively, it is expressed in Latin by a genitive; say
' custom of battle.'   7. ' send out '; make a compound verb to
express this.   8. ' scarcely had . . . when,' etc.; **135**.   9. Watch
the case with this preposition.

LESSON XXVI

CLAUSES OF CAUSE AND CONCESSION. ADVERSATIVE CLAUSES

140. Causal clauses are introduced in English by *because, since, inasmuch as, seeing that, in view of the fact that,* etc. They are translated into Latin by clauses introduced by **cum, quod, quoniam.**

a. **Cum** causal is joined with the subjunctive. Cause and time are often inseparably connected, and the least idea of cause is sufficient to throw into the subjunctive a clause that might naturally seem to refer to time alone. *Since they could not defend themselves, they sent envoys to Caesar,* **cum sē dēfendere nōn possent, lēgātōs ad Caesarem mittunt.** This may also be expressed *when they could not defend themselves,* etc., but the motive rather than the time of the main clause is the leading idea.

b. **Quod** causal is joined with the indicative, unless the writer or speaker wishes to indicate that the cause is not stated on his own belief or claim, but on another's authority, or from another's point of view; in other words, unless the writer or speaker wishes to indicate that he is quoting another. In the latter case it is joined with the subjunctive.

This had happened because they despised the legion, **id acciderat quod legiōnem dēspiciēbant**; *he blames them because* (as he claims) *he is not assisted by them,* **eōs accūsat quod ab iīs nōn sublevētur**; *the Haedui came to complain because* (as they said) *the Harudes were ravaging their lands,* **veniēbant Haeduī questum quod Harūdēs fīnēs eōrum populārentur.**

1. **Quod** is frequently strengthened by a preceding **proptereā**, *for this reason,* with no apparent change of force.

The Belgians are the bravest because they are farthest from civilization, fortissimī sunt Belgae, proptereā quod ā cultū longissimē absunt.

c. **Quoniam** expresses a real cause, known generally, or at least known to the person addressed.

Since I cannot save myself, I will look out for your lives, quoniam mē servāre nōn possum, vestrae vītae prōspiciam.

REMARK. No rule can be given to determine which of these conjunctions one should employ in stating a real cause. When ideas of time and cause are combined, **cum** must be used: a cause stated as a claim, or on another's authority or from another's viewpoint, must be rendered by **quod** with the subjunctive. The least common causal conjunction is **quoniam.**

d. Cause may also be expressed by a subjunctive clause introduced by a relative pronoun, especially when emphasis is to be thrown upon the antecedent of the relative as responsible for the act, rather than upon the act itself.

Caesar does him a wrong, since he is diminishing his revenues, Caesar iniūriam facit, quī vectīgālia dēteriōra faciat.

141. **Concessive and adversative clauses.**

a. Concessive clauses, which grant something for the sake of argument, are introduced in English by *granting that, granted that, conceding that, though, although.* In Latin such clauses are expressed by the simple subjunctive, or by a clause with **quamvīs** and the subjunctive (the negative is **nē**).

Granted that Pompey is esteemed above all men, antepōnātur omnibus Pompēius; *conceding that there are men who hate Carbo,* quamvīs sint hominēs quī Carbōnem ōderint.

b. Adversative or obstructive clauses, which give a fact in spite of which something else (the principal clause) is true, are introduced in English by *although, though, even though, even if, in spite of the fact that.* In Latin they are introduced by **etsī** (occasionally **tametsī**), **quamquam,** and **cum. Etsī** and **tam-**

etsī are conditional in their application, expressing *although* as *even if*. They introduce statements of fact and are regularly joined with the indicative. **Cum** and **quamquam** present objective obstacles and are joined respectively with the subjunctive and with the indicative. The principal clause is often introduced by a formal *still, yet, nevertheless,* **tamen**. The negative is **nōn**.

Although in such a situation this plan is not to be criticized, still it resulted badly, quod cōnsilium etsī in eius modī cāsū reprehendendum nōn est, tamen incommodē accidit; *though Cicero himself was in very feeble health,* ipse Cicerō cum tenuissimā valētūdine esset.

a. The concessive and adversative or obstructive ideas may also be expressed by a subjunctive clause introduced by the relative pronoun when the emphasis is thrown upon the personality of the antecedent.

Though even before this he had been ill-disposed toward us, he was much more incensed, ille, quī iam ante inimīcō animō in nōs fuisset, multō gravius exārsit.

142. VOCABULARY

fail,[1] **dēficiō, -ere, -fēcī, -fectum,** *w. acc. of person (with special reference to insufficiency).*

fail,[2] **dēsum, deesse, dēfuī, -futūrus,** *w. dat. of person (with special reference to failure in duty).*

fight, **pugna, -ae,** *f.*

gratitude, **grātia, -ae,** *f.; pl.,* thanks.

kingdom,[3] **rēgnum, -ī,** *n.*

lead away,[4] **dēdūcō, -ere, -dūxī, -ductum** *(with special reference to bringing men from one place to another).*

plan,[5] (arrangement), **ratiō, -ōnis,** *f.*

power,[6] **vīs, vīs,** *f.; pl.,* strength, **vīrēs, -ium.**

revolt, **dēfectiō, -ōnis,** *f.*

rise,[7] **orior, -īrī, ortus.**

IDIOMS

express thanks, thank, **grātiās agere,** *w. dat. ind. obj. of the person* and **prō** *w. abl. of the thing*

feel (*or* show) gratitude, **grātiam referre**

Synonyms. 1. revolt from, *w.* ā *and abl.* 2. be wanting. 3. royal power. 4. bring, lead, lead down. 5. order of arrangement; condition, terms. 6. force, violence. 7. begin (*intr.*), spring up.

143. 1. Since you are constructing a wall and a moat along[1] the river, the enemy will not be able to get across.[2] 2. Caesar placed Labienus in command of the cavalry, because he had never failed him in any emergency. 3. Strength was failing the soldiers because they had fought fiercely from dawn to sunset. 4. The Helvetii were eager for revolution because they were being hard pressed by their neighbors. 5. The soldiers expressed their[3] thanks to the general because he had permitted them to remain in camp that day. 6. The enemy seem to have fled for this reason, because they feared that an attack would be made at night on their fortifications and they would not be able to hold them. 7. The revolt arose among[4] the irregular troops, because they were being led away into another province. 8. The army refused to advance farther because their supplies had failed them. 9. The kingdom of the Belgae is by far the strongest of[5] all these regions, because it is farthest away from the province. 10. The cavalry suffered a great disaster, because in their enthusiasm[6] for a fight they had advanced too far into the neighboring forest. 11. *You* have done me this great wrong because you persuaded me to fight for the supremacy of this region.

---

12. Though I have the greatest confidence in you personally,[7] I demand that you bring cavalry only to the interview, because I certainly do not trust the Roman infantry, and I will not come on any other condition.[8] 13. Though the Gauls could not be compelled by force to retire out of the province, still they were at last persuaded to give hostages to the Romans so that they would not revolt.[9] 14. Though I am dismissing the hostages for your sake, Diviciacus, I am afraid your people will

revolt.   15. Although the route has been well reconnoitered, I am nevertheless sending scouts in advance, that the enemy may not attack us from ambush.   16. Although *I* have never found a man like Caesar, many Romans do not trust him.

1. **secundum** w. acc.   2. 'get across'; condense the phrase into its real meaning.   3. Omit; **38**.   4. The idea is that of source, 'from among'; hence ā w. abl.   5. **ex** w. abl.; the force is really selective, 'out of all these regions.'   6. Abl. of cause.   7. Express by a pronoun.   8. An attendant circumstance: hence abl.   9. Expresses the purpose for which the hostages were given.

LESSON XXVII

THE PARTICIPLE AS THE EQUIVALENT OF A CLAUSE

144. Participles, both in English and in Latin, may be regarded as brief and concise equivalents of relative clauses and of subordinate clauses of various kinds, and they are freely substituted for such clauses. Thus *a routed army* is *an army which has been routed; surrounded, they cut their way out* is equivalent to *though they had been surrounded, they cut their way out; this said, he went away* is merely a brief way of saying *after he had said this, he went away* or *after this had been said, he went away.*

145. Observe carefully the following sentences:

a. The Haedui, being weakened by losses, sent envoys.

b. The Haedui being weakened by losses (inflicted by some one other than Caesar), *Caesar attacked them.*

c. The Haedui being weakened by losses (inflicted by Caesar himself), *Caesar's opportunity had come.*

d. The arrival of the Haedui being known, Caesar resolved to fight.

In *a* the participle agrees directly with a word in the main structure of the sentence; that is, *being weakened* agrees with *Haedui*, which is the subject of the sentence.

In *b* the participle agrees with a noun which is represented in the main structure of the sentence by a pronoun. That is, *being weakened* agrees with *Haedui*, which is represented in the principal clause of the sentence by *them*, the direct object. This makes possible the reconstruction of the sentence into *Caesar attacked the Haedui weakened by losses*, and the elimination of the pronoun.

In *c* and *d* the participle agrees with a noun which not only has no syntactical connection with the main structure of the sentence, but which is not represented in the principal clause in any way whatever. Both the agreement and the reference of the participles *being weakened* and *being known* are absolutely restricted to their own clauses, and the construction is the one known in English as the nominative independent. The sentences may, however, be reconstructed as follows: *now that the Haedui had been weakened by losses* (inflicted by Caesar himself), *Caesar's opportunity had come,* which is equivalent to *now that he had weakened the Haedui, Caesar had his opportunity;* and *now that he had learned of the arrival of the Haedui, Caesar resolved to fight.* In these the concise participial expressions have been expanded into their real equivalents, true causal-temporal clauses (**140**, *a*), the subjects of which, whether logical (*c*) or actual (*d*), are identical with the logical or actual subjects of the principal clauses.

In translating such sentences into Latin, the participle must be made to agree like any other adjective with the noun to which it refers, as in *a* and in *b*, and the sentences must always be reconstructed, as above, to eliminate the pronoun. If, however, as in *c* and *d*, the noun and participle are entirely independent of the main structure of the sentence, then both the participle and the noun (or pronoun) with which it agrees stand in the ablative case, and the construction is known as the **ablative absolute**.

These sentences will thus appear in Latin as follows:

   a. **Haeduī, calamitātibus frāctī, lēgātōs mīsērunt.**

   b. **Haeduōs calamitātibus frāctōs Caesar aggressus est.**

   c. **Haeduīs calamitātibus frāctīs, Caesarī facultās data est.**

   d. **Cōgnitō Haeduōrum adventū, Caesar pugnāre cōnstituit.**

REMARK. The best type of *passive ablative absolute* constructions may be determined as follows: Turn the ablative absolute into an *active* **cum** clause with the pluperfect subjunctive. Then if the subject, real or logical, of the **cum** clause is identical with that of the principal clause, the ablative absolute construction is exactly correct.

This law has, however, no reference to *active ablative absolute* constructions, as can be seen in *he was not able to take this, though few defended it*, **id paucīs dēfendentibus expugnāre nōn potuit.**

146. The use of participles as equivalents of clauses is much more extensive in Latin than in English. Any English dependent clause of **time, cause, concession, manner,** or **attendant circumstance,** or the ' **if** ' **clause of any conditional sentence,** may be expressed in Latin by a participle, in agreement or in the ablative absolute, as the circumstances may require.

147. In English the participle *being* is used very freely in the nominative independent construction (**145,** *c*); as in *his army being cowardly, he was compelled to retire.* In Latin, however, the present participle of the verb *to be*, **esse**, passed out of use (except in the compound forms **absēns** and **praesēns**, which survived as the adjectives equivalent to the English *absent* and *present*); hence the Latin forms for such expressions as involve *being* in the nominative independent show only a noun and its predicate adjective or a noun and its predicate appositive.

   Caesar being alive (i.e., *while C. was living* or *in the lifetime of C.*), **Caesare vīvō**; *Pompey and Crassus being consuls* (i.e., *in the consulship*

of P. and C.), **Pompēiō et Crassō cōnsulibus;** *Caesar being absent*
(i.e., *in the absence of C.*), **Caesare absente.**

148. The tense of a Latin participle depends wholly on its
time relation to the principal verb. Thus, in the sentences
he retreated fighting, he retreats fighting, and *he will retreat
fighting,* the same participle is used in each instance, for the
action of the participle is represented as going on at the same
time as the action of the principal verb. That is, the action of
the participle is *present* in relation to the absolute time of the
principal verb, whatever that may be, and these sentences will
respectively appear in Latin thus: **pedem rettulit pugnāns,
pedem refert pugnāns,** and **pedem referet pugnāns.**

a. In translating an English dependent clause by an ablative
absolute, if it should be found that the participle to be employed
is *past* in reference to the time of the main verb, it is clear that
the construction of the clause must be changed to the passive,
since the Latin possesses no past active participle. Thus, to
employ a participial construction in the sentence *when he had
delivered this speech, he departed,* we must view it as *when this
speech had been delivered, he departed,* which is then easily rendered
into **hāc ōrātiōne habitā, discessit.**

149.   VOCABULARY

and not, **neque (nec); nēve** (*be-fore vowels*) ; **neu** (*before conso-nants*); *the last two used chiefly to connect a neg. dependent clause (mainly of purpose) with another dependent clause in the same construction.*

besides, **praetereā.**

especially,[1] **praesertim** (*introduces and emphasizes clauses, particu-larly causal clauses*).

rout, **pellō, -ere, pepulī, pulsum.**

Synonym. 1. particularly.

150. Every sentence of this exercise must contain, in its Latin
form, at least one participial construction.

1. When he had carried the town and slain many of the

enemy, he ordered the rest to march immediately home and never [1] to return into the province.   2. After the loss of their leader and many besides, the Gauls fled routed and conquered. 3. He came in three days from his fortified camp to the mountains, no one hindering him or delaying his march.   4. After the envoys had been summoned before him, the Roman general spoke as follows.[2]   5. He pitched camp near the river and tried to finish his defensive works [3] before the scouts of the enemy found him.   6. The scout reached camp that very night, avoiding the ambuscades [4] of the enemy.   7. Though a small garrison defended the town, the troops of the enemy could not carry it.   8. He will certainly execute Dumnorix, if he should be captured.   9. From these same mountains and forests a certain general in the consulship of Pompeius and Crassus had fled with the loss of a large part of his baggage.   10. The Roman army under the command of Caesar [5] accomplished great things in Gaul.   11. Dumnorix being an enemy of the Romans, Caesar could have no great confidence in the Haeduan cavalry which he [6] commanded. 12. The enemy, who had suffered great disasters in the war, sent envoys to Caesar to beg him for peace.   13. Though the enemy [7] attacked the camp of Caesar fiercely, they accomplished nothing, so valiantly did the soldiers defend themselves and their commander.   14. For three days the soldiers retreated through the forests, defending themselves all of this time against the charges of the savages.   15. Though he captured the largest town of the enemy, he found very little plunder, since the Gauls had set fire to the houses.   16. When he had received all the hostages, Caesar set out into the lands of the Remi.

1. 'and not ever.' 2. 'as follows' = 'thus.' 3. 'defensive works' — what are they? 4. Find a synonym. 5. 'Caesar being the commander.' 6. *I.e.*, Dumnorix; make this clear by using the proper pronoun. 7. This sentence will require considerable re-

arrangement. The main verb is ' defend ': ' accomplished ' should stand in a result clause with ' enemy ' as subject, and the ' though ' clause should be expressed by an ablative absolute.

LESSON XXVIII

THE PARTICIPLE AS THE EQUIVALENT OF A CLAUSE
(CONTINUED)

151. Treatment of English active participles.

If, in an English participial expression, the present participle active or passive is employed, care must be taken before attempting to translate into Latin to determine the time of the participle relative to the time of the main verb, since English usage is very lax in this regard and the English present participle is very commonly used to express time that is really past. Thus, in the sentence *he retired fighting*, the participle is a true present; but in *raising the flag, they charged*, the raising of the signal flag necessarily preceded the charge, and the participle really expresses a past act. Again, in *Caesar, being wounded, retreated*, the participle is also past, since the wounding preceded the retreat. Furthermore, while in English the emphasis of a present passive participle rests upon the state or condition resulting from an act (in the preceding example, the condition of being incapacitated by the wound), the Latin is compelled to throw the emphasis upon the performance of the act from which the condition has resulted (here the inflicting of the wound, a past event), because there is in Latin no passive participle of continued action or state in present time. The English past active participle has likewise no counterpart in Latin. Thus the lack of a present passive participle and of a past active participle in Latin forces the recasting of English clauses containing these participles into passive participial expressions in past time, in order that we may be able to employ in the Latin version that participial construction required by Latin usage, which will generally prove to be the ablative absolute.

Cotta is slain fighting, **Cotta interficitur pugnāns;** *raising a shout, the soldiers rushed to arms,* **clāmōre sublātō, ad arma mīlitēs concurrērunt;** *this fact being known, all the troops leave,* **hāc rē cōgnitā, omnēs cōpiae discēdunt;** *having discovered some little boats, they found safety,* **lintribus inventīs, salūtem repperērunt.**

a. If the English past active participle in such a construction is from a verb whose Latin equivalent is deponent, the necessity for the ablative absolute is obviated, because the perfect participle of a deponent is generally used actively.

Having encouraged the soldiers, he began battle, **cohortātus mīlitēs, proelium commīsit.**

152. Frequently in English two clauses, coördinate in form and joined by *and,* denote acts one of which necessarily follows the other in the order of time or thought. In such cases the clause coming first in logical succession should generally be translated into Latin in participial form. The Latin, singularly sensitive to order of time or thought, sees no coördination whatever in such clauses.

They discarded their javelins and fought hand to hand with swords, **rēiectīs pīlīs, comminus gladiīs pugnātum est.**

a. This principle may be extended to two verbs expressing successive acts affecting the same direct object.

These they surround and kill, **eōs circumventōs interficiunt.**

153.   VOCABULARY

afterward, **posteā.**

cut off[1] (*in sense of* barring from), **interclūdō, -ere, -clūsī, -clūsum,** *w. dir. obj. and abl. of thing or* **ā** *and abl. of place.*

far off,[2] **procul.**

far off from, **procul ā,** *w. abl.*

inflict, **dō, dare, dedī, datum.**

space,[3] **spatium, -ī,** *n.*

work,[4] **opus, -eris,** *n.* (*of the effort put forth or its result*).

wound, **vulnerō,** I.

IDIOM

take flight, take to flight, **sē fugae mandāre** (lit., *to intrust one's self to flight*)

Synonyms. 1. debar. 2. afar, at a distance, from afar. 3. distance, extent (*both of space and time*). 4. task.

154. Every sentence of this exercise must contain, in its Latin form, at least one participial construction.

1. At length, having inflicted and received many wounds, the enemy took flight and did not halt until they had crossed the river. 2. Raising a shout afar off, the enemy charged fiercely upon our line; but at length, repulsed, they were thrown into confusion and fled, with many of their number severely wounded. 3. Hurling their javelins at our advancing men, the Gauls threw our ranks into confusion, especially since they held the commanding positions. 4. Caesar, having pursued the fleeing troops of the enemy many miles, returned into camp toward sunset. 5. Accordingly, after conferring with the leaders of the irregular troops, he started with two companies and climbed the hill. 6. He afterwards surrounded a thousand Gauls in the forest and put them to death. 7. The small garrison which defends the town, having undertaken the task with great enthusiasm, will keep the enemy from carrying the defenses. 8. Having perceived the enemy in ambush, he led his army to Geneva by another and longer route. 9. He perceived the Gauls in the forest and at once attacked them. 10. Labienus received a large army from Caesar and marched rapidly through the mountains to attack Vesontio. 11. The Haedui were alarmed by the talk of their neighbors and feared to give the Romans grain, lest all the Gauls should attack them. 12. Caesar, having delayed a few days on account of the wounds of the soldiers, pursued the retreating[1] enemy with all his troops. 13. After[2] reporting Caesar's victory to Labienus and exhorting him not to fear that the Gauls would be able, by seizing the

crops of his allies, to cut him off from supplies, the messenger at once returned to Geneva. 14. Caesar's army, after making a forced march, carried the enemy's camp, pursued them a long distance, and killed a great number of them. 15. The Gauls, being induced by the talk of the traders to make war on the Romans and not to stand firm [3] in their allegiance, were defeated with the loss of a large portion of their army. 16. Caesar, being informed of the revolt of the Gauls, set out from Ocelum and led his army by forced marches among [4] the Remi.

1. cēdentēs.   2. Use a **cum** clause.   3. **permaneō**.   4. **in** w. acc.

LESSON XXIX

THE CONDITIONAL SENTENCE

155. A complete conditional sentence consists of two clauses: an *if* clause, called the **protasis** or *conditional clause*, and a conclusion clause, called the **apodosis** or *conclusional clause*.

156. The protasis is introduced in Latin by **sī**, *if*.

a. A negative protasis is introduced by **sī nōn**, *if . . . not*, or by **nisi**, *if . . . not, unless, except*.

1. **Nisi** negatives the entire protasis. *Unless aid be sent me, I cannot hold out*, **nisi subsidium mihi submittētur, sustinēre nōn poterō**.

2. **Sī nōn** negatives a single word. *If you think it not fair, why do you demand?* **sī nōn aequum exīstimās, cūr postulās ?**

3. **Sī nōn** introduces a negative protasis when the apodosis is emphasized by **at, certē, tamen**, *at least, still, nevertheless, yet*, or by any combination of these words. *If present danger is not to be feared, starvation at least is*, **sī nōn praesēns perīculum, at certē famēs est timenda**.

4. **Nisi** introduces a negative protasis when the apodosis also is negative. *He could not stop the fortifying unless he was willing to fight,* mūnītiōnēs prohibēre nōn poterat, nisi dēcertāre vellet.

5. For sī nōn or nisi, sī minus is sometimes used, especially if the verb of the protasis is omitted altogether, as in the formula *if not,* or if the protasis is much condensed. *Storm the fort and break down the bridge; if you can't, ravage the land,* castellum expugnāte pontemque interscindite; sī minus potueritis, agrōs populāminī.

REMARK. Sī nōn and nisi are often used with no perceptible difference in meaning.

b. An affirmative protasis in contrast to another protasis preceding is introduced by sīn, *but if.* We have two fully expressed conditional sentences set off one against the other in opposition.

If you will make peace with us, we will go; but if you persist in prosecuting the war, remember, sī pācem nōbīscum faciēs, ībimus ; sīn bellō persequī persevērābis, reminīscere.

c. An alternative protasis is introduced by sīve (also written seu), *or if,* often repeated, sīve . . . sīve (seu . . . seu), *if . . . or if, whether . . . or.*

In such sentences the single conclusional clause holds true in both the cases represented in the protases.

If trunks of trees, or if boats are sent drifting down, their force will be lessened, sī arborum truncī, sīve nāvēs erunt missae, eārum rērum vīs minuētur; *the thing is easy, whether you stay or go (if you stay or if you go),* facilis rēs est, seu manēbitis, seu proficīscēminī.

1. Sīve . . . sīve also expresses an alternation, in the conditional sphere, between two nouns or any two like parts of speech. *Whether by accident or design,* sīve cāsū, sīve cōnsiliō.

2. sīve . . . sīve : sī . . . sīn :: vel . . . vel : aut . . . aut.

157. Classification of conditional sentences.

Conditional sentences may be classified both in English and in Latin according to the time in which their action lies. There are two main classes : **Present and Past Conditions** and **Future Conditions**.

REMARK. Present and Past Conditions are classified together because present and past time constitute the realm of *fact :* there are no *facts* in future time, as its developments are necessarily unknown.

I. **Present and Past Conditions** are further classified as follows :

a. **Simple Conditions,** or *neutral conditions*, which contain no implication of the falsity of the supposition. Thus, *if you and the army are (were) in good health, it is (was) well* contains no hint that you and the army are (were) *not* in good health.

b. **Contrary to Fact Conditions,** in which it is implied by the form of expression that the supposition is false. *If our commander were here, we should be in no danger:* here the very form of expression *implies* (whether truly or falsely is immaterial) that the commander *is not* present and that we *are now* in danger. The condition clearly lies in *present time.* So also consider *if our commander had been present, we should not have been in danger:* here it is evidently *implied* that on some past occasion the commander *was not* present and that we *were then* in danger. The condition clearly lies in *past time.*

II. **Future Conditions** are further classified as follows :

a. **More Vivid,** in which the supposed future case is distinctly and vividly stated, the apodosis expressing what *will be* the logical result. *If the troops come, the siege will be raised.* (Note the apparent present tense characteristic of the English apodosis of this class, though the reference is clearly to the future.)

b. **Less Vivid,** in which the supposed future case is stated, not distinctly and vividly, but as remotely possible ; the apodosis expressing what *would be* the result in the case supposed. *If the troops should come, the siege would be raised.*

158. Forms of the conditional sentence in Latin.

English conditions of the various classes are to be translated into Latin in accordance with the following table:

Mode and Tense Usage in the Latin Conditional Sentence	**PRESENT AND PAST CONDITIONS**	*Simple.* Any required present or past tense of the indicative in both protasis and apodosis. Any imperative or hortatory form may stand in the apodosis. *Contrary to Fact.* Present time. Imperfect subjunctive in both protasis and apodosis. Past time. Pluperfect subjunctive in both protasis and apodosis.
	FUTURE CONDITIONS	*More Vivid.* Future indicative in both protasis and apodosis: but if the action of the protasis must be completed before the action of the apodosis can occur, the future perfect indicative stands in the protasis. Any form denoting or implying future time may stand in the apodosis of a future condition; as the imperative, either periphrastic form, and verbs of *necessity, possibility*, and the like. *Less Vivid.* Present subjunctive in both protasis and apodosis: but if the action of the protasis must be completed before the action of the apodosis can occur, the perfect subjunctive stands in the protasis. The apodosis variations noted for the more vivid condition may also occur in the less vivid.

Examples

Simple Conditions

If you and the army are (were) in good health, it is (was) well, sī tū exercitusque valētis (valuistis), bene est (fuit); *if you wish, come with us*, sī vultis, nōbīscum venīte.

Contrary to Fact Conditions

PRESENT TIME.   *If our commander were here, we would be in no danger,*
sī imperātor noster adesset, in perīculō nōn essēmus.

PAST TIME.   *If our commander had been present, we would not have
been in danger,* sī imperātor noster adfuisset, in perīculō nōn
fuissēmus.

Future Conditions

MORE VIVID.   *If the troops come, the siege will be raised,* sī cōpiae
venient, obsidiō dīmittētur; *if I capture the deserters, I will hold
them,* sī perfugās comprehenderō, eōs retinēbō (they must be
caught before they can be imprisoned.   The Latin is very exact
in its tense usage; the English, correspondingly careless); *if I see
the enemy, I intend to pursue them,* sī hostēs vidēbō, eōs persecū-
tūrus sum; *if I see the enemy, I shall be able to overtake them,* sī
hostēs vidēbō, eōs cōnsequī poterō.

LESS VIVID.   *If the troops should come, the siege would be raised,* sī
cōpiae veniant, obsidiō dīmittātur; *if I should capture the deserters,
I would hold them,* sī perfugās comprehenderim, eōs retineam.

Bennett's Classification of Conditional Sentences

The classification of conditional sentences given in **157–158** is
that of Allen and Greenough, and is here adopted because
identical with Goodwin's classification of conditional sentences
in Greek.   It is considered very advantageous to the student
that he shall have the same class of sentences in the two ancient
languages presented in the same way in each.   Many teachers,
however, prefer and have adopted the classification of Bennett,
and for such **B 157** and **B 158** have been prepared.   Those,
therefore, who prefer these paragraphs will omit **157** and **158**.

B 157.   The basis of classification in this system is the reality
of the supposed case, and the time element does not enter as
a consideration into the main divisions.   There are three
main classes or types:

First Type. *Nothing is implied as to the reality of the supposed case, and the condition may lie either in present, past, or future time.* Thus, *if you and the army are (were) in good health, it is (was) well* contains no implication of the state of health of the persons spoken of, and especially no implication that they are (or were) not in good health. So, *if the troops come, the siege will be raised* contains no hint as to whether or not the troops will come.

Second Type. *The supposed case is represented as contingent.* Here of necessity the condition lies in future time. The apodosis expresses what *would be* the result in the contingency indicated by the protasis; as in *if the troops should come, the siege would be raised.*

Third Type. *The supposed case is represented as contrary to fact.* The time of conditions of this type may be either present or past. Thus, in the sentences *if our commander were here, we should be in no danger* and *if our commander had been present, we should have been in no danger,* the language clearly *implies* (whether truly or falsely is immaterial) that the commander *is not* or *was not* present on the occasion alluded to.

B 158. Forms of the conditional sentences in Latin.

First Type. Any tense of the indicative demanded by the sense may be used in both protasis and apodosis. Any imperative or hortatory form, either periphrastic form, and verbs of *necessity*, *possibility*, and the like may stand in the apodosis when the sense demands it.

Second Type. The present subjunctive regularly stands in both protasis and apodosis; but if the action of the protasis must be completed before the action of the apodosis can occur, the perfect subjunctive stands in the protasis.

Third Type. The subjunctive regularly stands in both protasis and apodosis, the imperfect referring to *present time*, and the pluperfect referring to *past time*.

Examples. The student should take the examples given under **158** and refer each to its appropriate type.

159.   VOCABULARY

endure, **perferō, -ferre, -tulī, -lātum.**

enter,[1] **ineō, -īre, -īvī (-iī), -itum.**

extend,[2] **pertineō, -ēre, -uī, -tentum (— to, ad** w. *acc.*).

fortune,[3] **fortūna, -ae,** f.

short,[4] **brevis, -e.**

wing (of army), **cornū, -ūs,** n. (*lit.*, horn).

yield,[5] **cēdō, -ere, cessī, cessum.**

IDIOMS

conduct one's self,[6] **sē gerere**

form a plan, **cōnsilium inīre** (lit., *enter a plan*)

on the right wing, **ā dextrō cornū**

Synonyms. 1. begin, enter upon, form (a plan *or* course of action). 2. pertain, reach, tend. 3. lot, luck. 4. brief. 5. retreat. 6. behave.

160.[1] 1. If the troops on the right wing are standing firm, all is well. 2. In the same manner he drew up the left wing of the battle line; for unless cavalry is stationed on both wings, there is no protection to the flanks of the entire army. 3. If the general forms any plan about the route, we shall start at dawn with the entire column. 4. If a bridge did not reach to the lands of the Helvetii, we should be unable[2] to cross the river without boats. 5. If our battle line had been drawn up at a greater distance[3] from the mountains, the enemy would have had much less confidence in their commanding position. 6. If the lot of the Sequani were not harder than (that) of the rest, they would not have come here to complain of[4] it to Caesar. 7. If the enemy should delay for a brief space, until Caesar returns, we would defeat them easily; but if they should attack us now, we would be in very great danger. 8. If you can endure any fortune, whether favorable or adverse, you are a brave man. 9. If you are coming to see me to-morrow, I shall stay at home to wait for you. 10. Unless you behave differently

from what I have seen, I shall be compelled to dismiss you.
11. If you have weapons enough, send me a few.   12. If you do
not at once seize the top of the mountain, you will be compelled
to retire.   13. If your line shall extend to the river bank, the
river itself will defend you on that wing.   14. If you finish the
work of the fortifications before the enemy makes an attack
upon you, you can hold out a long time, for you have enough
provisions for the army.   15. I shall not join battle with the
enemy unless the commander arrives to-morrow.   16. If you
will not retreat, fight; for if you fight with me, I can whip you.

1. The sentences involving negative conditions in this exercise
may well be omitted with second-year students.   2. ' not be able.'
3. Abl., **34**, *f*.   4. **dē**.

LESSON XXX

THE CONDITIONAL SENTENCE (Continued)

161. **Mixed conditions.**
The protasis and the apodosis may lie in different times of
the same class, or even in different classes; but each clause
conforms strictly to the laws of its own time and class.   The
condition is then called a mixed condition.

If our commander had lived, we should now be free, **sī imperātor
noster superfuisset, līberī nunc essēmus;** *if I am not mistaken, he
will make a night attack on you*, **nisi fallor, vōs noctū aggrediētur.**

162. **Conditional clauses of comparison,** or *clauses of im-
aginative comparison*.
Clauses akin to conditions are those introduced by *as if, just
as if*, and called conditional clauses of comparison.   They are
introduced in Latin by **velut sī, ac sī, quam sī,** and have the
verb in the subjunctive, its tense being determined by the law
of sequence of tenses and not by the apparent class of the
condition.

They dreaded (dread) the cruelty of Ariovistus, though he was (is) absent, just as if he were present before them, **absentis Ariovistī crū-dēlitātem, velut sī cōram adesset (adsit), horrēbant (horrent).**

163. The protasis of any condition may be:
a. Implied, either by the context or in some special word.

Otherwise (implying if this had not been so) the Carnutes would not have adopted the plan, **neque aliter Carnūtēs cōnsilium cēpissent.**

b. Expressed by a participle, either (1) in agreement with a noun or pronoun in the main structure of the sentence, or (2) in the ablative absolute.

1. *Punishment must overtake him if condemned*, **damnātum poenam sequī oportēbat;** 2. *They will not be able to defend themselves if they give up their arms*, **sē dēfendere, trāditīs armīs, nōn poterunt.**

c. When a negative protasis is expressed by a participle or by an ablative absolute, the participle is preceded by **nisi.**

He had forbidden the lieutenants to leave unless the camp was forti-fied, **lēgātōs discēdere nisi mūnītīs castrīs vetuerat.**

REMARK. Similar implied and condensed protases occur in English, the condensed form usually being a participial phrase or a verbal introduced by *unless, except, without having, without being*, etc.; but it is not these alone that may be thus expressed in Latin.

164.   VOCABULARY

departure, **discessus, -ūs,** *n.*
hasten,[1] **contendō, -ere, -ndī, -ntum** (*to act quickly after starting*); **mātūrō,** I (*to start promptly*).
obtain[2] (a request), **impetrō,** I.

station[3] (troops), **dispōnō, -ere, -posuī, -positum** (*with special reference to tactical distribution*); **collocō,** I (*with special reference to locating a tactical unit, such as a cohort or a legion*).

Synonyms. 1. hurry. 2. gain a point, gain a request. 3. arrange, dispose, distribute.

165. Though many of the sentences in this exercise seem perfectly regular, each one should be written to illustrate some one of the peculiarities explained in this lesson. Usually the peculiarity is obvious, but think carefully over each sentence.

1. Are the troops on the right wing standing firm? If not, I will send two companies to their assistance. 2. I was compelled for many reasons to delay in the lands of the Remi. Otherwise I should have arrived here ten days ago. 3. If called to arms, we shall rally [1] to the standards as quickly as possible. 4. Did the messenger come to see *me?* If not, I shall not speak with him. 5. If you have not well fortified your camp, the enemy will certainly take it by storm. 6. I never allow men to seek rest from their labors without having stationed sentries. 7. If Ariovistus had defeated Caesar, the Germans would to-day be powerful in Rome itself. 8. If not already routed by Labienus, the Helvetii will soon arrive at this very hill to attack our one legion stationed far from the rest. 9. The enemy, if they have been informed of Caesar's departure, will hasten to attack [3] his winter camp. 10. Caesar hastened to Vesontio with all his troops and arrived there in three days. But for this,[4] the enemy would have captured all the grain there collected. 11. Unless Caesar be immediately informed of the Gauls' departure, he cannot overtake them. 12. You always advance bravely to the attack, just as if you surpassed the enemy in number. 13. They did their best to finish the work, just as if Caesar himself had been in command of them that day. 14. I shall attack Ariovistus fiercely, just as if the Germans were no braver than the Gauls. 15. I had forbidden the lieutenant to engage [5] the enemy if he were not in a commanding position. 16. The commander will never return home to Rome if he does not conquer the Gauls.

1. What does ' rally ' really mean? 2. ' in the city Rome itself.' 3. **85**, III, *a.* 4. Watch this phrase; analyze carefully and find a synonym. 5. Translate the meaning; do not be perplexed by mere form.

LESSON XXXI

SPECIAL IDIOMS IN VERB CONSTRUCTION

166. **Command and prohibition.**

a. A command is expressed in Latin by the imperative mode. Any command may, as in English, be accompanied by **tū, vōs,** or the vocative of a noun.

Leap down, fellow soldiers, **dēsilīte, commīlitōnēs.**

1. A command, in Latin as in English, is often put in the softened form of a request. The verb indicating the command (or request) is then in the subjunctive depending on the imperative of **cūrō, faciō, videō,** either alone or joined with **ut** (**89**), or on **volō** or **velim.** These expressions are equivalent to *see that you do, take care to do, I want you to do, I should like you to do* the thing requested.

See that you be a man, **cūrā ut vir sīs.**

b. The imperative cannot, in prose Latin, express a prohibition (negative command). Prohibitions in the second person are generally expressed by **nōlī** (pl., **nōlīte,** imperative of **nōlō**) with infinitive, by **cavē** (**cavēte,** imperative of **caveō,** *be on guard* or *beware*) followed by **nē** and the subjunctive, or by a subjunctive joined with **nē** and depending on a verb of requesting. (This last is a virtual, not a formal prohibition.)

Do not blunder, **nōlī committere** (lit., *do not wish to blunder*); *see that you do not go,* **cavē nē eās;** *I beg you not to pass too severe a sentence,* **obsecrō tē nē quid gravius statuās.**

167. Intention and likelihood.

Such expressions as *intend to, propose to, about to, going to, likely to,* etc., are translated into Latin by the forms of the active periphrastic conjugation.

What they were going to carry with them (or *intended to carry*), **quod sēcum portātūrī erant.**

168. Obligation and necessity.

Such expressions as *am to, deserve to, have to, must, ought to, should* (expressing duty), etc., are frequently translated into Latin by the forms of the passive periphrastic conjugation. These forms are always passive, and active English sentences of this kind must be recast into passive form in order to admit of being rendered by the periphrastic conjugation. The person on whom the obligation rests stands in the dative. This use of the dative is called the *Dative of Agent.*

Caesar had to do everything, **Caesarī omnia erant agenda** (lit., *everything was to be done by Caesar*).

a. The passive periphrastic of an intransitive verb is impersonal.

He decided that he must hurry, **mātūrandum sibi cēnsuit** (lit., *that haste-must-be-made by him*).

b. In the expression *ought to,* if the emphasis is on the sense of duty one feels or should feel toward a superior or to a principle, **dēbeō** with the infinitive is used. If moral or social obligation in general is expressed, existing whether felt or not, the impersonal **oportet** is used with the accusative and infinitive.

They fought fiercely, as brave men ought to have fought, **pugnātum ācriter est, ut ā virīs fortibus pugnārī dēbuit**; *they were able to decide for themselves what ought to be done,* **quid fierī oportēret ipsī sibi praescrībere poterant.**

c. Expressions depending on the verbs of duty, **dēbeō** and **oportet,** which involve the English perfect infinitive, employ the present infinitive in Latin, and the verb of duty or obligation is put in the perfect tense.

So that their lands ought not to have been laid waste, **ita ut agrī vāstārī nōn dēbuerint.**

REMARK. This idiom corresponds exactly to the incorrect English, often heard, *I had ought to go* for *I ought to have gone.*

169.   VOCABULARY

call,[1] **appellō, I.**

consume,[2] **cōnsūmō, -ere, -sūmpsī, -sūmptum.**

go forth,[3] **excēdō, -ere, -cessī, -cessum.**

one must,[4] **oportet, -ēre, -uit, —,** *impers., w. acc. and pres. inf.*

owe, ought, **dēbeō, -ēre, -uī, -itum,** *w. pres. inf.*

provide,[5] **prōvideō, -ēre, -vīdī, -vīsum;** *w. acc. and dat.; when intr., w. dat. of ref.; in verb construction, w. clause of purpose.*

Synonyms. 1. name. 2. destroy, use up. 3. depart, go out, leave (*intr.*). 4. one ought, it is necessary. 5. see that, see to, take care to.

170. 1. You ought not to have left the enemy's cavalry an approach to the camp. 2. You should never call yourself brave, nor boast of your achievements in war. 3. You must always construct a moat in front of the camp wall, even though your camp be pitched in a forest where there are many trees for an attacking force to fill this moat up with.[1] 4. Not only must you attack the camp to-day, but afterward you must also march against those chiefs who have fled far off into the mountains. 5. The army is going to march out of camp with a great pack train [2] and much baggage. 6. I intend to provide at once a supply of grain for my army, so as not to delay its departure against the Germans. 7. By right of war I propose [3] to seize the government of these provinces. 8. The reason for his departure was that [4] he proposed himself to march into these regions, sending all the cavalry quickly ahead. 9. I am going to leave to the enemy not even a single sword to fight with. 10. If I have to hasten into Gaul, give me three days to prepare. 11. If I've got to go, I'm going to go not only with plenty of supplies but with a pack train.

-----

12. Do not fortify your camp with a wall only, for fear [5] that the enemy will find some approach to it. 13. Do not proceed too far for fear your baggage will be lost. 14. Do not demand

more than you ought, and I am not afraid that you will not obtain your request.   15. You ought not to delay until all the crops of your allies are destroyed: attack the advancing enemy at once.   16. Don't try to leave us here alone in the midst of the enemy, for we're not going to stay: we're going to follow you.

1. Arrange to form a relative clause of purpose.   2. Devise a phrase for this: a pack train, of course, consists of horses or mules carrying packs.   3. ' I propose '; what is the real meaning ? 4. **quod**; **117**, *a*, 1.   5. **122**, *b*, 2.

LESSON XXXII

SPECIAL IDIOMS IN VERB CONSTRUCTION (CONTINUED)

171. Permission.

Expressions of permission, *you may, it is allowed, it is permitted*, etc., are regularly translated by the impersonal verb **licet** with the dative of the person to whom the permission is given and the infinitive of the act permitted. The person granting the permission is expressed by **per** with the accusative. The noun *permission*, so frequent in English, is not used in Latin: thus, *to ask permission* is *to ask that it be permitted; to grant permission* is either *to permit* (**patior**) or *to grant that one may ;* such a phrase as *you have my permission* is rendered *it is permitted to you through me.*

They asked permission to call a council, **petiērunt ut sibi concilium indīcere licēret**; *if you should permit*, **sī patiāris** or **sī per tē liceat.**

172. Ability.

Expressions of ability, *am able, can*, are translated by **possum** with the infinitive.

Nor, crowded as they were, could they avoid the spears, **neque tēla cōnfertī vītāre poterant.**

a. When **possum** is modified by **nōn**, the word order is always *infinitive, negative,* **possum**.

The ships could not ride except in deep water, **nāvēs nisi in altō cōnstituī nōn poterant.**

b. After the modal auxiliary verbs **licet** and **possum**, the infinitive usage conforms to **168,** *c.*

Here one might have seen a sudden reversal of fortune, **hīc subitam commūtātiōnem fortūnae vidēre licuit.**

c. If one of the modal auxiliaries is the apodosis verb of a past contrary to fact condition (**158**), it regularly stands in the perfect indicative in accordance with the above idiom.

Had he so desired, he could have escaped, **sī ita voluisset, perfugere potuit.**

173. Need.

Expressions of need, *I need, there is need,* are translated into Latin by the verb phrase **opus est.** The person who needs stands in the dative of reference. If the thing needed can be represented by a neuter pronoun, it stands as the subject of **est** (or **sunt** if plural), **opus** remaining unchanged in case and number. If the thing needed is a noun, it stands in the ablative of specification. A verbal noun or a brief phrase indicating an act needed is usually expressed by the ablative of the perfect participle. That for which a thing is needed is expressed by **ad** with the accusative.

If he needed anything, he would have come, **sī quid ipsī opus esset,** **vēnisset;** *whatever was needed for the siege,* **quaecumque ad oppugnātiōnem opus sunt;** *what need have I of citizenship?* **quid mihi cīvitāte opus est?** *if anything needed to be done,* **sī quid factō opus esset.**

a. When a need or necessity is indicated in English by a clause governing a verb construction, it is expressed in Latin by **necesse est** with an accusative or dative of the person and the infinitive. Such clauses are often indicated in English by the adverb *necessarily* or by some equivalent word or phrase.

Victory necessarily consists in the death of brave men, **fortium morte necess? est cōnstāre victōriam**; *we need not hurry to Gergovia*, **nōn necesse est nōbis Gergoviam contendere.**

174.   VOCABULARY

act, **agō, -ere, ēgī, āctum.**
also,[1] **quoque** (*adds a count or detail*).
consult,[2] **cōnsulō, -ere, -uī, -sultum** (*absol.; w. acc. of pers.*, to ask advice; *w. dat. of pers.*, to consult his interest, to take thought for*).
the day before (*adv.*), **prīdiē.**

necessarily, **necessāriō;** *often expressed by* **necesse est.**
need, **opus,** *indecl.*
there is need,[3] **opus est; necesse est.**
it is permitted,[4] **licet, -ēre, -uit (licitum est).**
visit,[5] **adeō, -īre, -īvī (-iī), -itum,** *takes acc. w. or without* **ad.**

IDIOM

ask permission to, **rogāre ut liceat,** *w. dat. of pers. and inf.*

Synonyms. 1. too. 2. deliberate, take counsel. 3. it is necessary, one needs. 4. it is allowed, one may. 5. go to.

175. 1. What do you need from me to-day? I need to be informed at once of your plans. 2. We need men and weapons for the siege immediately. 3. May we break camp and start for Ocelum to-day? 4. Yes; you might have started yesterday if you had been ready. 5. If you had sent forward scouts and had seized the top of the mountain, you could have defeated the enemy easily. 6. You will certainly be able to see the sea from the top of the hill. 7. Alarmed by the surrender of their friends, they necessarily retired across the river for fear[1] that they too would be unable to resist us. 8. They had been able to build in three days this great bridge, which they had needed for the safety of their forces. 9. You may take what you need and as much as you need. 10. You might have seen your friend here, if you had arrived two hours ago. 11. You seem able to show courage whenever there is need. 12. Your army needs action, not deliberation. 13. If you should be allowed to go to Rome to-morrow, what would you do there? 14. You can send him a letter by one of these messengers if there is need of haste. 15. You may dispose your troops as you please; but try to place them to the advantage of the republic.

---

16. But start as soon as you can and march to the bank of the Rhine: pitch camp there in a suitable place and wait three days: then, starting at dawn every day, advance twenty miles from where you halted the day before.

1. **Nē** . . . **nōn** is used if the verb of fear is negative, or if the negative in the dependent clause emphasizes a particular word.

LESSON XXXIII

CORRELATION

176. Groups of words presenting the same idea in different relations are called **correlatives**. Thus the *size* or *quantity* idea may be presented **interrogatively**, *how great?* **indefinitely**, *rather great;* **demonstratively**, *so great;* **relatively**, *as great as;* and as a **relative indefinite**, *however great*. These ideas are expressed in Latin by words from the same root, varying in prefix and suffix. Thus the correlatives of the size idea, as presented above, are **quantus? aliquantus; tantus; quantus; quantuscumque.**

177. The clause following a demonstrative correlative, of whatever meaning, is introduced in English simply by *as;* in Latin it must be introduced by a relative word of kindred meaning. The Latin cannot say simply *my house is as large as yours;*

it must be thought of as *my house is so-large, as-large-as yours,* **mea domus tanta est quanta tua**; so also, *that the enemy might be injured as much as the soldiers could injure (them),* **ut tantum hostibus nocērētur quantum mīlitēs efficere poterant.**

a. *As* or *that* following *the same* must be expressed in Latin by the relative pronoun.

They did not exhibit the same energy as in fights on land, **nōn eōdem studiō, quō in pedestribus proeliīs ūtēbantur.**

b. Apparent correlative expressions involving *as* with an adjective or adverb and a verb of ability or possibility are really superlative expressions of the nature of **69,** *c.*

Having laid in supplies as quickly as he was able, **rē frūmentāriā quam celerrimē potuit comparātā.**

c. The demonstrative member of a demonstrative-relative correlation is sometimes not expressed.

He pursued the enemy as far as the time of day permitted, **secūtus hostēs quantum diēī tempus est passum** (the full form would have been *pursued so-far, as-far-as,* **tantum, quantum**).

178. A few of the more important groups of correlatives are here given in the same order as above: interrogative; indefinite; demonstrative; relative; relative indefinite. Other groups may readily be developed as need arises.

Person: **quis,** *who?* **aliquis,** *some one;* **hīc,** *this one;* **quī,** *who;* **quī-cumque,** *whoever.*

Place where: **ubi,** *where?* **alicubi,** *somewhere;* **ibi,** *there;* **ubi,** *where;* **ubicumque,** *wherever.*

Place whence: **unde,** *whence?* **alicunde,** *from somewhere;* **inde,** *thence;* **unde,** *whence;* **undecumque,** *whencesoever.*

Place whither: **quō,** *whither?* **aliquō,** *somewhere;* **eō, hūc,** *thither, hither;* **quō,** *whither;* **quōcumque,** *whithersoever.*

Time: **quandō,** *when?* **aliquandō,** *some time;* **nunc, iam, tum,** *now, then;* **quandō,** *when;* **quandōcumque,** *whenever.*

179.   VOCABULARY

.ormer, **superior, -ius;   prior,**
  prius.

repair, **reficiō, -ere, -fēcī, -fectum.**

so [1] (*adv.*), **tam** (*w. adj. and adv.
  only*); **sīc** (*w. verbs only*);
  ita (*w. verbs, adj., adv.*).

so far, **tantum.**

so great, **tantus, -a, -um.**

so long (time), **tam diū.**

so much (*adv.*), **tantum.**

so often, **totiēns.**

such (kind), **tālis, -e;** *also* **eius
  modī** (cf. **106**).

the . . . the (*w. comp.*), **quantō
  . . . tantō; eō . . . quō** (*abla-
  tives of degree of difference*).

Idioms

be displeased at, **graviter ferre** (*always of a thing or act as obj., never
    a person*)

intend,[2] **in animō esse,** *w. a dat. of ref. of the person and the inf.*

recover from, **sē recipere ex,** *w. abl.*

Synonyms. 1. thus. 2. have the intention, have in mind, propose.

180. 1. The plan of battle of the Gauls is the same as that
of the Belgians. It is this: they stand firm in the same position
until the enemy advance; then they rush out and charge them
as fiercely as they can. 2. This place is as unfavorable for a
battle as any place that I have ever seen. 3. Our commander
is such a man as all commanders ought to be. 4. The more
fiercely the enemy attacked us, the more bravely our troops
resisted, until at last they drove them away with ranks in confusion. 5. This small band which he had sent forward advanced as far as the forces of the enemy had gone, and then
encamped. 6. As long as the enemy fought, so long our soldiers
had no rest from their labors. 7. The more displeased he became [1] at what the enemy were doing, the less he was able to
stop them. 8. As often as any company charged, so often it
had to retire fighting. 9. I intend to attack the enemy as
fiercely as I can. 10. The Romans intended to march through
the lands of the Cimbri, doing as much damage as they had

themselves done to the province. 11. As long as Caesar remains with the army, so long it has no fear. 12. A great disaster has befallen the enemy, such as they cannot recover from in many months. 13. These are the same wagons that we used in our former march against the Helvetii; the oftener you repair them, the less likely[2] are you to use them. 14. The more you thank me for what I have done, the less likely am I to do it for you again. 15. I advise you to march with as much speed as you can; for the faster you go, the better[3] it will please me. 16. Either go by the same route as before or by some shorter one.

1. Express by the tense employed in the idiom. 2. **167.** 3. **magis.**

LESSON XXXIV

THE ENGLISH VERBAL IN –ING

181. English expressions involving the use of the verbal in *-ing* are, in general, translated into Latin, in the oblique cases, by the gerund or by the gerundive participle.

a. The verbal in *-ing* is rarely used in the nominative or as a simple objective. When it is so used, it must be rendered into Latin by a present infinitive. *Reading is useful* is the same as *to read is useful;* so, *I like reading* is equivalent to *I like to read.*

182. The gerund and the gerundive as equivalents of the verbal in *-ing*.

a. If the verbal is not syntactically connected with a noun, it is represented by the gerund.

I will take a day for deliberating, **diem ad dēlīberandum sūmam.**

b. If the verbal governs an object, the gerund is sometimes used governing an object; but most frequently the object noun itself assumes the case relation of the verbal, and the gerundive participle stands in agreement with this noun.

More ready for facing danger, **ad perīcula subeunda parātiōrēs** (lit., *more ready for dangers to-be-faced*).

c. There is no difference in meaning between the gerund and the gerundive constructions, and they are generally interchangeable; but no gerund governed by a preposition can itself govern a noun : in this case a gerundive must be used instead. Thus we translate *he devoted himself to writing* by **sē contulit ad scrībendum**, a gerund; but *he devoted himself to writing verse* must be expressed by **sē contulit ad versūs scrībendōs**, a gerundive; **ad scrībendum versūs** would be barbarous.

d. The gerundive when used with the genitive of the personal pronouns admits no distinction of gender or number. (Cf. **85**, III, *b*, 1 and example.)

183. Case relations of the verbal.

a. When the verbal in English stands in a phrase modifying a noun or completing the meaning of an adjective, it is expressed in Latin by the genitive of the gerund or gerundive.

A chance of standing (i.e., *a chance to stand*), **cōnsistendī potestās**; *fond of fighting* (or *of warfare*), **cupidī bellandī**.

b. When the verbal indicates a purpose or motive, introduced by *for*, *for the purpose of*, *for the sake of*, etc., one of the purpose constructions of the gerund or gerundive is employed (**85**, III, *a*, *b*).

For the carrying out of these plans Orgetorix is chosen, **ad eās rēs cōnficiendās Orgetorix dēligitur.**

c. When the verbal (or an infinitive) in English depends on a verb of tendency or on an adjective of fitness or preparation, it is expressed in Latin by **ad** with the accusative of the gerund or gerundive.

Which tend to weaken the character, **quae ad effēminandōs animōs pertinent;** *in a place suitable for drawing up a line*, **locō ad aciem** īnstruendam idōneō (cf. **17**, and note the difference when the adjective of fitness governs a single noun without a verbal).

d. When the verbal expresses cause, manner, means, etc., the ablative of the gerund or gerundive is used in the Latin, either alone or with the appropriate preposition.

Busy reaping, in **metendō occupātī**; *by passing along weapons and by carrying turf,* **tēlīs subministrandīs et caespitibus comportandīs.**

1. The same clause or phrase in English may sometimes be translated into Latin either by the ablative of the gerund or gerundive or by the ablative absolute. If the emphasis of thought rests on the act, use the gerund or gerundive; if the emphasis rests on the time or circumstances of the act, use the ablative absolute.

e. The English infinitive governed by a noun is expressed in Latin by the gerund or gerundive (usually in the genitive), especially if in English the verbal in *-ing* may replace the infinitive.

An opportunity to fight (i.e., *an opportunity of fighting*), **pugnandī potestās.**

184.   VOCABULARY

attend to,[1] **administrō,** I.

busy,[2] **occupātus, -a, -um,** *w.* in *and abl.*

but (*in sense of* except), **nisi.**

magistrate, **magistrātus, -ūs,** *m.*

necessary (*adj.*), **necessārius, -a, -um,** *w. dat. of pers.;* **ad** *and acc. of thing or act.*

opportunity,[3] **facultās, -tātis,** *f.*

power,[3] **potestās, -tātis,** *f.*

surrender,[4] **dēdō, -ere, -didī, -ditum; trādō, -ere, -didī, -ditum;** *always tr.; the intr. Eng. use requires a reflexive pron. object in Latin.*

tower, **turris, -is,** *f.*

IDIOMS

give opportunity, **facultātem dare** *or* **potestātem facere,** *w. dat. of pers. and gen. of thing or act*

present an appearance,[5] **speciem praestāre**

Synonyms. 1. administer, carry out (orders). 2. engaged in, occupied in. 3. chance (*in sense of* opportunity), permission. *The two Latin words are practically interchangeable.* 4. give up. 5. give an impression, make a show.

185. 1. Caesar had given the necessary orders,[1] but his men had no opportunity to carry them out. 2. The soldiers had no chance to make a stand on the wall, for the enemy were hurling a swarm of javelins over it. 3. The enemy had built an earthwork for the purpose of protecting[2] themselves from the attacks of our men. 4. In a place suitable by nature for drawing up a line of battle, they at last halted and resisted bravely as long as they could. 5. They gave the impression of fighting by carrying weapons to whatever part of the line they were ordered and by leading the wounded out of the fight. 6. By moving forward[3] a tower against[4] the wall, they enabled us to take the city much more quickly than any one supposed possible. 7. We have reported to you our achievements for the purpose of comparing ourselves with those other auxiliaries who do nothing else[5] but make a show of fighting. 8. We are fond of surpassing our allies in fighting. 9. The soldiers were busy building fortifications when the enemy attacked them sharply. 10. Daily drawing up his line of battle in front of their camp, he gave them the chance to fight. 11. All this[6] tends to make the minds of men savage. 12. By feeding your pack animals well, you can render them capable[7] of the greatest labor. 13. The place is most unfavorable for pitching a camp, for it is at the edge of a swamp which affords us no chance of obtaining provisions from the region behind us. 14. The enemy tried to drive us from our intrenchments[8] by collecting trees with which to fill up the moat and by hurling javelins over the wall. 15. By finding a place suitable for pitching camp, the scouts will enable us to obtain a whole night's[9] rest, which we need greatly. 16. By marching all day and the greater[10] part of the night, the men were greatly exhausted; but nevertheless this forced march compelled the magistrates to surrender the town to us at once.

1. 'had ordered the necessary things': when in English a noun phrase is used with verbal force, the verb whose idea the noun expresses is usually employed in Latin. 2. 'defending.' 3. Make a compound verb out of the two ideas 'move' and 'forward.' 4. **ad**. 5. 'no other thing' or 'nothing other.' 6. Plural. 7. Cf. **106**, example. 8. Find a synonym. 9. Say 'a rest of a whole night'; see **106**. 10. Superlative in Latin.

LESSON XXXV

TREATMENT OF THE ENGLISH INFINITIVE

186. The chief uses of the infinitive in English are:

a. To complete the meaning of another verb; the complementary infinitive.

b. As the subject or object of another verb.

In both these uses it is translated by the infinitive in Latin.

a. He hastened to set out from the city, **ab urbe proficīscī mātūrāvit**; *b. it is better to suffer than to be killed*, **praestat patī quam interficī**; *I wish to go*, **īre volō**.

187. Subject of the infinitive.

Contrary to English usage, the infinitive in Latin takes a subject freely, and this subject stands in the accusative case. The infinitive with subject accusative, as well as the simple infinitive, may stand in Latin as the subject or object of a verb or as an appositive.

For the Germans to grow accustomed to cross the Rhine was dangerous, he perceived, to the Roman people, **Germānōs cōnsuēscere Rhēnum trānsīre populō Rōmānō perīculōsum vidēbat**; *he orders Crassus to set out*, **Crassum proficīscī iubet**; *it seemed best to send Procillus*, **commodissimum vīsum est Procillum mittere**.

a. A neuter adjective may agree with an infinitive in Latin, or with an infinitive and its subject. Cf. **187**, first and third examples.

b. The nearest approach the English makes to a subject of the infinitive is in such expressions as *for him to do this is an advantage to us*, where *him* is really the subject of *to do* and the whole infinitive phrase introduced by *for* is the logical subject of *is;* and also where a noun or pronoun is associated with an object infinitive, as in *I order you to go*. Cf. **187**, first and second examples.

c. In narrative Latin the present infinitive with subject nominative is sometimes used to express continued or repeated action in past time, as a substitute for the imperfect indicative, to secure swiftness and vividness of style. This construction is called the historical infinitive.

Day after day the Haedui kept putting off, **diem ex diē dūcere Haeduī.**

188. *a.* Many of the verbs which in English take an object infinitive are construed with a subjunctive clause in Latin (cf. **89**).

b. Verbs which in English in the active voice take an object infinitive with a noun as its subject (cf. **187**, *b*) take in the passive voice a personal construction in which the noun becomes the subject of the passive verb and the infinitive is retained; as in *he ordered the man to charge* and *the men were ordered to charge*. Similarly, many verbs in Latin which in the active voice govern an infinitive with subject accusative admit the personal construction in the passive.

He ordered the soldiers to attack, **mīlitēs impetum facere iussit,** and *the soldiers were ordered to attack,* **mīlitēs impetum facere iussī sunt.**

1. This construction is even extended to admit a neuter pronoun as a sort of secondary object.

They do what they were ordered, **quod iussī sunt, faciunt.**

189. *a.* The English infinitive with adjectives of emotion, *glad to, sorry to,* etc., is rendered by the indicative, and the adjective may remain, or may become an adverb. Prose Latin avoids an infinitive depending on an adjective.

They are delighted to leave, **laetī discēdunt;** *men are glad to believe what they desire,* **libenter hominēs id quod volunt crēdunt.**

b. The English infinitive with such adjectives as *easy, good, pleasant, strange,* and their contraries is rendered in Latin by the supine in -ū limiting the adjective.

It is very easy to do, **perfacile factū est;** *the best thing to do* (or *to be done*), **optimum factū.**

c. For the English infinitive governed by a noun, see **183,** *e.* For the English infinitive with a word of tendency or fitness, see **183,** *c.*

190. The English representative subject.

It, which introduces so many clauses in English with the verbs *be, seem,* and impersonal expressions with adjectives and passives, and to which the real subject stands in predicate apposition as an infinitive or clause, has no equivalent whatever in Latin. The infinitive or clause there stands as the actual subject of the verb.

It is dangerous to cross (i.e., *to cross is dangerous*), **perīculōsum est trānsīre;** *it furthered their plans that the Nervii had long ago made these entanglements as good as a wall,* **adiuvābat eōrum cōnsilium quod Nervii antīquitus effēcerant ut īnstar mūrī hae saepēs essent.**

REMARK. The real subject in both languages is, of course, the infinitive or the explanatory clause. This may readily be determined in the English by putting the sentence in the form of a question, and then answering it. Thus in the examples above, the answer to *what is dangerous?* is *to cross,* which is evidently the subject of *is:* and the answer to *what furthered their plans?* is *that the Nervii had,* etc., so that the **quod** clause is clearly the subject of **adiuvābat.**

191. The English infinitive, either ungoverned or in a phrase with *for*, following a comparative, expresses an act or state prevented by the circumstance stated in the comparative clause. It is therefore used to express a real result of a negative character, and the clause must be recast as a result clause before translating. The comparative is often not expressed at all in the Latin.

A calm settled too great (for them) to stir out of the spot, **tanta malacia exstitit, ut sē ex locō movēre nōn possent.**

REMARK. Probably no Latin result clause would be thus translated into English by any student, nor is it advisable to do so.

192.   VOCABULARY

believe, **crēdō, -ere, -didī, -ditum,**
  w. dat. of pers. and acc. of thing
  believed.
dangerous, **perīculōsus, -a, -um.**
difficult,[1] **difficilis, -e.**
easy, **facilis, -e.**

glad,[2] **laetus, -a, -um.**
gladly,[3] **libenter.**
plunder, **populor, I,** *dep.*
show,[4] **ostendō, -ere, -ndī, -ntum.**
unwilling,[5] **invītus, -a, -um.**

IDIOM

against my (your, his) will, **mē (tē, eō) invītō** (*abl. absol.*)

Synonyms. 1. hard. 2. willing. 3. freely, willingly. 4. make plain, reveal. 5. reluctant, reluctantly, unwillingly. *Often an English adverb may be well expressed in Latin by an adjective of emotion in agreement with the subject of the verb.*

193. 1. I was unwilling to tell you this, but circumstances compel me to reveal everything. 2. I am glad to see you. You must come to see[1] me often. 3. It is easy for the Germans to cross the Rhine and come into the province. 4. It was dangerous to Italy for the Gauls to assemble at[2] one place for the purpose of consulting with one another. 5. To accomplish all this is a very easy thing to do; for the men will believe us, since all men are always glad to believe what they wish. 6. I am never reluctant to believe what I wish. 7. To construct a bridge over the Rhine is a very difficult thing to do on account of the breadth, swiftness, and depth of the river. 8. It hindered the plans of those who were eager for revolution that Labienus, as soon as he had been informed of the new war, had with the greatest hardship led back over the mountains the troops which Caesar had given him to take [3] home to the province. 9. The best thing to be done now is to retire with the loss of as few men as possible. 10. Against my will the lieutenant joined battle, and the victory of the enemy is harder to bear for this reason. 11. The enemy suddenly collected an army, took the field against Caesar, joined battle, and retired to Ocelum, plundering on the way.[4] 12. Caesar ordered his men to hold the mountain even against the fiercest attacks of the enemy. 13. The soldiers were ordered to retire after the battle commenced,[5] so as to lead the enemy into an ambuscade. 14. To climb a very high mountain so swiftly, and there to attack an intrenched [6] enemy, is (a task) [7] of the severest labor. 15. To keep the enemy from attacking us before we are ready is the duty [7] of the cavalry we have sent ahead. 16. For a man to believe everything he wishes is too dangerous to him to be often done.[8]

1. ' come to see ' may be expressed literally or may be condensed into ' visit.' 2. in w. acc. 3. ' lead.' 4. ' march.' 5. ' began.' 6. Find a synonym. 7. Cf. **105** and **106**. 8. Do not overlook the idea of obligation involved: recast to introduce *ought*.

LESSON XXXVI

QUOTATION

194. Quotation may be *direct* or *indirect;* **ōrātiō rēcta** or **ōrātiō oblīqua** are the respective Latin terms.

a. **Direct quotations** use the exact words of the original speaker.

" *Leap down, comrades,*" *said he,* " *unless you wish to betray our eagle to the enemy,*" " **Dēsilīte,**" **inquit,** " **commīlitōnēs, nisi vultis aquilam hostibus prōdere.**"

b. **Indirect quotations** in English, depending on active verbs of speech or thought, are introduced by the quotation particle *that:* within the quotation occur certain changes of tense and person in the verbs and such changes in its pronouns as are thereby rendered necessary. In brief quotations, however, *that* is often omitted.

Caesar said (that) he would go with the tenth legion alone: Caesar's actual words were, " *I will go,*" etc.

1. If an indirect quotation in English depends on a passive verb, the construction may be personal or impersonal. The personal construction requires the dependent verb to be in the infinitive; the impersonal construction requires a clause with *that.*

Personal: *Caesar is said to have conquered.* Impersonal: *It is said that Caesar conquered.*

195. Indirect quotation in Latin is wholly different. **No equivalent for the quotation particle *that* exists in Latin**; but indirect quotations are expressed in accordance with the following

Laws of Indirect Discourse

In dependence on verbs and expressions of saying, knowing, thinking, perceiving:

1. **The verbs of all assertions (affirmative or negative) in principal clauses become infinitive with subject accusative.**

2. **The verbs of questions in principal clauses become subjunctive.**

3. **The verbs of commands and prohibitions in principal clauses become subjunctive.**

4. **The verbs of all dependent clauses become subjunctive.**

5. All subjunctives in indirect discourse obey the Law of Sequence of Tenses, and take sequence from the verb which introduces the quotation.

6. In all changes involving finite modes only, between direct and indirect discourse, the stem of the changed verb forms never changes.

Examples. In the following examples the sentence is given first in direct discourse, then in indirect discourse depending on a primary tense; the secondary tense and sequence are bracketed. In practice it should be noted that the English *says, thinks* is usually rendered in Latin by a perfect tense, and that the verb of *saying* introducing a *direct* quotation is regularly **inquit**, *says he, said he*, and not **dīcit** or **dīxit**, which are reserved for indirect quotation. The numbers attached to the examples refer to the divisions under **195**.

    1. *a.* " *I will come,*" *says* (*said*) *Caesar*, " **Veniam,**" **inquit Caesar·**

    b. *Caesar says* (*said*) *that he*[1] *will* (*would*) *come*, **Caesar dīcit (dīxit) sē ventūrum esse.**

    2. *a.* *Caesar asks* (*asked*): " *What do you*[1] *wish?* " **Caesar rogat (rogāvit): "Quid vīs?"**

    b. *Caesar asks* (*asked*) *what he*[1] *wishes* (*wished*), **Caesar rogat (rogāvit) quid ille velit (vellet).**

    3. *a.* " *Remember,*" *says* (*said*) *Caesar*, " **Reminīscere,**" **inquit Caesar.**

    b. *Caesar says* (*said*) *he must remember*, **Caesar dīcit (dīxit)**[2] **reminīscātur (reminīscerētur).**

    4. *a.* " *Labienus,*" *says* (*said*) *Caesar*, "*who has conquered the Gauls, has arrived,*" " **Labiēnus,**" **inquit Caesar, " quī Gallōs vīcit, pervēnit.**"

[1] It will be seen from the above examples that careful attention must be paid, both in English and in Latin, to the changes in the person of pronouns in passing from direct to indirect discourse. Thus **ego** and **nōs**, **meus** and **noster** of the direct discourse regularly, in indirect discourse, become **sē** and **suus** respectively, while **tū** and **vōs** become **ille** or, if not emphatic, **is**.

[2] In practice a very short imperative sentence would be rendered by **imperat ut** with subjunctive or by **iubet** with infinitive, and not as a quotation.

b. Caesar says (said) that Labienus, who has (had) conquered the Gauls, has (had) arrived, **Caesar dīcit (dīxit) Labiēnum, quī Gallōs vīcerit (vīcisset), pervēnisse.**

REMARK. A relative clause explaining some fact or allusion, especially a geographical fact, and lying within a quotation, but not a part of the quoted words, regularly stands in the indicative. *Caesar was informed that all the Belgians, which we said constituted the third division of Gaul, were conspiring,* **Caesar certior fīēbat omnēs Belgās, quam tertiam esse partem Galliae dīxerāmus, coniūrāre.**

196. *a.* The tense of the infinitive in an indirect quotation is to be determined by the time of the original statement. Thus if the original statement lies in present time, the present infinitive is used; if in past time or if the action is completed, the perfect infinitive is used; if in future time, the future infinitive is used.

1. In the rare instances where a future perfect must be represented by an infinitive, it is to be expressed by **fore** followed by a subject clause with **ut** and the perfect or pluperfect subjunctive.

b. The future infinitive active of a verb which has no supine stem, and the future infinitive passive of all verbs, are represented by **fore** followed by a subject clause with **ut** and the present or imperfect subjunctive, according to the sequence.

He says that he will be willing, **dīcit fore ut velit;** *he said that many would be slain,* **dīxit fore ut multī interficerentur.**

c. When the verbs *hope, promise, undertake* refer to a future act, their Latin equivalents take the future infinitive with subject expressed.

Lentulus promises not to fail the state, **Lentulus reī pūblicae sē nōn dēfutūrum pollicētur.**

197. In Latin, as in English, a personal and an impersonal construction are admitted in indirect discourse in dependence on the passive of certain verbs. In Latin those verbs which in the active govern the infinitive with subject accusative usually admit the personal construction in the passive. The chief verbs admitting this construction are: **iubeō**, *command, order;* **vetō,** *forbid;* **videō,** *see,* passive *seem;* **dīcō,** *say;* **exīstimō,** *think;* **iūdicō,** *judge,* in all persons; **ferō,** *say, report;* and **trādō,** *report, circulate rumor,* in third person only. In compound tenses and periphrastic forms, verbs of *saying* and *thinking* more commonly take the impersonal construction.

Personal construction: *he charges him to check the Germans, who were said to have been called in,* **huic mandat Germānōs, quī arcessītī dīcēbantur, prohibeat.** Impersonal construction: *one part, which it has been said that the Gauls hold,* **ūna pars, quam Gallōs obtinēre dictum est.**

198. It is in indirect discourse especially that the somewhat uncertain and variable use of the direct and indirect reflexive is most frequently found (cf. **39,** *b*). The following example well illustrates the usage.

As to Caesar's declaring to him (Ariovistus) *that he* (Caesar) *would not overlook the wrongs done to the Haedui, no one had ever fought with him* (Ariovistus) *without his* (the opponent's) *destruction,* **quod sibi Caesar dēnūntiāret sē Haeduōrum iniūriās nōn neglēctūrum, nēminem sēcum sine suā perniciē contendisse.**

a. **Ipse** in oblique cases may stand alone for an emphatic reflexive. Ambiguity in reflexive usage may often be avoided by the judicious employment of **ipse,** especially where an original first person of the **ōrātiō recta** is indicated.

b. If there is a reflexive in the direct discourse, it must be represented by a reflexive in the direct.

199. VOCABULARY

ascertain,[1] **comperiō, -īre, -ī, -tum.**
assure,[2] **cōnfīrmō, I.**
bring word, **dēferō, -ferre, -tulī, -lātum.**

feel,[3] **sentiō, -īre, sēnsī, sēnsum.**
guide, **dux, ducis,** *m.*
hope, **spērō, I;** *w. dir. obj.; in verb constructions w. fut. inf.*

know, **sciō, scīre, scīvī, scītum** (*most general term*); **intellegō,**[4] **-ere, -lēxī, -lēctum** (know thoroughly, know by reason); **cōgnōscō,**[5] **-ere, -gnōvī, -gnitum** (*in perf. system,* know by senses *or* by hearsay).

make plain, **dēmōnstrō,** I; **ostendō, -ere, -ndī, -ntum.**

notice, **animadvertō, -ere, -tī, -sum.**

oath, **iūs iūrandum, iūris iūrandī,** *neut. compound.*

pay, **persolvō, -ere, -solvī, -solūtum.**

promise, **pollíceor, -ērī, -citus,** *w. dir. obj.; in verb constructions w. fut. inf.*

punishment,[6] **supplicium, -ī,** *n.*

say, **inquam,** *defective; third sing.* **inquit** (*used to introduce direct quotations*), said he.

say not,[7] **negō,** I (*not* **dīcō** *w. neg.*).

take, **sūmō, -ere, sūmpsī, sūmptum.**

think, **putō,**[8] I (*most general term*); **arbitror,** I, *dep.* (*of deliberate decision*); **exīstimō,** I (*of reaching a conclusion*); **cōgitō,** I (*of the act of thinking*).

IDIOMS

inflict punishment on,[9] **supplicium sūmere dē** (— — for, **prō**)

suffer punishment for, **supplicium dare prō, poenās persolvere prō,** *or w. gen. of the crime*

the result will be that, **futūrum est ut,** *w. clause*

Synonyms. 1. discover, find out.   2. assert, declare.   3. know (by sense and feeling), realize.   4. know well, understand.   5. find out, learn.   6. penalty.   7. deny.   8. consider, suppose.   9. punish.

200. 1. The scout said to us that he knew the Germans would be called in for assistance by the Belgae.   2. I hope you will dismiss your forces and return home before I am compelled to attack you.   3. The Remi promised to rescue from the hands of the enemy the scouts who had been captured.   4. I demand of you an oath that you will never again make war on me or on the Roman people.   5. I promise, and confirm it by oath, that we will at once choose a guide to lead you out of these forests back into the province.   6. Considius made it plain to him that he would never be able to find the road to the mountain which they could hardly see in the distance.[1]   7. I well know that you all feel that the best thing to do is to retreat to-day to the place you started from yesterday. 8. I noticed that you were doing nothing that [2] the others were doing. 9. The scouts kept bringing word that the enemy were building a bridge over the great river which was not more than two miles from our camp, in order to lead their forces over it and storm our fortifications. 10. I learn by inquiry [3] that the Germans have retained in camp as captives the envoys we sent to them on a message of peace [4] and have inflicted a severe punishment upon them. 11. You don't suppose, do you,[5] that our men in winter quarters are struggling against [6] a scarcity of grain? I have made diligent [7] inquiry about them, and I think, from what I hear, that they have enough grain for the winter. 12. I knew that Ariovistus was a savage man, but I never thought he was so barbarous as to put to death the hostages given him by the Gallic tribes. 13. I think the result of [8] this will be that Caesar will send ahead the cavalry to ravage the country of the Germans and to make them pay the penalty for their attacks on him. 14. I hear you are going to Rome to-morrow to stay two weeks.[9] 15. I know that all you have told me is true; but not even thus am I persuaded to go from home. 16. Tell me you know I am your friend. No! but I'll tell you this: that not even an oath could make me believe you.

1. ' in the distance,' a single adverb. 2. Not **nihil, quod**, which would indicate that the others also were doing nothing: say ' nothing of these things which,' etc. 3. ' by inquiring.' 4. ' on a message of peace '; form a simple prepositional phrase to fit the real meaning. 5. **52**, *b*. 6. Use abl. alone or abl. with ā or ē; the phrase denotes the cause of the struggling. 7. Use adv., **dīligenter**. 8. Be careful about this preposition; what is its force here? 9. The Romans had no word for ' week ' as a time unit. It is, however, a very easy thing to devise an expression that will accurately translate the idea here. How will you do it?

LESSON XXXVII

INDIRECT QUESTIONS

201. Indirect questions in Latin include (1) the indirect quotation of a formal question; (2) subordinate statements implying a question that might have given rise to all statements. The subject of indirect questions is thus much broader in Latin than in English: for in Latin, not only is the following an indirect question, *he asked where Caesar was going*, which is the quotation form of *where is Caesar going?* but this also, *he told them where Caesar was going;* because to give rise to the statement, the question *where is Caesar going?* is implied, though it may never have been asked. The verbs of all indirect question clauses are subjunctive by **195**, 2; and the word that introduces them — pronoun, adjective, or adverb — is interrogative and not relative, as it is regarded in English.

(1) (*He asked*) *why they distrusted their own valor,* (rogāvit) cūr dē suā virtūte dēspērārent; (2) *he tells what his plan is,* ostendit quid suī cōnsilī sit.

a. Sometimes the same English expression may be translated indifferently by an indirect question or by a relative clause. The entire character of the clause and the nature of the word which introduces it depends in these cases wholly on the presence or absence of an expressed antecedent. Thus, *find out what is going on among them* may be expressed in Latin in two ways, either **quae apud eōs gerantur cōgnōscite**, where **quae** is an interrogative pronoun, or **ea, quae apud eōs geruntur, cōgnōscite**, where **quae** is identified as a relative by the presence of an antecedent, **ea**.

1. Even when the clause is relative, as in the second example, the verb is often subjunctive as a relative clause of characteristic or by attraction.

REMARK. There are frequent exceptions to the law of sequence of tenses in indirect questions in Latin literature, but with these the student will not be called upon to deal in this book. The exercises are so constructed that he should observe the law of sequence strictly.

202. **Whether** in indirect single questions is translated by **num** or **-ne** without essential difference; or by **sī** if any idea of *trial, effort,* or *expectation* is involved.

The problem is whether they want to lead away the soldiers, **est cōnsilium velintne mīlitēs dēdūcere;** *they tried whether they could break through,* **sī perrumpere possent cōnātī sunt.**

203. **Indirect double questions** are introduced as are direct questions of the same type.

Their old women determined by divination whether it was advantageous or not, **mātrēs familiae vāticinātiōnibus dēclārābant utrum ex ūsū esset necne.** (See **53,** *b.*)

204. Clauses depending on affirmative expressions of doubt are really indirect questions. They are introduced in English by *whether* or by an interrogative pronoun, and in Latin by **an, num, utrum . . . an, -ne . . . an,** etc., or by an interrogative pronoun, adjective, or adverb.

Not even you doubt what the outcome of the war will be like, **quālis ēventus bellī sit futūrus, nē vōs quidem dubitātis;** *it is doubtful whether Ambiorix did not mass his troops on his own judgment, or was prevented,* etc., **iūdiciōne Ambiorīx cōpiās suās nōn condūxerit, an prohibitus (sit) dubium est,** etc.

205. VOCABULARY

ask,[1] **quaerō, -ere, quaesīvī, -sītum.**

difficulty, **difficultās, -tātis,** *f.*

diligence, **dīligentia, -ae,** *f.*

perpetual, **perpetuus, -a, -um.**

safe,[2] **incolumis, -e** (*unharmed*); **tūtus, -a, -um** (*not exposed to harm*).

servitude,[3] **servitūs, -tūtis,** *f.*

test,[4] **experior, -īrī, -pertus.**

Synonyms. 1. inquire. 2. unharmed, uninjured. 3. slavery. 4. try if, try whether.

206. 1. I don't understand what you're complaining about.[1]
2. I will make plain to you what I am directing you to do.
3. I have now been busy for three hours fortifying the camp, and
I can't see what I've accomplished. 4. He inquired of Caesar
whether he should send some [2] or whether all should go to the
assistance of the camp. 5. I shall certainly be informed before
night what is delaying our forces. 6. When are you going to
inform the envoys what requisition you will make upon their
province? 7. I shall try with the utmost diligence whether I
can cut the enemy off from supplies. 8. He inquired whether
all his men had come back safe into camp after making the sortie, which had been a task of great difficulty. 9. Try whether
you can capture the enemy's camp to-night.[3] 10. Do not ask
me a single thing and I will tell you all you wish to know.
11. Try if you can find out whether the Gauls will attack us
to-morrow or whether they will wait until the rest of their forces
arrive. 12. I have asked him what he is going to do, but
he will [4] tell me nothing. 13. Ascertain, if you can, what
the enemy's plans are. 14. I cannot determine what is the
best thing to do, whether to remain in camp and withstand
their attack there, or to go out and fight them. 15. It is
difficult to tell [5] what is to be done. 16. Tell me, if you please,
what your plan is, for I am in doubt what to do, to fight
or to retreat.

1. 'what . . . about,' an adverbial accusative, **quid**. 2. 'some'
is here equivalent to a noun: what does it really mean? 3. There
is no adverb for 'to-night,' such as **hodiē**, *to-day;* but note the ele-
ments of which **hōdiē** is composed, **hōc diē**, and then make a phrase
for 'to-night.' 4. What does 'will' signify here? certainly not mere
futurity, but rather the expression in brief form of an unwillingness
to give the information requested. 5. This is a rather curious,
though extremely common, use of 'tell': what does it really mean?
The appropriate verb to use here will have no reference whatever to
speech.

LESSON XXXVIII

CONDITIONAL SENTENCES IN INDIRECT DISCOURSE

207. The subject of conditional sentences in indirect discourse will present no difficulties if such sentences be regarded as fixed forms subjected to a uniform external force — the verb of quotation — producing, of course, fixed results. That is, the same class of condition always appears in the same form in indirect discourse.

208. **Changes in form of conditional sentences in passing from direct to indirect discourse.**

a. **Changes in protasis.**

All protasis verbs stand in the subjunctive in Latin in indirect discourse, obeying the law of sequence of tenses, except that the tenses of contrary to fact conditions can never become primary.

b. **Changes in apodosis.**

All apodosis verbs, except those of commands and prohibitions, will become infinitive forms, as follows :

1. All indicatives become infinitives, the tense of which is determined by **196**, *a.*

2. All *active* subjunctives become future infinitives or the substitute form, **fore** with **ut** and the subjunctive, except that in the past contrary to fact condition the apodosis is expressed by a compound infinitive formed by joining **fuisse** to the future participle of the verb ; but if the verb has no supine stem, use **futūrum fuisse** followed by **ut** and the imperfect subjunctive.

3. All *passive* subjunctives become **fore** (**futūrum esse**) followed by a clause with **ut** and the subjunctive ; except that in the past contrary to fact condition **futūrum fuisse** is substituted for **fore**.

4. Apodosis verbs of command and prohibition become subjunctive.

5. Since the introducing verb of indirect discourse is usually secondary rather than primary (**dīxit** rather than **dīcit**), the imperfect and pluperfect subjunctive are the tenses commonly met with.

Examples

Simple Conditions

These men can find out if they inquire, **hī, sī quaerunt, reperīre possunt**, becomes in primary sequence, **hōs, sī quaerant, reperīre posse**, and in secondary sequence, **hōs, sī quaererent, reperīre posse**.

Contrary to Fact Conditions

I think Caesar is gone: otherwise the Carnutes would not have formed the plan, nor would the Eburones, if he were here, now be swarming to the camp, **Caesarem arbitror profectum: neque aliter Carnūtēs cōnsilium cēpissent, neque Eburōnēs, sī ille adesset, ad castra venīrent**, becomes in *any* sequence, **dīcit (dīxit) sē Caesarem arbitrārī profectum: neque aliter Carnūtēs cōnsilium fuisse captūrōs, neque Eburōnēs, sī ille adesset, ad castra ventūrōs esse**. So also for passive conditions of this class: *had not announcement of Caesar's victory been brought in, it* (the town) *would have been lost*, **nisi nūntiī dē Caesaris victōriā essent allātī, (oppidum) āmissum esset**, becomes in *any* sequence, **dīcit (dīxit) nisi nūntiī dē Caesaris victōriā essent allātī, futūrum fuisse ut āmitterētur**.

Future Conditions, More Vivid or Less Vivid

If hostages be given, I will make peace and *if hostages should be given, I would make peace*, **sī obsidēs dabuntur, pācem faciam** and **sī obsidēs dentur, pācem faciam** become in primary sequence, **dīcit sē, sī obsidēs dentur, pācem factūrum**, and in secondary sequence, **dīxit sē, sī obsidēs darentur, pācem factūrum**. Thus it appears that it cannot be determined *by the form* whether a Latin future condition in indirect discourse represents an original more vivid or an original less vivid condition in the direct discourse.

209. **Table of changes in protasis tenses in the narrative Latin of Caesar.**

Direct Discourse	Indirect Discourse	
	PRIMARY SEQUENCE	SECONDARY SEQUENCE
Present	Present Subjunctive	Imperfect Subjunctive
Imperfect	Imperfect [1] Subjunctive	Imperfect Subjunctive
Future	Present [2] Subjunctive	Imperfect [2] Subjunctive
Perfect	Perfect Subjunctive	Pluperfect Subjunctive
Pluperfect	Pluperfect Subjunctive	Pluperfect Subjunctive
Future Perfect	Perfect [2] Subjunctive	Pluperfect [2] Subjunctive
Present	Present Subjunctive	Imperfect Subjunctive
Imperfect	Imperfect Subjunctive	Imperfect Subjunctive
Perfect	Perfect Subjunctive	Pluperfect Subjunctive
Pluperfect	Pluperfect Subjunctive	Pluperfect Subjunctive
Present	Present Subjunctive	Imperfect Subjunctive

Indicative Mode — Present, Imperfect, Future, Perfect, Pluperfect, Future Perfect.
Subjunctive Mode — Present, Imperfect, Perfect, Pluperfect.
Imperative Mode — Present.

210. 1. I have already told you that, if I had not been informed of the advance of the Gauls, a great part of the army

1. Takes sequence from the perfect infinitive into which the apodosis changes.
2. Often employs an active periphrastic form.

would have been slain. 2. He said that if he captured the
leader of the revolt, he would be executed. 3. I cannot believe
that if you had known the situation here you would have come
to my assistance. 4. If you should receive aid from me, you
say you would be friendly to the Romans in the future. 5. He
told them if they wanted to fight, to draw up their forces on the
next day. 6. The general told the envoys not to come near
the camp if they expected peace. 7. Caesar said that if you
were his enemy, he did not know it. 8. Caesar told the Haedui
that if they had already given the grain which they had promised,
he would not ask them for anything more. 9. He said to me
that if he had held Dumnorix in perpetual slavery, this would
not have occurred. 10. All he said was, that if you were in
command it was well. 11. Tell them I say that if they want
anything, they must come back to-morrow. 12. He assured
them on oath[1] that if all his men came back safe from the
march, he would give them a rest from their labors for[2] the
remainder[3] of the summer. 13. He promises to place all[4]
the bravest centurions in command of a legion within two
years, if they find Ariovistus in his camp and capture him.
14. He told Labienus that if he had not ascertained that
Ariovistus was then in Ocelum and what he was doing there,
he would have sent him ahead to assault the town. 15. If you
are doing your best to inform me about the enemy's forces,
I have nothing to say; but I wish to make it plain to you
that if you fail the state now, I will throw you all into perpetual slavery. 16. He replied that he had not the slightest
idea[5] what Caesar was going to do if he came back to camp
and found them still there.

---

1. 'on oath'; that is, by means of an oath. 2. What time relation here? 3. Say 'remaining part of.' 4. **49**, *e*, 1. 5. 'had
not . . . idea,' a phrase equivalent to a verb. Cf. **185**, n. 1: say
'by no means knew.'

LESSON XXXIX

THE RELATIVE SENTENCE: ENGLISH CONSTRUCTIONS FOR WHICH A RELATIVE SENTENCE MAY BE EMPLOYED IN LATIN

211. The relative word cannot of itself exert any influence on the mode of the verb of its clause. If the verb of a relative clause in Latin is subjunctive, it is the result of a force imposed on it by some governing verb, or the result of the influence of some subordinate conjunction, or else it is the result of some necessity of expression within the relative clause itself.

212. A verb may impose its force on the verb of a relative clause:

a. **By throwing it into indirect discourse.**

b. **By attraction.** A relative clause, included within another clause whose verb is in the subjunctive, often has its own verb subjunctive for no apparent reason other than that it is regarded as an integral and logically necessary part of the subjunctive clause in which it lies.

To cut Caesar off from the supplies which were being brought from the Sequani, **utī commeātū, quī ex Sēquanīs supportārētur, Caesarem interclūderet.**

213. The necessities of expression laid upon the verb of a relative clause may be:

a. Purpose. **79**, II, *c.*   *d.* Concession. **141**, *a.*

b. Result. **95**, *a.*   *e.* Character. **214**.

c. Cause. **140**, *d.*

214. **The relative characteristic,** or *descriptive relative.*

When a relative clause refers its antecedent to a type, asserting a fact which is characteristic of that type, the clause is said to be a relative clause of *characteristic* or *description*, and its verb is in the subjunctive. A characteristic clause *defines* the antecedent as *of such a character* that the statement made is true not only of this antecedent but of all others of the same class or type. This characterizing force is most apparent when the antecedent is indefinite or general, but the usage was finally extended to defining particular antecedents in clauses which differ only slightly from statements of fact.

a. If the antecedent is negative or approaches a negative (as *only*, *alone*, **ūnus**, **sōlus**), if it is interrogative, or if it is wholly indefinite, especially in expressions of existence and non-existence (as *there are some who*, *there is none who*), the relative clause is necessarily to be regarded as characteristic. *There was not one man of the soldiers in the fort who was not wounded*, **in castellō nēmō fuit omnīnō mīlitum quī nōn vulnerārētur** (in such sentences **quī nōn** often unite into **quīn**); *he was the only one who could not be induced*, **ūnus erat quī adducī nōn potuerit**; *there were some who were of the opinion*, **erant quī cēnsērent**.

REMARK. Relative clauses having **ūnus**, **sōlus**, **prīmus**, etc., as antecedents are also called *Limiting Clauses*.

b. It is often optional with the writer whether or not he shall regard as characteristic a relative clause with an apparently definite antecedent. *The number of those who were able to bear arms*, **numerus eōrum quī arma ferre possent**: here **possent** indicates the type, *such as were able;* had **poterant** been used, it would have signified those individuals who, as an actual fact, possessed the requisite strength and skill. So, *the things which tend to weaken character* is expressed by Caesar, **ea quae ad effēminandōs animōs pertinent**: an actual fact is stated and a definite list of outlawed goods is implied; **pertineant** would have expressed *such things as tend to weaken*.

c. Clauses of characteristic are closely akin to relative clauses of result. Indeed it is often impossible to say positively that a given clause expresses a result rather than a characteristic.

This is especially true after comparatives, where the same clause may be introduced either by **quam ut** (result) or **quam** *and a relative* (characteristic). *The enemy were no further away than a spear could be thrown* (or *not too far away for a spear to be thrown,* **191**), **nōn longius hostēs aberant quam quō tēlum adigī posset**; here **quam ut** could have been used.

1. This close relationship between result and characteristic is not confined to comparative sentences. In Ariovistus' boast to Caesar, *I am not such a novice in affairs that I do not know,* **nōn tam imperītus sum rērum ut nōn sciam**, the subjunctive clause might with equal propriety have been written **quī nōn sciam** or **quīn sciam**.

215. 1. A man who fails the state at a critical[1] time ought to be put to death.   2. I am the only man here who has kept the savages from laying waste my land.   3. All who were able to bear arms assembled immediately in the Gauls' camp.   4. " Who is the man who has made war against me? " asked Caesar in the council of the Gauls; and there was no one who replied to this.   5. You are doing me a great injury in attempting[2] to debar me from supplies.   6. You, whom I have even put in command of a legion, have allowed the enemy to cut you off from your camp, and you have not even shown any diligence in preparing for battle.   7. I cannot trust a man who has handed his weapons over to the enemy.   8. The two lines were now no further distant from each other than[3] a man could throw a javelin.   9. Who starts from Rome for Gaul who does not go through the mountains with great danger?   10. There is no tribe in Gaul that I fear more.   11. He is the only barbarian I have ever seen who cannot be persuaded to kill a captive.   12. There was no other soldier who doubted whether his commander was able to conquer the enemy's bands.   13. It happens that there is a certain Gaul here who knows the way.   14. Where is the soldier who does not wish to capture a town which has begun to be besieged by his commander? 15. There are some who seem to fear that I shall be unwilling to return home with my legions after the war. 16. There are certain soldiers who are always trying whether they can dodge [4] the weapons or not.

1. A critical time is a time of danger or need; hence, 'dangerous' or 'necessary.' 2. Arrange as a relative clause. 3. Say 'than whither,' **quam quō**. 4. Find a synonym.

LESSON XL

ENGLISH CONSTRUCTIONS RENDERED BY AN INDEPENDENT SUBJUNCTIVE

216. Though the subjunctive mode in Latin is essentially dependent, there are certain kinds of clauses in English which are to be rendered into Latin by the subjunctive as an independent mode. Clauses such as these belong chiefly to forms of discourse other than narrative, and they represent an act or state as *willed*, as *desired*, or as *possible*.

217. I. **Clauses representing an act or state as willed.** These may express:

a. **Exhortation**, in the first person plural of the present tense only. The negative is **nē**.

Let us go, **eāmus**; *let us not go*, **nē eāmus**.

b. **Command**, in the third person, singular or plural. The negative is **nē**.

Let him go, **eāt**; *let them not go*, **nē eant**.

c. **Questions of doubt or indignation**, usually rhetorical and not expecting an answer. The negative is **nōn**. The present tense is used referring to present time; the imperfect refers to past time.

What shall I do? or *what am I to do?* **quid faciam**? *what was I to do?* **quid facerem**?

1. Note that *am to, was to* here denote doubt, not obligation (cf. **168**).

d. **Concession**, something granted for the sake of argument. The negative is **nē**. The present tense refers to present time; the perfect, to past time.

Granting that Caesar is famous, **sit Caesar clārus**; *granting that this was not true*, **nē fuerit hoc vērum.**

II. **Clauses representing an act or state as desired.** The negative is **nē**. These clauses are frequently introduced by **utinam**, *oh that, would that*.

a. The present tense is used in wishes which deal with the future.

Oh, that Caesar may come, **utinam Caesar veniat**; *may the enemy not conquer*, **nē hostēs vincant.**

b. The imperfect tense expresses a wish contrary to fact in present time.

Would that Caesar were present, **utinam Caesar adesset.**

c. The pluperfect tense expresses a wish contrary to fact in past time.

Would that Caesar had been present, **utinam Caesar adfuisset.**

REMARK. **Utinam** is used chiefly with the imperfect and pluperfect wishes. Note that the tense usage in clauses indicating a wish exactly conforms to that of the corresponding classes of conditional sentences.

III. **Clauses representing an act or state as possible.** The negative is **nōn**. The present and perfect tenses are used without appreciable difference of meaning. *Some one may say*, **dīcat aliquis** or **dīxerit aliquis.** Be careful not to attempt to render other uses of *may* by this construction.

218. 1. Some one may ask why Caesar did not make greater haste[1] on the march. 2. Let no one complain because I did not bring the cavalry with me. 3. Let us all retire to the camp, for we have suffered a great disaster to-day. 4. What was he to say?   Caesar[2] came to him suddenly and inquired why the line of battle had not yet been drawn up, which indeed ought to have been done two hours before. 5. Come with me, men! Let us attack the enemy at once. 6. Grant that Ariovistus is savage and brave. Why should we fear him? 7. Would that Caesar had not been wounded; for we would have pursued[3] the enemy with all speed. 8. May the night come quickly. We have been fighting all day and we are exhausted. 9. May the enemy not make a charge on the camp before the walls are finished. 10. "Don't attack," some one may say. Why shouldn't I attack when the enemy are exhausted and our men are eager for fighting? 11. Where am I to send Labienus? Let him take his stand on the right wing. 12. Let the town not be given up until[4] every soldier of the garrison is killed. 13. Let us die but never[5] surrender.[6] 14. "What am I to do with the prisoner?" you ask of me. Let him die. 15. Let us make a fierce attack on the enemy's camp before the dawn has come.[7] 16. "Let us go to visit Caesar in his camp," some one may say. No! Let us not go, say I. May I never see him again,[8] even granting that he was my friend in former years.

1. **185**, n. 1; say 'hasten more.'   2. Indicate logical connection of sentences where such connection exists.   Thus Caesar's coming to him was the reason for his embarrassment; therefore introduce this sentence by 'for.'   Also Latin prefers to employ subordinate clause constructions where any logical subordination exists, and thus to avoid the succession of apparently coördinate clauses so common in English. The correct form for this sentence is 'For Caesar, when he had come . . . , inquired,' etc. 3. **163,** *a.* 4. 'before'; **126,** *c.* 5. Say 'not ever.' 6. The verb is transitive only: in such expressions use a reflexive object. 7. Watch the tense. 8. 'again' here means 'hereafter,' **posthāc.**

PART II

EASY EXERCISES IN CONNECTED LATIN WRITING

THE STORY OF THE FIRST FIVE YEARS OF THE GALLIC WAR

EXERCISE 1

bring together,[1] cōgō, -ere, coēgī, coăctum.

case[2] (at law), causa, -ae, *f.*

court, iūdicium, -ī, *n.*

narrow, angustus, -a, -um.

plead (a case), dīcō, -ere, dīxī, dictum.

powerful (*adj.*), potēns, -entis.

previously,[3] anteā, ante.

shut in,[4] contineō, -ēre, -uī, -tentum.

summon, vocō, I.

trial, iūdicium, -ī, *n.*

vassal,[5] cliēns, -entis, *m.*

Synonyms. 1. assemble, collect. 2. cause. 3. before. 4. bound. confine, hem in. 5. retainer.

When Caesar arrived in Gaul he at once heard that all the Helvetii were preparing to leave their territories because their land was shut in on all sides by high mountains and they considered[1] their territories too narrow. A few years previously[2] a certain Orgetorix had persuaded them to try to get control of the government of all Gaul. But there is no doubt[3] that he also tried to make himself too powerful, so that[4] the Helvetii, after[5] learning of his plans, summoned him before[6] the court. He was unwilling to plead his case, and accordingly he brought together to the trial all his vassals and escaped.[7] A short time afterward he died.

1. Use **arbitror**. 2. In expressions involving measure of difference (**71**), **ante** and **post** are used, not **anteā** and **posteā**. 3. **121**. 4. Use a result clause or a clause with **quam ob rem**. 5. Abl. absolute. 6. **in** w. acc. 7. Say 'rescued himself.' Apply **218**, n. 2 here and throughout.

EXERCISE 2

down (a river), **secundum**, *prep.* *w. acc.*	narrow pass, **angustiae**, -**ārum**, *f.* task, **negōtium**, -**ī**, *n.*

The Helvetii nevertheless prepared to go forth. They tried to persuade the nearest states to allow them to go through their boundaries, for on account of the high mountains and narrow passes their neighbors could easily prevent them. Caesar feared for the Province[1] if the Helvetii should settle near it, and accordingly assembled his legions to check them. He fortified one bank of the Rhone for some distance[2] from Geneva and so prevented them from[3] crossing the river. They marched down the Rhone ravaging the lands of the Haedui and Allobroges, who were allies of the Romans, and they were crossing the Arar when he overtook them and defeated one division which had not yet crossed the river. He then pursued the rest of the Helvetii and, though[4] he lost one opportunity[5] to finish[6] his task through the fear of Considius, he finally defeated them and compelled them to return to their own territories.

1. Dat. of ref., **18**.   2. **aliquantum spatium**.   3. **120**.   4. Use **quamquam** or **cum**; an abl. absolute should not be used with a modifying phrase added to it.   5. Use **occāsiō**, -**ōnis**, *f.*   6. Gen. of the gerundive.

EXERCISE 3

cruelty, **crūdēlitās**, -**tātis**, *f.*	spread,[1] **vagor**, I, *dep.*
indeed, **quidem**.	treat, **afficiō**, -**ere**, **affēcī**, **affectum**.
king, **rēx**, **rēgis**, *m.*	
land (*as opposed to water, or in national sense*), **terra**, -**ae**, *f.*	word, **verbum**, -**ī**, *n.*

Synonyms.   1. wander, roam.

Hardly had he finished the Helvetian war when[1] he heard some alarming news,[2] for his friend Diviciacus the Haeduan came to him to complain that Ariovistus, king of the Germans, had crossed the Rhine and was ravaging the land of Gaul; that he had seized the greater part of the territory of the Sequani and was treating them with the utmost[3] cruelty. He urged the Sequani, many of whom were present, to tell him about their ill-treatment[4] by Ariovistus,[5] but they were so terrified that they dared not say even one word. He understood, indeed, that for the Germans to cross the river whenever they wished was a great danger[6] to Gaul, because the Germans were a great and barbarous nation, and if they became accustomed to live in Gaul they would spread over the whole land. He therefore sent ambassadors to Ariovistus to request that he should name[7] a place where[8] they might meet for a conference.[9] Ariovistus, however, refused to speak with him.

1. Omit 'when' and write first clause as an abl. absolute. 2. 'certain things which alarmed him'; use **commoveō** or **perturbō**. 3. 'greatest.' 4. 'injuries.' 5. **22,** *d*. 6. **77.** 7. **dīcō.** 8. **79,** II, *c*. 9. 'for the sake of conferring,' **85,** III, *b*; **86; 183,** *b*.

EXERCISE 4

as (= in what manner), quō-modō, quem ad modum.

govern, imperō, I, *w. dat.*

huge, ingēns, -entis.

incredible, incrēdibilis, -e.

instructions, mandāta, -ōrum, *n.*

join, coniungō, -ere, -iūnxī, -iūnctum, *w. dir. obj. and* cum.

reply, respōnsum, -ī, *n.*

restore,[1] reddō, -ere, -didī, -ditum.

subjects, victī, -ōrum, *m. (lit.,* conquered ones).

Synonyms. 1. give back, return.

Caesar again sent commissioners to say to Ariovistus that, since he had refused to confer with him, he was compelled to make the following demands upon him[1]; that he should lead no more[2] Germans into Gaul, and that he should restore to the Romans' allies the hostages which he held. Ariovistus replied to this[3]: " You govern your subjects as you wish; I shall do the same. Attack me when you wish; you'll know then what my troops can do [4] in war." Caesar then, after hearing this reply, resolved to make war on Ariovistus before larger forces of Germans could cross the Rhine and join [5] him. Caesar's soldiers asked the Gauls many questions [6] about the Germans, and they [7] always replied that they were huge men and of incredible bravery in war. This scared the soldiers awfully,[8] so that many of them even asked permission of Caesar [9] to go back to Rome. Caesar told them to go back [10] if they wanted to, and he would attack the Germans with the tenth legion alone. " For in this legion," said he, " I have the utmost confidence."

1. 'to demand these things from him.' 2. An adv., **amplius**; 'should not any more lead,' etc. 3. **ad haec.** 4. Omit 'do'; use **possum** alone. 5. 'join themselves with him.' 6. 'inquired many things from the G.' 7. Rel. clause: arrange word order to bring the antecedent, 'Gauls,' nearer than 'Germans' to the rel. 8. **maximē.** 9. 'asked of C. that it be permitted to them.' 10. Jussive subjv. in indirect discourse.

EXERCISE 5

business, **negōtium**, -ī, *n.*
embassy, **lēgātiō**, -ōnis, *f.*
important (most), **summus**, -a, -um.
listen to, **audiō**, -īre, -īvī, -ītum.
the other, the others (*of more than two*), **reliquus**, -a, -um; *when pl. often* **cēterī**, -ae, -a.

satisfy, **satisfaciō**, -ere, -fēcī, -factum, *w. dat.*
seize (a person), **comprehendō**, -ere, -ndī, -nsum.
soon, **iam.**
take back, **recipiō**, -ere, -cēpī, -ceptum.
treat (with), **agō**, -ere, ēgī, āctum, *w.* **cum** *and abl.*

Courage then returned and took possession [1] of their minds. First the soldiers of the tenth legion thanked him for his kind words about them,[2] and assured him that they were ready to accompany [3] him even across the Rhine, if he wished, and to fight any [4] number of Germans. Then the other legions also did their best to satisfy Caesar in respect to their courage. Caesar listened to their speech and promised to take them back again into favor. He then hastened by forced marches against the Germans. For, as he said, he wished to know whether fear or duty prevailed among them. They soon approached Ariovistus, who sent an embassy to say to Caesar that he wished to confer with him on [5] most important matters.[6] Caesar went to the conference with certain soldiers of the tenth legion whom he had mounted [7] on the horses of the Gallic cavalry, for he had no great confidence in the Gauls. In the beginning of the conference Ariovistus asked Caesar what business he had [8] in Gaul at all, and in a short time his cavalry attacked Caesar's, but were unable to terrify them. Caesar retired to his army before any one [9] was killed, and prepared for battle. A few days afterward, however, Ariovistus again asked for a conference. Caesar refused, but sent to him two commissioners to treat with him. These Ariovistus seized and held.[10]

1. 'occupied.'   2. 'because he had spoken (subjv.) so well about them.'
3. 'go with.'   4. **49**, *c.*   5. **dē**.   6. 'things.'   7. 'placed on,' **impōnō** w. dat.   8. 'what of business was to him.'   9. Note the implication that no one was killed; **49**, *b.*   10. 'retained.'

EXERCISE 6

cease,[1] **dēsistō, -ere, -stitī, -stitum,** *w. inf.*

dense,[2] **dēnsus, -a, -um.**

deserter, **perfuga, -ae,** *m.*

moon, **lūna, -ae,** *f.*

new, **novus, -a, -um.**

Synonyms.   1. stop (an act), desist.   2. thick.

Ariovistus held himself within his fortified camp and would [1] not fight although Caesar daily led out his forces and gave him the opportunity to fight.[2] Caesar, when he had captured a few deserters, asked them why Ariovistus would not fight. They replied that he had no hopes of victory if he fought [3]

before new moon. Caesar then drew up his battle line and
assaulted the camp of Ariovistus. Thus he was compelled to
fight, and a long and fierce battle ensued [4] until sunset. The
Germans were defeated with heavy loss [5] and fled across the
Rhine into the dense forests. They were indeed so terrified
that they did not stop running [6] until [7] they had come from the
place of the battle to the bank of the Rhine, about five miles.
All this distance Caesar's cavalry pursued them and slew a
great number of the fugitives.[8] In this flight Caesar found his
two commissioners whom Ariovistus had seized. By this [9]
battle Caesar had finished two very serious [10] wars in one summer.
Accordingly he led [11] the legions into winter quarters and himself returned into the Province.

1. ' was unwilling to,' or simply ' did not.'   2. Gen. of gerund.
3. Watch the tense.   4. Impers. construction, ' it was fought long and
fiercely.'   5. ' many being killed,' abl. absol.   6. ' cease to run.'   7. ' before.'   8. Pres. ptc., ' of the fleeing.'   9. Rel.   10. ' great.'   11. Abl.
absolute.

EXERCISE 7

blame, **accūsō, I;** *w.* **quod** *and*
  subjunctive if followed by verb
  phrase.
carry to, **afferō, -ferre, attulī,**
  allātum, *w.* **ad** *and acc.*

conspire, **coniūrō, I.**
frequent, **crēber, -bra, -brum.**
rumor, **rūmor, -ōris,** *m.*
take up (arms), **capiō, -ere, cēpī,**
  captum.

While the Roman army was in winter quarters, frequent
rumors were carried to Caesar that all the Belgae were conspiring against Rome for fear that [1] Caesar would make war on
them after conquering all the rest of Gaul. He was also informed what states were likely to take up [2] arms and what their
war strength was.[3] Accordingly he determined that he must
hasten against them. He [4] did not wish to fight with them all
at one time, so he persuaded the Haedui, his allies, to lead their
troops into the boundaries of one of the Belgian tribes and

ravage their fields, so that the tribe might attack them and not be able to join the other Belgians against his army. Meanwhile Caesar marched against certain of the Belgae who were attacking a town of the Remi, his allies, which Iccius commanded, and which was of great use [5] to him for carrying on the war, since in it were supplies of every kind. Having beaten the enemy and driven them from the town, he hastened on against the Nervii, the bravest and fiercest of the Belgae, who blamed the rest of the Gauls for surrendering to Caesar, and declared that they would never accept any terms of peace.

1. 'for-fear-that,' **nē**. 2. Fut. periphrastic. 3. 'what they were able (to do) in war.' 4. Make this a causal clause: 'since he, etc. . . . he persuaded. . . .' 5. Dat. of service: that for which a person or thing is of use is expressed by **ad** w. acc. of noun, gerund, or gerundive.

EXERCISE 8

fierce,[1] **ācer, ācris, ācre.**	success, **fortūna, -ae,** *f.*; **fēlīcitās, -tātis,** *f.*
oppose, **oppōnō, -ere, -posuī, -positum,** *tr. and intr.*	varied,[2] **varius, -a, -um.**

Synonyms. 1. keen, sharp. 2. changing, varying.

The Nervii had persuaded other tribes to conspire with them, and the whole army had halted across a small river and were awaiting there the arrival of Caesar. They had hoped to be able [1] to attack his troops encumbered with all their baggage, but before he was very near them he drew up six legions in advance of [2] the baggage and behind it he stationed his two new legions as a guard for the baggage and the rear of his line. The Nervii first made so fierce an attack on our cavalry that they threw them into confusion. Under such circumstances [3] a commander has everything to do quickly: he must draw up his line of battle against the enemy, and must see to it that an attack cannot be made on the flank. The soldiers also must be able to do many things for themselves,[4] so that, even if the commander himself be not present at some crisis,[5] they may know what is best to do.[6] The battle raged with varying success, since the legions, some in one part, others in another, were resisting the enemy as [7] best they could without their general. Caesar hastened from one legion to another to exhort them to stand firm and fight bravely. Finally the tenth legion under Labienus,[8] having gained possession of the enemy's camp and having defeated the forces opposed to it, came to the aid [9] of the other legions and put the enemy to flight with great slaughter.[10]

1. When a verb has no fut. inf., **fore** must be used followed by **ut** and a substantive clause w. the subjv. 2. 'before.' 3. 'at these times.' 4. Dat. of ref. 5. 'necessary time.' 6. Supine in -ū limiting **optimum**. 7. 'as ' = 'in what manner.' 8. 'Labienus (being) the leader,' abl. absol. 9. 'for aid to.' 10. 'many being killed,' abl. absol.

EXERCISE 9

artillery, **tormenta, -ōrum,** *n.*

believe (*in sense of* be confident), **cōnfīdō, -ere, -fīsus.**

betake one's self, **sē cōnferō, -ferre, contulī, collātum.**

build (*of military construction*), **exstruō, -ere, -strūxī, -strūctum.**

coast (*adj.* = on *or* near the coast), **maritimus, -a, -um.**

decree, **dēcernō, -ere, -crēvī, -crētum.**

god, **deus, -ī,** *m.*

happen to, **contingō, -ere, -tigī, -tāetum.**

honor, **honor, -ōris,** *m.*

lay down,[1] **dēpōnō, -ere, -posuī, -positum.**

mound, **agger, -eris,** *m.* (*for military purposes*).

move up (*or* forward), **prōmoveō, -ēre, -mōvī, -mōtum.**

pacify,[2] **pācō, I.**

reduce, **redigō, -ere, -ēgī, -āctum.**

shout,[3] **conclāmō, I.**

splendidly, **ēgregiē.**

thanksgiving, **supplicātiō, -ōnis,** *f.*

unexpected, **imprōvīsus, -a, -um.**

Synonyms. 1. lay aside. 2. subdue. 3. call to.

Caesar next marched against the Aduatuci, who were coming with all their forces to the aid[1] of the Nervii. When they[2] learned of this battle they betook themselves into a town splendidly fortified both by hand and by the nature of its location, since it was situated on the top of a hill. At the arrival of our army the enemy made frequent sorties from the town and attempted to drive us away by unexpected attacks. Caesar, however, moved up his artillery and began to build towers and a mound with which to assault [3] the town. When they saw these things being built,[4] they shouted to us: " Why do you build that thing so far away? [5] With whose [6] hands do you believe you'll move it to the wall? It's too big, and you're too little." But when they saw our tower move [7] easily, they were terrified and shouted again that they knew we waged war by the aid of the gods, and that they would surrender immediately and lay down their arms. But that night they tried to make a rush from the town. Caesar slew many of them and gave the rest into slavery. He then reduced many of the coast states into the power of the Roman people, and having led the army into winter quarters, he set out for Italy, since he thought Gaul was pacified. When these things were announced at Rome by letters of Caesar the Senate decreed a thanksgiving of fifteen days, an honor which had never previously fallen to the lot of [8] any man.

1. ' for aid to.' 2. Rel. pron. 3. Rel. purpose clause. 4. Pres. inf. pass. 5. **ab tantō spatiō**. 6. The enclitic **-nam** appended to the interrog. pron. emphasizes the question. 7. Pres. inf. pass. 8. ' fallen-to-the-lot-of ' = ' happened to.'

EXERCISE 10

burst forth, **ērumpō, -ere, -rūpī, -ruptum.**

despise, **dēspiciō, -ere, -spēxī, -spectum.**

forbid (*tr.*), **interdīcō, -ere, -dīxī, -dictum,** *w. dat. of person and*

abl. of thing; in verb construction, dat. of pers. and **nē** *w. subjv.*

fresh, **integer, -gra, -grum.**

heights, **loca superiōra,** *n. pl.*

money, **pecūnia, -ae,** *f.*

be open, **pateō, -ēre, -uī,** —.

overhang, **impendeō**, -ēre, —, —.

panic-stricken, **perterritus**, -a, -um.

rest,[1] **sē reficiō**, -ere, -fēcī, -fectum.

stronghold, **oppidum**, -ī, *n.*; **cas-tellum**, -ī, *n.*

succeed,[2] **succēdō**, -ere, -cessī, -cessum, *w. dat.*

unexpectedly, **imprōvīsō**.

wearied,[3] **dēfessus**, -a, -um.

a little while, **paulisper**.

Synonyms. 1. recover, refresh one's self.   2. take the place of.   3. exhausted, tired out.

The nations which extend from the boundaries of the Allobroges to the summit of the Alps had forbidden the road through the Alps to merchants unless they gave them much money. Caesar, however, wished these roads to be open.   Accordingly he sent Galba among[1] these nations to lift the blockade[2] of the roads and to winter there with a legion if he thought there was need.   Galba defeated them in several battles, captured many of their strongholds, and resolved to winter in the village of Octodurus.   He began to have[3] supplies brought[4] into the town.   Suddenly the Gauls seized the mountains which overhung the town and fiercely attacked Galba's troops, whom they despised because they were so few. The Romans were not able to give even wounded men a chance[5] to rest, while the enemy when they were wearied left[6] the battle, and others with fresh strength took their places.   Finally Galba realized that the only hope of safety was to make[7] a sortie and take the Gauls by surprise.[8]   He accordingly ordered the soldiers not to fight for a little while, and when they had rested to burst forth at the giving of the signal[9] and attack the barbarians with the utmost valor.   They did as[10] they had been ordered, and, making a fierce sortie from all the gates, they slew a large part of the enemy and drove the rest back so panic-stricken that they dared not make a stand even on the heights.

1. 'into.'   2. 'free the roads from blockade.'   3. **85**, III, *a*, 1.
4. **cōnferō.**   5. **183**, *e.*   6. 'went out from.'   7. Use an apposition clause w. **ut** and subjv.; this clause can also be expressed as a condition.   8. 'attack unexpectedly.'   9. Abl. absol.   10. 'what'; rel. pron.

EXERCISE 11

blockade (v.), **obsideō, -ēre, -sēdī, -sessum.**

coast (n.), **ōra, -ae,** f.

in detail (i.e., one at a time), **singulī, -ae, -a.**

fleet, **classis, -is,** f.

offer, **praebeō, -ēre, -uī, -itum.**

officer, no general term; use **praefectus** or **tribūnus.**

seacoast, **ōra maritima.**

In the beginning of winter,[1] since he thought Gaul subdued, Caesar started for Illyricum, for he wanted to learn the region. He had sent Crassus with the seventh legion to winter near the coast. In these regions there was a scarcity of grain, so Crassus sent certain of his officers into the neighboring tribes to seek supplies for[2] the winter. The Veneti, who inhabited the seacoast and had many ships, in the use of which they surpass all the nations of these regions, seized two of them and detained them as prisoners. The other tribes likewise held the officers who had come to them, and they gave oath to one another that they would join together against the Romans and liberate themselves from slavery. This region offers great difficulty for infantry because of the many rivers, and the Romans had no ships in which they could[3] besiege the towns on the seaward side[4] and prevent the enemy's flight.[5] When the towns had been blockaded on the land side, Caesar hastened with the greater part of his army to the assistance of Crassus, from whom he had received letters. He had as many ships as possible assembled from nations already pacified. When these had assembled he fought a great battle with the enemy's ships and captured almost their entire fleet. For his own ships were able to move[6] faster[7] than the heavier ships of the enemy, so that he was able to attack and capture them in detail. By this[8] battle the war of the entire seacoast was ended.[9] For after the loss of their ships[10] the enemy had no place to retire to[11] nor any means of flight.[12]

1. Abl. absol.   2. **ad**.   3. Rel. clause of purpose or characteristic.   4. **ā mari, 31**.   5. 'prevent (*or* cut off) the enemy from flight.'   6. Use the pass. voice.   7. 'more swiftly.'   8. Rel.   9. 'finished.'   10. Abl. absol.   11. Rel. clause.   12. 'nor by what manner they might flee.'

EXERCISE 12

absent, **absēns, -entis**, *adj.*

bad,[1] **malus, -a, -um**.

challenge, **ēvocō**, I.

circumstances, **occāsiō, -ōnis**, *f.*; *of situation or opportunity*

brought about by chance.

favorable, **aequus, -a, -um**.

increase [2] (*tr.*), **augeō, -ēre, auxī, auctum**.

run, **currō, -ere, cucurrī, cursum**.

Synonyms.   1. evil, wicked.   2. augment.

While all this was going on [1] among the Veneti, Caesar sent Sabinus with a detachment [2] of his army among the Venelli to keep them in order and prevent Viridovix, who was in command of them, from revolting. But Viridovix had already raised [3] an army from the neighboring nations, which had been increased by a multitude of rascals [4] who had fled from the cities into the forest to escape the punishment of the laws. He pitched his camp against Sabinus at a distance of less than two miles.[5] He daily led his army to the camp of the Romans, and challenged Sabinus to [6] come out from his fortifications and fight him. Sabinus did not think he ought to fight in Caesar's absence [7] except under the most favorable circumstances.[8] Accordingly he kept himself in the camp until the enemy thought he was afraid of them.[9] He also sent out a certain Gaul whom he trusted to go over to the enemy and say that he had fled from the Romans' camp and that the very [10] next night Sabinus intended to go out from the camp with all his troops and march to Caesar, because in the camp he had no provisions. The enemy shouted that they ought at once to storm the camp, which had been pitched on top of a hill. So they ran quickly up the hill [11] to the very gates of the camp in the hope of gaining possession of it easily, and they arrived there tired out. Sabinus, when he saw them now not far off, made a sudden attack upon them. They did not even attempt to make a stand, but fled in confusion. Our soldiers and cavalry, pursuing them,[12] slew many of them, leaving few [13] who gained [14] the forests in safety.[15]

1. **128**, *a*. 2. 'part.' 3. 'assembled.' 4. 'bad men.' 5. **72**, *a*; **73**; ā **mīlibus passuum minus duōbus.** 6. Clause of purpose or imv. in ind. discourse. 7. Abl. absol. 8. Abl. of attendant circumstance. 9. 'feared them.' 10. Use the proper dem. pron. 11. Cf. an idiom in **75**. 12. Use rel. pron. at head of clause. 13. Abl. absol. 14. 'arrived at.' 15. 'safe.'

EXERCISE 13

escape, **effugiō, -ere, -fūgī, —**.	press on (in pursuit), **īnsequor,**
hurl back,[1] **rēiciō, -ere, -iēcī,**	**-sequī, -secūtus.**
-iectum.	way (*in sense of* manner *or* plan),
insufficiently, **nōn satis.**	**ratiō, -ōnis,** *f.*; **modus, -ī,** *m.*

Synonym. 1. drive back (*with or without the idea of* defeat).

About the same time Crassus had arrived in Aquitania and in a cavalry battle with the Sotiates he was nearly caught in an ambush. For when their cavalry retreated and ours pressed on, the infantry suddenly attacked our men. There was a long, fierce fight, though our troops finally drove them off. Crassus then besieged one of their large towns for several days and captured it. The chieftain of the enemy attempted to escape in the night with a great number of his retainers in whom he had the utmost [1] confidence. These were always with him, and to them he gave a share [2] of all his goods, but on this condition : that if anything happened to him, they also would die. The flight of him and his band was discovered by the noise, and they were hurled back into the town. Other nations then joined them, and envoys were even sent to Spain to seek auxiliaries and leaders who knew [3] and could use our methods of fighting.

When they [4] came, they began to wage war in a far different manner ‹from [5] the rest of the barbarians. For they seized commanding positions [6]; they fortified camps; they tried to cut our men off from supplies; and they held off their troops from battle. Crassus tried in every way to make them fight, but finally was compelled to attack their fortified camp. This he carried by assault, by sending his cavalry to attack it where it was insufficiently defended. The greater part of Aquitania then surrendered to Crassus and sent hostages. After a brief expedition [7] against the Morini, Caesar ordered all his lieutenants to lead their forces into winter quarters.

1. ‘greatest.’   2. ‘part.’   3. Subjv. in rel. clause of characteristic. 4. Rel. pron. should begin sentence.   5. **ac.**   6. **loca superiōra.**   7. Abl. absol., ‘a march of not many days being made,’ etc.

EXERCISE 14

call in (*in sense of* remove), dēdūcō, -ere, -dūxī, -ductum.

good will, grātia, -ae, *f.*; voluntās, -tātis, *f.*

march on, prōcēdō, -ere, -cessī, -cessum.

sentry, custōs, -tōdis, *m.*; *pl.*, custōdēs, -um, guard.

During [1] that winter certain German tribes, harassed for many years by the Suebi, who were the most powerful of all the Germans, crossed the Rhine. When they had first come to the Rhine and were prevented from crossing by the Menapii, who dwelt in these places, they retreated at night a short distance into the forests. The Menapii thought they had gone home and accordingly called in their sentries. The Germans suddenly returned and defeated the Menapii, whose boats they used to cross [2] the Rhine. Caesar hastened to the army and began to march toward the Germans. Commissioners came to him from them when he was not far distant, who spoke as follows [3]: “If you want our good will, we can do much [4] for you. Give us lands in Gaul, or allow us to retain those [5] we have seized.

The Suebi alone are more powerful than we: there is no other nation whom we cannot [6] conquer." Caesar replied: " There can be no friendship between us [7] if you remain in Gaul. Return across the Rhine and settle in the lands of the Ubii. I will obtain this for you from the Ubii." They then begged Caesar not to advance farther until they had reported what he had said to their people and had returned to him. Caesar made no promises,[8] but marched on against them.

1. Abl. of time within which.   2. A purpose construction.   3. ' thus,' or ' these things.'   4. ' many things,' n. pl.   5. Do not omit rel.   6. Subjv. in rel. clause of characteristic.   7. ' to me with you.'   8. ' promised nothing.'

EXERCISE 15

destroy (*in sense of* break down, break to pieces), **rescindō, -ere, -scidī, -scissum.**	elder, **maior nātū**; *pl.,* **maiōrēs** (**nātū**), the elders. strong, **fīrmus, -a, -um.**

Then they attacked the cavalry of the Romans, which Caesar had sent ahead. Even then these did nothing else than [1] defend themselves, as they had been ordered by Caesar. The next day the German elders came into camp to say that they had not been able to restrain their men from fighting. Caesar detained them in camp, and, attacking the army of the Germans, routed it with great slaughter. Caesar now saw that the Germans were too easily induced to cross the Rhine, and he wished to show them that the army of the Roman people was able and also dared to cross the Rhine, and to make them fear for themselves and for their own lands. In order still better to show them the power of the Roman people, he determined that he must build a bridge over the Rhine, a thing which [2] had never before been seen or heard of. Finishing the bridge in a few days, he led the army over. Leaving a strong guard at both ends [3] of the bridge, he marched against the most powerful German tribes. These quickly retired into the densest forests,

where Caesar was unwilling to follow them, lest in his absence
an attack be made on the guard of the bridge. Besides, he
had accomplished all he had come for,[4] for the Germans had
fled at his approach. So he returned into Gaul and ordered
the bridge to be destroyed, so that the Germans might not
avail themselves of it.[5]

1. 'nothing other except.'   2. 'which thing.'   3. **ad utramque partem.**
4. 'for the sake of which he had come.'   5. 'use it.'

EXERCISE 16

damage,[1] **frangō**, -ere, **frēgī, frāctum.**

disembark, (ex) **nāvī ēgredī.**

harbor,[2] **portus, -ūs,** *m.*

island, **īnsula, -ae,** *f.*

ocean, **ōceanus, -ī,** *m.*

plan,[3] **cōgitō,** I, *absolute, w. dir. obj. in neut., or w.* **dē** *and abl.*

suitable, **opportūnus, -a, -um.**

take risk, **perīculum facere.**

warship, **nāvis longa.**

water, **aqua, -ae,** *f.*

Synonyms.   1. break, ruin, wreck.   2. port.   3. plot, think about.

A great island was situated in the ocean not far from Gaul.
The traders called it Britain; nor did any one except the traders
ever go there, and *they* knew no part of it except those regions and
nations which are nearest the sea. Caesar especially desired to
visit this island and to see the sort of men who dwelt in it and
to learn what was the nature of the land and its harbors. Before
he took any risk, however, he sent Volusenus with a warship
to find out everything he could. Meanwhile he distributed his
troops in suitable places in Gaul, that the Gauls might not
revolt in his absence. The Morini, the only tribe which was
still in arms, now surrendered to him and sent hostages. Caesar
now proceeded to Britain with all his ships, and when he approached the island he saw all the forces of the enemy drawn up
to prevent him from disembarking. When the ships came
nearer, the barbarians even ran out into the sea and threw their

weapons at our men disembarking. It was a thing of great difficulty, for the soldiers had to fight in deep water where they could scarcely stand. At last they drove away the enemy and reached land. They then pitched camp, for they could not pursue the enemy very far, since the ships which were bringing the cavalry were driven back by a storm. Envoys, however, came from the Britons to seek peace. But that very night many ships were damaged by a great storm, so that already on the next day the Britons began to plan a revolt. Caesar used the damaged ships to repair the others, and, after defeating the Britons in front of his very camp, where they had come to attack him, he returned to Gaul.

EXERCISE 17

award,[1] **attribuō, -ere, -uī, -ūtum.**
deserve,[2] **mereor, -ērī, meritus.**
free, **līber, -era, -erum.**
haul ashore, **subdūcō, -ere, -dūxī, -ductum.**

postpone,[3] **differō, -ferre, distulī, dīlātum.**
revolution, **rēs novae,** *f. pl.*
shape,[4] **figūra, -ae,** *f.*
storm, **tempestās, -tātis,** *f.*

Synonyms. 1. assign. 2. earn, merit. 3. defer. 4. figure.

In the beginning of the next summer Caesar, after defeating several tribes who had revolted and after awarding the kingdom of the Treveri to that one of the two chiefs who, he thought, deserved it, assembled his ships at[1] a suitable port, and prepared to start a second time[2] for Britain. Just at this juncture[3] Dumnorix, the brother of his friend Diviciacus, who had always been eager for a revolution, asked Caesar to be allowed to stay in Gaul because he feared the sea. Caesar, because he did not wish to leave an enemy behind him, refused. Dumnorix then urged certain chiefs of the Gauls to remain in Gaul with their troops, since Caesar would certainly put them to death if they fell[4] into his hands in any place whatsoever outside of Gaul. He said, besides, that he had always been free and intended to remain so. When he had persuaded many of them by such talk,[5] he deserted [6] with them. Caesar postponed his departure and sent cavalry with orders [7] to bring him back. When he resisted them, they killed him. Leaving Labienus in Gaul, Caesar then set out. He landed without opposition [8] and quickly pitched camp. That night, just as in the preceding year, a storm did much damage to his ships. Although it was a task of great difficulty, he hauled all the ships ashore and fortified them by throwing a wall around [9] them. He then investigated the shape of the island itself and the customs of its inhabitants.[10] Having conquered the troops of the Britons in many battles, he received hostages from them and returned to Gaul.

1. **in** w. acc.   2. 'again.'   3. 'at this very time.'   4. 'came.'   5. 'this (**is**) speech.'   6. 'departed.'   7. 'with these orders, that,' etc.   8. 'no one preventing,' abl. absol.   9. 'by a wall thrown around.'   10. 'those who inhabit it.'

EXERCISE 18

Caesar distributed his troops for the winter among more states than usual.[1] The Eburones, under the leadership of Ambiorix, formed the plan of attacking the winter quarters of the legions in detail. They first came to the camp of Sabinus and Cotta. The soldiers bravely defended the camp and repulsed them. Then they shouted to our men to send [2] some one to confer with them. Two men were sent. These [3] Ambiorix endeavored to persuade to leave the camp with all the baggage and march to the nearest winter quarters of another legion. It was the best thing to do,[4] he said, and he would grant [5] them a safe march through his lands, for he had attacked the camp because he was compelled by his state, not because he was himself an enemy to Caesar. His people wished their lands to be freed from winter camps. When these things were reported to the generals, one said he would never leave a fortified camp, nor do any other thing, on the advice of an enemy.[6] The other had great faith in Ambiorix, and said they must do as he had advised. In two days they could reach the nearest winter camp, before any harm [7] was done. At last the opinion of this man prevailed, and orders were given [8] to march out at daybreak. When they were no great distance from camp and were marching through a dense forest, the enemy suddenly attacked them. When they had fought long and fiercely and very many had been slain, a few opened the way to their camp with swords. Others ran from the battle line into the forest, where they were overtaken by the enemy and slain. The rest died fighting. That night those who had reached the camp, since they saw no hope of safety, killed themselves.

1. 'than he had been accustomed.' 2. Clause of purpose, or an ind. discourse form of an original imperative. 3. Rel. pron. 4. Supine in -ū following neuter adj. 5. 'give.' 6. Abl. absol., 'an enemy the adviser (auctor).' 7. 'evil,' or 'injury.' 8. Impers., 'it was ordered.'

EXERCISE 19

arm, armō, I.
conceal, abdō, -ere, -didī, -ditum, *used chiefly of physical objects.*
deed, factum, -ī, *n.*

news (message), nūntius, -ī, *m.*
prove, probō, I.
sight, cōnspectus, -ūs, *m.* (*a limiting gen. may be subj. or obj.*).

Elated by this victory, the Eburones sent envoys to many other tribes of Gaul to persuade them to revolt, and they themselves with the Nervii hastened with all their forces to the camp of Cicero before any news of [1] the death of the two generals had reached him. When they came, they said the same things they had said to Sabinus and Cotta. Cicero replied: " I will never accept terms from an armed enemy. Lay down your arms and send envoys to Caesar to ask him for what you desire." Then they besieged the camp fiercely. Cicero and his men fought day and night, and Cicero himself was present in all places of the camp exhorting his men and fighting, though he was by no means well.   Many brave deeds were witnessed in this siege.   Two centurions in the legion were always in keen rivalry for promotion.[2]   One[3] day when they were fighting on the wall, one of them cried to the other: " Come, now; prove your courage!" and he rushed out from the gate into the thickest[4] (of the) enemy.   The other hastened to his aid, and both,[5] after killing several of the enemy, retired safe inside the fortifications.   Cicero sent many men to tell Caesar of the siege, but they were all captured and killed in sight of our soldiers.   Finally he persuaded a certain Gaul in whom he had the greatest confidence to carry to Caesar a dispatch[6] concealed in a javelin.   A Gaul among Gauls, he was not recognized, and he reached Caesar.

1. ' message concerning.'   2. Express the *facts* in common-sense terms; *e.g.*, ' always were contending with each other concerning honor.'   3. ' a certain.'   4. ' densest.'   5. Use **ambō** here.   6. ' letter.'

EXERCISE 20

apprehend (suspect), **suspicor**, I, *dep.*

fire, **ignis**, **-is**, *m.*

praise, **laudō**, I.

report, **fāma**, **-ae**, *f.* (*in sense of* rumor).

send back, **remittō**, **-ere**, **-mīsī**, **-missum**.

tie to, **dēligō**, I, *w. dir. obj. and* **ad** *and acc. of the thing to which.*

uprising, **tumultus**, **-ūs**, *m.*

Caesar quickly sent messages to the nearest winter quarters that the generals should join him as quickly as possible, and he showed them in what great peril Cicero was.   He also sent back the Gaul to Cicero with a letter that he was himself coming to his assistance.   The Gaul tied the letter to a javelin and threw it over[1] the wall.   It was not found for three days.   Then a soldier saw it and carried it to Cicero, who announced to the army: " Caesar has our letter and is coming."   With a great shout they began to fight even more bravely than before. The Gauls then abandoned the siege and hastened against Caesar, the light of whose fires they now could see at night. Caesar held himself in camp, since he knew that Cicero was no longer [2] in danger, and by this impression [3] of fear lured the enemy to charge [4] up to [5] the very gates. Then, making a sortie from all the gates, he put them to flight and killed the greater part of them. When he had come to Cicero's camp, he praised all for their magnificent defense of the camp.[6] The report of Caesar's victory reached Labienus with incredible swiftness through the forest by some system [7] of signals which the barbarians used, so that, though Labienus' camp was about sixty miles distant from Cicero's, and Caesar had reached Cicero's camp about three o'clock in the afternoon,[8] Labienus was informed of the battle before midnight.[9] All the Gauls then returned home; but Caesar apprehended an uprising of all the states in [10] the next summer.

1. **trāns** or **per** w. acc. 2. 'not now.' 3. 'opinion.' 4. 'brought it about that the enemy charged.' 5. **ūsque ad**. 6. 'because they had defended the camp magnificently (**ēgregiē**).' 7. **aliqua ratiō**. 8. The Roman day extended, approximately, from 6 A.M. to 6 P.M. without distinction of morning and afternoon, and was measured by hours: make your own expression for 3 P.M. 9. 'the middle of the night.' 10. Cf. **59**, III.

PART III

EXERCISES IN TRANSLATING IDIOMATIC ENGLISH

NOTES[1] ON THE BALKAN[2] WAR

EXERCISE 1

The entire Balkan peninsula,[3] as that part of Europe is called which begins[4] at the Danube River and faces the southeast,[5] is divided[6] among six nations, Greeks, Servians, Bulgarians, Roumanians, Montenegrins, and Turks.[7] Of these, the Servians, Bulgarians, and Montenegrins are of Slavonic[8] stock. Their allies, the Greeks, though of far different stock, yet made common cause with them[9] against the Turks. Greece, indeed, can hardly be said to form[10] a part of the Balkan peninsula; still, because the Greeks joined with the Balkan nations and because it is situated in the country bounded by a line[11] drawn[12] from the Black Sea[13] to the Adriatic[14] following-the-direction-of[15] the Balkan chain,[16] it may be included in[17] the same name as the others. The origin[18] and history[19] of the Greeks are well known, so that this subject need not be here treated.[20]

1. Cf. the title Caesar gave to his work.   2. **Balkānus, -a, -um** : except where the classic name of a place has given rise to its modern name, terms thus coined will be used.   The ancient name of the Balkan chain, **Haemus,** does not even suggest the modern term.   3. **paenīnsula, -ae,** *f.*   4. Cf. Caes. *B. G.*, I, 1.   5. 'south' = **merīdiēs, -ēī,** *f.*; to form 'southeast,' remember how Caesar forms 'northeast.'   6. **distribuō,** w. dat. ind. obj.   7. **Graecī, Serbī, Bulgāriī, Rūmānī, Nigromontānī, Turcī.**   8. **Sclāvēnicus, -a, -um.**   9. In all such instances form a phrase expressing the facts : here, *e.g.,* 'joined themselves in common plan.'   10. 'to be.'   11. **līnea, -ae,** *f.*

12. 'which extends.'   13. **Pontus**, -ī, *m.*   14. **mare Hadriāticum**.   15. **secun-dum**, prep. w. acc.   16. **iugum**, -ī, *n.*   17. 'called by.'   18. 'beginnings.'   19. 'things accomplished,' **rēs gestae**.   20. Again seek a common-sense expression of the facts; *e.g.*, 'so that it need not be spoken about it,' **ita ut hīs dē rēbus nōn opus sit dīcī**.

EXERCISE 2

Of the Slavonic nations, of which stock three of the states now fighting in the Balkans are offshoots,[1] it is necessary to speak somewhat [2] more fully.[3]   The Slavs [4] seem to have had their first home [5] in the region of the rivers Vistula and Dniester,[6] which extends northeast from the Carpathian [7] mountains. In the first century [8] A.D.[9] came [10] probably [11] the first important Slav migration.[12]   The great migrations and movements [13] of the Goths [14] so occupied the attention [15] of men that no notice was paid to the fact [16] that the Slav races also were gradually [17] migrating.   The Goths certainly dominated [18] them, and for a time [19] occupied the same territories.   This [20] was probably the reason for the Slav migrations, for, although the Slavs were the equals [21] of the Germans in warfare, they were less able to combine [22] and act for their common safety.

1. **prognātus** (n. or adj.) w. abl. alone or w. **ab**, **ex**.   2. **aliquantō**.   3. 'more carefully,' comp. of **accūrātē**.   4. **Sclāvī**.   5. Either as written, using **domicilium**, or thus: 'seem to have anciently (**antīquitus**) inhabited.'   6. **Danaster**, -trī, *m.*   7. **Carpatēs**.   8. **saeculum**, -ī, *n.*   9. **post Chris-tum**.   10. Not **veniō**: what does 'came' mean here?   11. Use a paren-thetic clause, 'as it seems.'   12. **dēmigrātiō**; or reconstruct the whole clause: 'a great number of Slavs, as it seems, first began to migrate.'   13. **mōtus**, -ūs, *m.*   14. **Gothī**.   15. 'minds.'   16. 'that it was not no-ticed (or 'that this thing was not noticed') 'that the Slav races,' etc. Use an acc. and inf. depending on the verb 'noticed.'   17. **paulātim**.   18. **dominor**, followed by **inter** w. acc., 'exercised control among them.'   19. **aliquamdiū**.   20. 'This, as it seems, was to the Slavs a cause of migrating.'   21. **pār**, **paris** (adj.), w. dat.   22. **inter sē societāte et foedere coniungere**; literally, 'join among themselves in association and treaty.'

EXERCISE 3

The first mention [1] of the Slavs in literature is in the beginning of the sixth century.   This means [2] that by this time they had spread [3] far enough to attract the notice of [4] the Empire,[5] for they had crossed the Balkans and had appeared [6] as a new terror to Byzantium.   By the beginning of the seventh century the Slavs had overrun [7] the entire Balkan peninsula together with [8] Greece.   Religion [9] was probably the leading cause for [10] their breaking up [11] into the beginnings of the kingdoms of to-day.[12]   They were in the earliest times [13] savages,[14] and their greatest god was thunder.[15]   But whenever [16] they came into contact [17] with Christian peoples, these endeavored to convert [18] them to the true God.   Thus those who settled in the western [19] portions of the peninsula became adherents of [20] the Roman church,[21] while those who remained in the eastern part adopted [22] the Greek.   By far the greater part of the Slavs had become Christians before their conquest [23] by the Bulgars.

1. Avoid rendering a real verb action by a verbal noun, a very common English idiom; say 'The Slavs are first named (nōminō) in letters.'   2. sīgnificō.   3. vagor.   4. A result clause; ' that they were noticed by.'   5. Imperium.   6. 'were present.'   7. pervagor w. in and abl. of place or w. acc. dir. obj.   8. ūnā cum.   9. religiō, -ōnis, f.   10. 'why (quārē) they should,' etc.   11. dissolvō.   12. An impossible phrase in Latin; say ' the kingdoms which exist (exstō) to-day.'   13. 'anciently.'   14. ferus, -a, -um often used as subst.   15. tonitrus, -ūs, m.   16. utcumque or quotiēscumque w. indic.; or cf. 136.   17. occurrō, III, w. dat.   18. convertō.   19. occidentālis, -e, adj.   20. 'joined themselves with,' or more simply, ' favored ' (faveō w. dat.).   21. ecclēsia, -ae, f.   22. cōnsequor.   23. Cf. note 1.

EXERCISE 4

The Servians were the largest and most powerful clan [1] of the Slav stock.   In the beginning of the sixth century they had descended [2] from their northern [3] home [4] across the Balkans to

the shores [5] of the Black Sea [6] and thence had spread west-
ward [7] along the Danube and had settled in the devastated
northwestern [8] provinces of the Balkan peninsula. The history [9] of Servia as [10] a nation begins [11] towards [12] the middle of
the seventh century. The Servian forces were conquered by
the Turks in 1389 [13] and Servia became a Turkish province.
Servia enjoyed [14] a brief independence [15] from 1804 to 1813,
when it was again subjugated by the Turks. It finally became
a free and independent kingdom [16] in 1830.

1. gēns, gentis, *f*.   2. dēscendō.   3. septentriōnālis, -e.   4. domicilium.   5. lītus, -oris, *n*., or ōra, -ae, *f*.   6. Pontus, -ī, *m*.   7. in occidentem
sōlem.   8. Cf. Caes. *B. G.* I, 1.   9. memoria, -ae, *f*.   10. tamquam.
11. 'takes beginning,' or use incipiō.   12. sub w. acc., or in this instance ab
w. abl.   13. annō dominī mīlēsimō trecentēsimō octōgēsimō nōnō, or
A.D. MCCCLXXXIX.   14. ūtor.   15. lībertās.   16. 'a free and independent (*i.e.*, autonomous) kingdom' is best rendered by rēgnum nōminis
suī atque iūris: 'independent' may also be expressed by potēns suī.

EXERCISE 5

The Bulgars, savage men of Tatar [1] stock, first appeared
on the banks of the river Pruth [2] in the latter part of the seventh
century. They were wild [3] and barbarous horsemen, polyg-
amists,[4] and despotically [5] governed by their chiefs and nobles.
Their original abode was in the tract between the Ural [6] Mountains and the Volga.[6]   In 679 they crossed the Danube,[7] subjugated the Slavonic population of Moesia, and advanced to
the gates of Constantinople [8] and Saloniki.[8]   The eastern
Roman Emperors [9] were compelled to cede [10] to them the province of Moesia and to pay [11] tribute.[12]   The enemy had,
however, come in no large number, so that during the next two
hundred years [13] they became merged [14] in the Slavonic population and adopted its language, customs and local institutions.[15]
Not a trace [16] of Tatar speech is found among the Bulgars to-

day. They also became Christians and supporters [17] of the Greek church.

1. **Tatar, -aris.** 2. **Porata.** 3. **immānis, -e.** 4. Use rel. clause and the word ' wife ' (**uxor**). 5. **superbē et crūdēliter.** 6. **montēs Urālēs, Volga**; cf. Ex. **1**, n. 2 : the ancient names were **Rhimmicī** and **Rhā**, the latter indecl. 7. **Dānuvius.** 8. **Constantīnopolis, Thessalonīca.** 9. ' Roman Emperors of the East,' **Imperātōrēs Orientis** or **Eurōpae Orientālis.** 10. **cēdō.** 11. **pendō.** 12. **stīpendium, -ī,** *n.* 13. ' in these 200 years.' 14. ' were merged ' (**cōnfundō,** w. **in** and acc.). 15. ' institutions of each place.' 16. **nē paululum quidem.** 17. Cf. Ex. **3**, n. 20.

EXERCISE 6

The Montenegrins are offshoots of the Servians. Every-where [1] in this region are great mountains to which an approach is most difficult, so that it offers to a brave race the very best [2] opportunities for defense. It originally formed a portion of the Roman province of Illyria. In 493 it was conquered by the Ostrogoths,[3] and fifty years later came under the rule of Byzantium. The Serb race occupied the country about the middle of the seventh century ; and after the defeat of the Serbs by the Turks in the fierce battle at Kossovo [4] in 1389, which extinguished [5] the freedom of Servia for [6] four hundred years, a Servian chief, George [7] Balsha, escaped [8] to the mountains and founded [9] the little nation of mountaineers, every man of whom is a soldier, which has ever since [10] engaged in ceaseless [11] warfare with the Turks.

1. **passim**, or devise a still stronger expression. 2. **quam** w. superl. 3. **Ostrogothī.** 4. Indeclinable, or treat as an **-on** stem. 5. ' took away ' (**ēripiō**) or ' destroyed ' (**dēleō**). 6. **per** w. acc. 7. **Georgius.** 8. **effugiō.** 9. **condō.** 10. ' always from that time '; cf. **137.** 11. **perpetuus, -a, -um.**

EXERCISE 7

The Balkan War is really the outcome [1] of long-standing [2] rivalries [3] among the Bulgars, Serbs, Montenegrins and Greeks, who were striving [4] severally [5] to obtain ascendancy [6] in Macedonia, the population of which is a composite [7] of all four races. They also distrusted and even hated [8] one another because of religious differences,[9] which always powerfully affect [10] rude [11] and only partially civilized [12] peoples.   Let us briefly glance at [13] the situation [14] of these Balkan states at the outbreak [15] of the war.   In [16] the first place, holding the balance of power [17] in the situation, and prepared to seek good for herself by favoring either party,[18] is Roumania.·   She is the best governed of all the Balkan states and possesses a large and well-disciplined [19] army.   Bulgaria, moreover, for reasons of her own, hates Roumania, because at the close[20] of the Russo-Turkish [21] War, Russia assigned to Roumania certain territory to the south [22] of the mouths [23] of the Danube, which from the nature of the region properly belongs to Bulgaria.[24]   Had Roumania joined forces with the Turks[25] in making war on Bulgaria, the latter would have been in the utmost danger in having [26] an enemy both in front and rear.[27]   Roumania, however, held off [28] from actual [29] war, but kept her army in readiness [30] as a hint [31] to the victors that she would look out [32] for herself in the final settlement [33] after the war.

1. 'comes out from' (ēveniō, w. ex and abl.); cf. Ex. 3, n. 1.   2. vetus, -eris, adj.   3. certāmen, -inis, n.   4. nītor.   5. 'each for (prō) itself.'   6. What is the real meaning in simple words?   7. compōnō or permisceō, w. ex and abl.   8. 'not only did not trust but also hated' (ōdī).   9. 'diversities (varietātēs) of religions,' or ' religions which differ from each other.'   10. 'are very powerful among.'   11. dūrus, -a, -um.   12. parum hūmānus.   13. 'notice.'   14. Here 'state' or 'condition,' status, -ūs, m., or condiciō, -ōnis, f.   15. Abl. absol., coörior.   16. Recast into one this and the following sentence: 'In the first place (imprīmīs) R., which is the best governed . . . and possesses . . . holds . . . and is prepared . . .'   17. This phrase cannot be rendered literally; look for the facts: 'is able to bring about any desired (quīvīs) outcome (exitus, -ūs, m.) of war.'   18. 'either (utervīs) part.'   19. exercitātus, -a, -um.   20. Abl. absol., cōnficiō.   21. Rel. clause.   22. 'which extends to the south from.'   23. ōstium, -ī, n.   24. 'ought to be of B.'   25. 'made war on B. along

with (ūnā cum) the T.' 26. Causal clause w. verb in subjv. 27. ā fronte et ā tergō. 28. abstineō. 29. Omit. 30. parātus, -a, -um. 31. 'by which she would indicate' (indīcō, I). 32. prōvideō or prōspiciō. 33. 'in things to be determined (gerundive) after the war.'

EXERCISE 8

West of Bulgaria lies Servia, in the most dangerous [1] position of all the Balkan states, for she lies across Austria's path to the Aegean,[2] and to the Aegean [3] Austria intends finally to go. Between Servia and the sea a Slavonic population inhabits the provinces of Bosnia and Herzegovina, which were seized by Austria a few years ago; so that Servia fears for her own interests [4] also, since she has small confidence in her powerful neighbor. Below [5] these provinces lies Montenegro, the little kingdom of the mountains,[6] which is completely [7] hemmed in by Turkey [8] and Austria and has but a few miles [9] of seacoast. The land there will [10] not now support [11] the population, and Montenegro needs [12] land for agriculture and a port where she may sell [13] her own goods and buy food.[14] Her ambition [15] is to possess Scutari.[16] At the lowest [17] part of the peninsula lies Greece. Within the ring [18] of these provinces lie the possessions of European Turkey,[19] often called by the one name, Macedonia, but divided into several lesser provinces. Between Servia and Montenegro is the Turkish province of Novi-Bazar,[20] which is really the main issue [21] in the Balkan question.[22] For it extends in a northwesterly direction and is bounded on that side by Bosnia, so that it offers to Austria a highway [23] to Saloniki and the Aegean. It is therefore a constant menace [24] to the Slavonic nations from the Germanic.

1. perīculōsus, -a, -um. 2. prohibet (dētinet) enim Austriam quōminus ad Aegaeum perveniat, quō, etc., or both clauses may be condensed into obvia enim est Austriae, quae ad Aegaeum, etc. 3. Avoid the rhetoric; say simply 'whither,' or else so reconstruct the sentence as to require a relative pronoun only (cf. n. 2). 4. rēs. 5. īnfrā w. acc. 6. Use an

adj., **montānus**.   7. ' all,' **tōtus**.   8. **Turcia**.   9. ' a few miles only '
(**tantum**).   10. No ref. to fut. time; say ' cannot ' or ' does not.'
11. **sustineō**.   12. **egeō** w. abl.   13. **vēndō**.   14. **rēs frūmentāria**.   15. Cf.
Ex. **3**, n. 1.   16. **Scodra**.   17. **īnfimus, -a, -um**.   18. **orbis, -is,** *m.*   19. **Turcia
Eurōpaea**.   20. Indecl.   21. ' the question (**quaestiō**) itself.'   22. **in rēbus Balkānīs**.   23. ' easy road.'   24. ' perpetual danger.'

EXERCISE 9

Macedonia is inhabited by many races, especially Greeks,
Bulgarians and Servians. The Greek youth,[1] however, have in
great part [2] abandoned the land and gathered in the cities, and
Bulgarian peasants [3] have spread over Macedonia and have thus
come to be in the majority.[4] Bulgaria claims [5] Macedonia
because from 893 to 1277 it was ruled [6] by Bulgarian kings and
the bulk [7] of its inhabitants are of Bulgarian stock. The Servians claim it because the great King Dushan who reigned
from 1336 to 1356 held Macedonia in his vast [8] kingdom and
styled himself Czar [9] of Macedonia and Great King of the
Serbs, Greeks, and Bulgars ; and, moreover,[10] that part of Macedonia called Old [11] Servia is inhabited by people of their own
race. Greece claims Macedonia because Alexander the Great
and Philip ruled it many ages [12] before Servia and Bulgaria
were heard of,[13] and very many of the Macedonians to-day are
Hellenes. As a result of this race rivalry [14] armed bands of
Greek and Bulgarian desperadoes [15] have for more than twenty
years harried Macedonia, the one killing [16] all the Bulgarians
they could find, the other all the Greeks. The Turkish government [17] did not try to stop them, for as long as Christians were
killing one another,[18] they could not combine [19] against the
Turks. Sometimes,[20] however, the Turks themselves would
raid [21] the unfortunate [22] provinces and kill every Christian of
whatever race. Furthermore, they cruelly overtaxed [23] and mis-
governed [24] them, nor would they obey [25] the demands [26] of the
Great Powers to improve conditions.[27]

1. iuventūs, -ūtis, *f.*   2. magnam partem; cf. Caes. *B. G.* IV, 1.
3. agrestis, -is, *m.*   4. 'become the greater part (*or* number).'   5. petō.
6. regō, *tr.;* rēgnō, *intr.*   7. What is meant here?   8. ingēns, -entis.
9. Caesar.   10. praétereā.   11. vetus.   12. saeculum.   13. Impers.; 'before
it had been heard about S.,' etc.   14. ' from (ex) this rivalry (certāmen) of
races it came out that.'   15. latrō, -ōnis, *m.*   16. ' of whom the one (alterī)
killed,' etc.   17. imperium.   18. ' other Christians were killing others.'
19. ' join themselves.'   20. aliquandō.   21. incursiōnēs facere, imperfect
indic.   22. miser, -era, -erum.   23. 'imposed too great taxes' (stīpendia).
24. 'governed badly.'   25. pāreō w. dat.   26. postulātum *or* praeceptum
followed by purpose clause.   27. ' govern better.'

EXERCISE 10

The Great Powers themselves, who similarly [1] fear and distrust one another, have always rendered the Balkan situation
more uncertain and difficult.   The six great powers of Europe,
Germany, Austria, Italy, Russia, France and England, have
formed [2] treaties of peace and friendship in groups of three.[3]
The former of these two groups [4] calls itself the Triple Alliance [5];
the latter, the Triple Entente.[6]   They have united, as they say,
for [7] defense and for preserving the peace of Europe.   Each
group seeks to prevent the other from gaining [8] influence [9] or
advantage [10] in any way or in any place.   When, therefore, they
seek to coerce [11] or restrain or advise Turkey, or to compel her
to cease from killing and abusing [12] her Christian subjects, [13]
she never obeys, well knowing [14] that the Powers will not take
active measures.[15]   So on this occasion, when the war clouds
were gathering,[16] the Powers were able neither to prevent the
Allies from declaring [17] war nor to compel Turkey to grant reforms,[18] since they could not adopt any common plan of action.[19]
The Great Powers could not say to the Balkan States: " You
shall not aid [20] the Christian population to [21] escape persecu-
tion [22] and maladministration," [23] nor could they order the
Turks to grant the demands of their enemies [24] and [25] give free-

dom to Macedonia, Albania and Old Servia. This would have been useless,[26] because, first, the Turks would certainly have refused; and next, even if Turkey should yield,[27] the Powers well knew that they could themselves never agree[28] as to how[29] they should enforce[30] their demands. Moreover, the Turks, a warlike[31] nation, believed themselves invincible,[32] and nobody[33] believed that the turbulent[34] Balkan States could ever join in an alliance.[35]

1. 'in the same manner.' 2. cōnfīrmō. 3. Use distributive numeral. 4. pars. 5. Societās Triplex. 6. Cōnsēnsiō Triplex. 7. ad w. gerundive. 8. cōnséquor. 9. auctōritās. 10. ūtilitās. 11. coerceō. 12. vexō. 13. cīvis. 14. Causal clause w. cum. 15. 'will do (agō) nothing.' 16. Avoid the figure; say 'when war was breaking out.' 17. indīcō, III. 18. sē melius gerere. 19. agō, gerund. 20. adiuvō. 21. ad w. gerundive. 22. vexātiō. 23. 'cruel rule.' 24. 'to do the demands (postulātum) of their enemies,' or 'to satisfy (satisfaciō w. dat.) their enemies demanding.' 25. Clause of purpose w. ut, expressing the substance of the demand. 26. inūtilis, or an adv., 'in vain' (frustrā). 27. What tense? 28. inter sē cōnsentīre. 29. quem ad modum. 30. persequor. 31. cupidus bellandī. 32. invictus. 33. 'nor did anybody' (nec quisquam). 34. tumultuōsus. 35. 'join in friendship and treaty' (foedus, -eris, n.).

EXERCISE 11

Then the incredible happened. Laying aside their jealousies,[1] since they realized that thus only[2] could they obtain any advantage[3] for themselves, they suddenly concluded a firm alliance[4] and made preparation against the common enemy. Turkey was exhausted[5] by the Italian war in Tripoli[6] and the Allies believed[7] that they would quickly prove victorious and divide the spoil.[8] Thus there has suddenly appeared[9] in Europe a new Great Power, the Balkan Confederation. I shall now briefly indicate the size[10] of the forces of each state and their efficiency[11] for war. For its size, Bulgaria has the best equipped[12] and most efficient army[13] in Europe. Every sixth man [14] is a soldier, hardy [15] and enduring [16] and well drilled,[17] and the officers are brave and skillful.[18] She was believed at the outbreak of the war to be able to put in the field [19] about 250,000 men and 500 guns.[20]   The Servians had for many years been strengthening [21] their army to meet [22] the danger from Austria, and were estimated [23] at 200,000 men. Their infantry is excellent,[24] their artillery [25] mediocre,[26] their cavalry of no great value.[27]   Greece claimed to be able to furnish 200,000 men.   The Montenegrin army is the nation under arms.[28]   There was no organized [29] army prior to the present war, but every man was always armed; and the old [30] king would often require his subjects [31] whom he met [32] in the streets of Cettinje or on the mountain trails [33] to show him their weapons that he might see if they were well cared for.[34]

1. **inimīcitia**, *pl.*   2. ' not otherwise.'   3. ' anything of good.'   4. ' established peace and friendship with one another.'   5. **dēfessus**.   6. **Tripolis, -is**, *f.*   7. **cōnfīdō**.   8. **praeda**.   9. ' is present,' or ' has been made.' 10. ' how great are the forces.'   11. ' what they can (do) in war.'   12. **armātus** or **īnstrūctus**.   13. ' best adapted for (**aptus ad**) war.'   14. **sextus quisque**; note word order.   15. **dūrus**.   16. **labōris patiēns**.   17. **exercitātus**.   18. **perītus reī mīlitāris**.   19. **cōnficiō**.   20. **tormentum**. 21. **augeō**.   22. **ad**.   23. **aestimō** w. **ad**.   24. ' the best.'   25. **tormentāriī**.   26. **mediocris**.   27. **valeō** w. adverbial acc.   28. ' the nation wholly (**tōtus**) armed '; avoid the use of a noun modified by a prepositional phrase.   29. **iūstus**.   30. **senex**.   31. ' citizens.'   32. **incidō** w. **in** and acc., or **obviam fīō** w. dat.   33. **sēmita montāna**.   34. **cūrō**.

EXERCISE 12

Montenegro was the first to declare [1] war, induced probably by the fear that Russia would forbid it.   On the 8th of October, 1912, King Nicholas issued the following proclamation [2] at Cettinje: " Montenegro had hoped to be able to secure the liberation [3] of the Serbs in Turkey without bloodshed,[4] but, since all her efforts [5] have proved unavailing,[6] no recourse [7] is

left but ⁸ to take up arms in their behalf. Montenegro attacks
Turkey, not from motives of arrogance,⁹ but inspired ¹⁰ by a
noble resolve ¹¹ to prevent the extermination ¹² of her brethren."
Within a week ¹³ the Montenegrin army, led by King Nicholas
in person, had invaded ¹⁴ the Turkish ¹⁵ province of Novi-Bazar ¹⁶
and stormed a number of strongly ¹⁷ fortified positions, and
the soldiers were hailed ¹⁸ as liberators ¹⁹ by the Slavs dwelling
there. At the same time the armies of Servia, Bulgaria and
Greece mobilized ²⁰ and moved forward ²¹ to the Turkish fron-
tier.²² The parliaments ²³ of these nations voted liberal credits ²⁴
and with one voice the people demanded ²⁵ war to ²⁶ the death
with Turkey. To the Allies' demands ²⁷ for immediate reforms
in Macedonia, Turkey replied by mobilization,²⁸ and on October
17 declared war against Bulgaria and Servia. Hardly had the
notes ²⁹ of the Allies been delivered ³⁰ to the Porte,³¹ when the
Powers tried to coerce the little states and to persuade Turkey:
but it was too late.³² Turkey, indeed, on October 14 replied
to the representations ³³ of the Powers and declined to allow
any intervention by Europe ³⁴ in her system ³⁵ of administering
Macedonia.

1. 'first declared.' 2. 'thus proclaimed' (prōnūntiō). 3. 'to bring it
about that the S. be liberated.' 4. 'blood' (sanguis, -inis, *m*.). 5. 'attempts' (cōnātum). 6. 'have come forth badly' (male prōficere).
7. 'nothing.' 8. nisi followed by ut w. subjv. clause. 9. ex arrogantiā.
10. impulsus. 11. 'by this noble (nōbilis) plan, that' (ut w. subjv.).
12. 'prohibit her brothers from extermination' (interneciō). 13. 'seven
days'; the week was unknown as a time unit in Rome. 14. ingredior
w. in and acc. 15. Turcicus. 16. Indecl. 17. ēgregiē. 18. appellō.
19. līberātor. 20. omnibus rebus parātī (*or* īnstrūctī); omit 'and.'
21. 'advanced.' 22. fīnēs, *pl.* 23. senātus. 24. 'decreed much money
for (ad) the war.' 25. dēpōscō. 26. ūsque ad. 27. 'to the Allies
demanding that in M. it should be better ruled (impers.) immediately.'
28. cōpiīs ad bellum comparandīs. 29. In this case 'letters.' 30. dēferō.
31. ad Portam. 32. sērō, sērius. 33. 'demands.' 34. 'declined (negō)
to allow Europe to intervene' (interveniō w. dat.). 35. ratiō, here w. gen.
of gerundive.

EXERCISE 13

Ten days after the declaration of war,[1] the first Bulgarian army took by assault the city of Mustapha Pasha,[2] and all the allied troops began to move forward. Strict censorship both by Bulgaria and by Turkey kept the world ignorant of the Allies' aims and movements.[3] Soon, however, the plans of campaign[4] worked out[5] by the General Staffs[6] in Sofia, Belgrade and Athens[7] began to unfold[8] in the actual campaigning.[9] The plan of the whole war was that Montenegro should attack and capture the important city of Scutari and generally[10] seduce[11] Northern Albania to revolt from Turkey. The Bulgarian armies under King Ferdinand in person,[12] with Savov as his commander in chief,[13] were[14] to invade Thrace : the Servian armies under the general command[15] of Prince Alexander were[14] to pierce[16] Macedonia through the provinces of Kossovo[2] and Monastir,[2] while the Greek forces under Crown Prince[17] Constantine should[14] advance through the mountains with the object[18] of driving the Turks out of Epirus and striking at[19] Saloniki. The Bulgarian, Servian and Greek lines were[14] finally to converge on[20] Constantinople. These plans were carried out[21] with amazing[22] dash[23] and precision.[24] Scutari was at once invested by the Montenegrin army and completely isolated[25] ; and though the Turks by their fierce resistance[26] held the bulk of the Montenegrin army engaged[27] before this stronghold[28] during the entire war, the troops of King Nicholas achieved notable successes[29] elsewhere[30] in Novi-Bazar.[2]

1. ' after war declared ' (perf. ptc.). 2. Indecl. 3. An impossible sentence : war correspondence and press censorship were unknown to the Romans, and the statement must be recast ; *e.g.*, ' Both T. and B. most diligently concealed (**cēlō**) their plans and movements (**rēs gestae**), nor permitted any letters to be sent out from the armies, so that men in Europe were ignorant of (**īgnōrō**) everything.' 4. **ratiōnēs bellī gerendī.** 5. **praeparō.** 6. **Concilium dē rē mīlitārī.** 7. **Sofia, Alba Graeca, Athēnae.**

8. ' to be shown *or* understood.' 9. ' by waging (gerundive) the war itself.'
10. ' by every means' (ratiō). 11. sollicitō. 12. 'F. himself leading,
along with Savovius.' 13. Here lēgātus; imperātor cannot be used of a
commander whose military superior is in the field. 14. The movements of
all these armies are to be expressed by purpose clauses dependent on the
phrase, " the plan . . . was." 15. ' Prince A. being commander in chief '
(imperātor). 16. ' invade,' or ' go into.' 17. Prīnceps Rēgius. 18. ' with
this plan, that they should,' etc. 19. ' attacking '; here petō rather than
oppugnō, as the emphasis is on its being the objective point sought in
the campaign. 20. conveniō w. ad. 21. exsequor. 22. ' incredible.'
23. alacritās. 24. dīligentia. 25. ' cut off.' 26. ' by fiercely resisting.'
27. ' occupied.' 28. arx, arcis, *f.* 29. ' fought many successful battles,'
or ' things proceeded well (optimē prōcēdō) for the troops ' (dat. of ref.).
30. ' in other places.'

EXERCISE 14

After the capture of Mustapha Pasha, the northern door [1]
to Adrianople, the main [2] Bulgarian army under Savov invested
this ancient [3] capital [4] of Thrace, while [5] the second Bulgarian
army made a detour eastward [6] and took Kirk-Kilisseh,[7] which [8]
closed the door [9] to any Turkish aid from the east. Adrianople was then regularly [10] besieged. The Bulgarian General
Staff pushed on [11] with two other armies into Thrace,[12] and
soon had command of [13] the roads to Constantinople. Meanwhile the Servian invasion of Turkish territory had begun.[14]
Within a few days King Peter took the town of Pristina, stormed
the stronghold [15] of Novi-Bazar,[7] the capital of the province
of the same name, and after a heavy engagement [16] carried the
ancient strategic [17] city of Uskub.[7] Greece also had begun her
campaign [18] by the dispatch of her fleet [19] to attack the Aegean
islands. The Greek army advanced through Miluna Pass,[20]
defeating the Turks in a sharp engagement. A few days later
the important city of Elassona was taken by the army of King
George. The Bulgarians meanwhile were hotly [21] besieging
Adrianople, while [5] the Turks carried on a dogged resistance.[22]

On October 27 the Bulgarian troops captured the town of Eski-Baba, which gave them control of the Orient Railway [23] which connects [24] Vienna and Constantinople.

1. Avoid the figure; say ' which offered access to A. from the north.' 2. **prīnceps**, adj. 3. **antīquus**. 4. **caput**. 5. ' while ' is often equivalent to a mere conjunction, ' and,' ' and also.' 6. ' set out toward the east by a circuit ' (**circuitus**). 7. Indecl. 8. The antecedent is here not a word, but the entire idea of the army's movement and successful action.   In such cases the rel. clause is always introduced by **id quod** or **quae rēs**. 9. Avoid the figure: say ' prevented any T. aid,' etc. 10. ' as is the custom of war.' 11. **contendō**. 12. **Thrācia**. 13. ' occupied.' 14. ' the S. had begun to march into,' etc. 15. **arx** or **castellum**. 16. A phrase in abl. absolute. 17. No word for ' strategic '; translate the idea : ' which offered great opportunities for waging war.' 18. No special word for ' campaign '; ' began to make war ' (**bellum īnferre**). 19. Abl. absolute. 20. **per quāsdam angustiās montium Milūnam appellātās.** 21. ' with great violence *or* valor.' 22. ' resisted obstinately ' (**obstinātē**). 23. ' brought it about that they were able to control (**praesum**) the O. R. ' (**via ferrea Orientis**). 24. **iungō**, w. acc. dir. obj. and dat. ind. obj. or w. **cum**.

EXERCISE 15

Three days later, after a terrific battle, the Turks were driven from the fortifications of Lule Burgas, a place of great strategic importance.[1]   The terrible fight here lasted five days, the Bulgarian forces opposing [2] a great Turkish army of 130,000 men with 300 guns and 65 squadrons [3] of cavalry.   The Turkish right wing attacked the Bulgarians repeatedly [4] in deep column,[5] but failed.[6]   The Bulgarians repelled these attacks with unexampled [7] bravery and used the bayonet [8] much both here and throughout the war, proving [9] that, in spite of [10] the theories of military writers, cold iron [11] is still the King of Battles.[12]   The Bulgarian artillery also was most admirably and accurately served,[13] and from charge after charge [14] the enemy was compelled to retire, leaving the field covered with the dead.[15]   On the third day of the fight the Bulgarian center [16] advanced, the infantry storming the fortified positions of the Turks with the bayonet and then scourging [17] their panic-stricken enemy with artillery. On the fifth day the Bulgarian left wing made the decisive attack [18] and drove the Turks in headlong flight.[19] The Turks are said to have lost 40,000 men killed and wounded, the Bulgarians 15,000; for no matter how [20] they expose themselves to danger, the victors [21] never suffer like the vanquished. After this dreadful battle was over there was an interval of twenty-four hours when both sides were too exhausted to fight. [22]

1. ' which is of great use (77) for waging war,' quod oppidum (or quī locus) magnō ūsuī est ad, etc.; cf. also n. 17, Ex. 14.   2. ' when the B. forces were drawn up against,' etc.   3. turma.   4. etiam atque etiam.   5. longō (or cōnfertissimō) agmine.   6. What does this word mean here?   7. 'incredible.'   8. ' weapons tipped with iron ' (arma ferrō praefīxa).   9. ' by which they proved.'   10. No word for ' in-spite-of '; use an abl. absolute and say ' neglecting (neglegō) the theory (ratiō) of military writers ' (scrīptor).   11. ferrum frīgidum.   12. The figure is impossible : say ' is still of most value in fighting battles,' etiam nunc plūrimum valēre in proeliīs pugnandīs.   13. optimē atque accūrātissimē administrō.   14. This is not a Latin idiom; ' from many charges,' or ' having made many charges.'   15. ' leaving heaps (acervus) of corpses (cadāver) everywhere ' (passim) : there is no word for ' battlefield ' in Caesar.   16. medium.   17. vexō.   18. impetus ultimus.   19. ' gave the T. headlong (praeceps) into flight.'   20. ' in whatever manner victors expose (obiciō), etc., they never so (ita) suffer (calamitātem accipiō) as (ut) the conquered (do).'   21. victōrēs.   22. ' a space of 24 hours followed when both armies were more exhausted (dēfessus) than that (ut w. subjv. in result clause) they should fight.'

EXERCISE 16

The Bulgarian advance [1] then continued without giving [2] the Turks a chance to rest [3] further. On November 1 the invaders [4] captured Demotica, and next the Turks were driven back after a terrific three days' [5] battle at Tchorlu.[6] Nazim Pasha's [6] forces were so battered [7] in this fight, it is reported, that the entire command,[8] excepting [9] only the higher officers, fled in confusion to escape the pursuing Bulgars. Pushing on in spite of [10] bad roads with his almost exhausted troops, the Bulgarian commander forced his way [11] eastward along the swampy [12] peninsula at the end of which Constantinople is situated, the Turks in full retreat [13] before him, in order to cut off the enemy from the impregnable [14] fortifications at Tchataldja which extend from the Black Sea to the Sea of Marmora [15] and are less than twenty miles from Constantinople. The Tchataldja lines [16] are marvelously [17] constructed [18] for defense and are considered almost the best fortified position in Europe. On one flank is the Black Sea, on the other the Sea of Marmora : they are defended on the right front [19] by Lake Derkos [20] and on the left front by an inlet,[21] and along [22] the shore they are still further [23] protected [24] by extensive marshes. Thus that portion of the peninsula through which [25] an army can march, even with nothing to hinder, is only sixteen miles in width, and every mile of this space is fortified with every device [26] known to military science.[27] At last, however, the Turkish commander succeeded [28] in leading his shattered [7] troops within the Tchataldja lines, where they made a last [29] stand and where they were aided [30] by rest and reënforcements, though these reënforcements were raw [31] Asiatics while those received by the Bulgarians were Servian veterans.[32] Exhausted [33] by the war and hopeful of action by the Powers,[34] on whose aid she relied,[35] Turkey on November 3 had requested the ambassadors of the Great Powers to intervene in the war. The next day the reply came refusing intervention [36] and advising Turkey to deal [37] with the Balkan Powers direct.[38]

1. Cf. Ex. **3**, n. 1.   2. 'nor did they give.'   3. 'of rest' (**quiēs**).   4. Omit : no need to repeat the principal subject.   5. **trīduum**.   6. Indecl.   7. **frangō**. 8. ' army.'   9. **excipiō**, abl. absol.   10. Cf. Ex. **1**, n. 10, and note the essential difference in meaning : **neglegō** would be wholly wrong here, as they did not neglect the roads but traveled them : accordingly say ' over very bad

roads,' abl. of means or **per** w. acc.   11. **contendō** or iter difficile **faciō**.
12. **palūster.**   13. Abl. absolute.   14. **inexpugnābilis** or simply **ēgregius.**
15. **Propontis, -idis,** *f.*   16. 'fortifications.'   17. **mīrē.**   18. **exstruō.**
19. **ā fronte dextrā** or **ā fronte ad dextrum cornū.**   20. **Lacus Derkos;**
treat as second declension nominative in -os.   21. **aestuārium.**   22. **secun-**
dum w. acc.   23. **melius etiam.**   24. **prōtegō.**   25. 'where': an adverb
regularly replaces a rel. pron. governed by a prep. in phrases of place and
time.   26. 'kind of fortification.'   27. **scientia rērum mīlitārium.**   28.
'was able to.'   29. Adverbial acc. modifying the verb.   30. **adiuvō.**
31. **imperītus.**   32. **veterānus.**   33. **dēfetīgātus.**   34. 'hoping that the P.
would act.'   35. **nītor.**   36. 'they replied that they would not intervene.'
37. **agō.**   38. A pronoun.

EXERCISE 17

The Bulgarians meanwhile were making desperate attempts
to carry the Tchataldja lines by assault, but though they succeeded in capturing the outer defenses, they were unable to
dislodge the Turks from the main works.   At this time also the
Servian army was advancing south to join the Greeks who had
started across Albania to take the port of Durazzo.[1]   The
Greeks also, after a series of [2] successful battles in which they
steadily [3] drove the Turks before them, entered Saloniki on
November 8 and at once turned north to meet the Servians.
On November 18 Monastir surrendered to the second Servian
army after a three days' battle in which twenty thousand Turks
were killed and wounded.   By this victory the last coherent [4]
portion of the Turkish army of the west was destroyed.   Eighty
thousand Turks held the fortifications of Monastir, but so fierce
was the Servian attack that they were everywhere [5] beaten.
About half [6] of the surviving [7] army was captured; and what
escaped, escaped as a broken mob [8] and not as military units.[9]
A few days later the Servian army occupied Durazzo.   Asiatic
cholera [10] had now broken out [11] in the Turkish army both at
Tchataldja and at Adrianople, which was still holding out.[12]
When therefore on November 14 the aged [13] Kiamil Pasha, the

grand Vizier,[14] instructed Nazim Pasha, the commander in
chief in the trenches [15] behind the last defenses of Constantinople, to negotiate [16] with the generals of the Allies for [17] a
fourteen-day truce,[18] the end of this astonishing [19] six weeks'
war [20] was in sight,[21] in which the Allies had never suffered a
single reverse.[22]

1. **Dyrrachium.** 2. ' many ': abl. absol. 3. **cōnstanter.** 4. **composi-**
tus or **quae sub iūstō imperiō erat.** 5. ' in all parts.' 6. **dīmidium.**
7. Rel. clause w. **supersum.** 8. **turba disiecta.** 9. Must be paraphrased;
nūllō certō ōrdine. 10. **cholera Asiātica.** 11. **exārdēscō.** 12. **sustineō.**
13. **senex.** 14. **Prīnceps Cīvitātis.** 15. **fossa.** 16. **agō.** 17. ' about ' (**dē**).
18. ' a truce (**indūtiae**) of fourteen days.' 19. **mīrus.** 20. ' war of forty-
two days.' 21. ' was near ' (**subsum, īnstō**). 22. ' had been defeated not
even once ' (**semel**).

EXERCISE 18

Turkey on November 23 rejected [1] the terms proposed by the
Allies for an armistice,[2] and the war went steadily on.[3] Finally,
early in December an armistice was signed [4] by the Allies and
the Turks on the following terms [5]: First; that hostilities
should be ended [6] until peace was established. Second; that
supplies should be sent to Adrianople, Janina and Scutari to
the Turkish troops cut off by the Allies' armies. Greece refused
to join the Allies in this truce, so that she might not be compelled to interrupt [7] her naval operations [8] in the Aegean where
she was blockading [9] the Bosporus and gaining possession of
many of the islands which she had possessed in ancient times.
The peace negotiations [10] opened in London [11] on December 16,
Greece sending commissioners along with the other Balkan
states, though she had refused to join the armistice. Day after
day [12] the Turks, according to their habit, prolonged [13] the conference and delayed [14] the commission's task, alleging first one
question then another [15] about which they claimed they had
to [16] seek instructions at [17] Constantinople. This they did

hoping to secure [18] better terms by delay, or even intervention [19] by the Powers.   One condition the Allies laid down [20]
without which a treaty was impossible.[21]   This was the surrender [22] of Adrianople.   The Turks refused this with equal
firmness,[23] till finally, when, compelled by Russia, they promised
to give up their ancient and holy [24] city, a revolution [25] broke
out in Constantinople, the cabinet was overthrown,[26] Nazim
Pasha the commander in chief was assassinated, [27] and the new
cabinet reiterated their firm resolution [28] never to give up
Adrianople.   The so-called Young Turk party [29] which had come
into power [30] by this crime [31] soon found that the responsibility
of conducting[32] the war had lessened[33] their confidence.   The populace of Constantinople cared nothing for the government, but
only for their own suffering and starvation.[34]   The army, in
which [35] Nazim Pasha had been very popular,[36] was on the
point of mutiny.[37]   No military or diplomatic advantage had
resulted from their rash act.[38]

---

1. recūsō.   2. 'terms of truce.'   3. 'it was fought continuously'
(continenter).   4. obsīgnō.   5. 'these terms: first (prīmum) . . . then'
(deinde).   6. 'that it should not be fought more' (amplius).   7. intermittō.
8. bellum nāvāle.   9. obstruō.   10. 'conference concerning peace.'
11. 'was begun (incipiō, passive) in London' (Londinium, loc. case).
12. diem ex diē.   13. prōdūcō.   14. dēmoror.   15. Cf. Caes. B. G. I.,
39.   16. oportet.   17. 'from.'   18. obtineō.   19. Express by an object
clause w. ut depending on 'secure.'   20. prōpōnō.   21. 'there could be
no treaty' (foedus).   22. Express by clause.   23. cōnstantiā parī.
24. sānctus.   25. mōtus or tumultus.   26. administrī imperiī ex officiō
ēiectī sunt.   27. occīdō.   28. 'kept saying that they had entirely (plānē)
resolved.'   29. 'the party (pars) of the Younger (iuvenis) Turks, as they
were called.'   30. 'gained possession of power.'   31. facinus.   32. 'the
serious business (or burden, onus) of directing' (dīrigō).   33. 'made
less.'   34. Vulgus autem Constantīnopolītānum imperium nihilī fēcit, ac
dē dolōre suō et famē sōlum cōgitābat.   35. Dative.   36. acceptus.
37. 'were not much distant but that (quīn) it should revolt.'   38. 'To
them acting rashly nothing of advantage had resulted (prōcēdō) either
(aut) with (apud) the army or with the embassies.'

EXERCISE 19

Meanwhile the deadlock [1] in London caused the adjournment [2] of the peace conference on January 6. Affairs with the Turks went from bad to worse,[3] and at last the diplomats of the Great Powers formally [4] advised Turkey to cede Adrianople. This was met by a curt refusal, and on January 30 the Allies notified Turkey that the armistice would be terminated [5] on February 3. On this date they fiercely renewed the attack on both Adrianople and Tchataldja, and a few days afterwards the Turkish Ambassador at London requested the British Foreign Minister [6] to invite the Powers to end the war. Turkey evidently still hoped for intervention. Meanwhile the Greeks, who had not accepted the armistice, were battering away at Janina, and the Montenegrins had renewed the attack on Scutari on the very day of the expiration of the armistice. Early in March the Greeks under Crown Prince Constantine captured Janina with 32,000 Turkish troops. A strong force of Servians was now dispatched to the assistance of King Nicholas in the siege of Scutari, against the vehement [7] objection [8] of Austria, who positively denied Scutari to Montenegro or any outlet [9] to the sea to Servia. By the middle of March the Allies informed the Powers that they would accept peace on the following conditions: First; [10] that the boundary of the Turkish Empire should be a line drawn [11] from Rodosto on the Sea of Marmora to Cape [12] Malatra on the Black Sea, and that all land to the west of this line except the peninsula of Gallipoli be given to the Allies. Second; [10] that the islands in the Aegean Sea be ceded to the Allies. Third; [10] that Turkey renounce all interest in Crete.[13] Fourth; [10] that an indemnity [14] be paid [15] by Turkey, the amount [16] to be settled [17] after the conclusion of peace. Fifth; [10] that the status [18] of the citizens of each state in the territories of the other be regulated.[19]

1. pertinācia.   2. differō.   3. 'proceeded even worse.'   4. 'by letters.'
5. tollō or dirimō.   6. administer Britannus rērum aliēnārum.   7. vehe-
menter.   8. recūsō.   9. aditus.   10. prīmum . . . deinde . . . deinde . . .
deinde . . . dēnique.   11. dēscrībō.   12. prōmuntōrium.   13. 'that there
be nothing of interest (negōtium) at all in Crete to Turkey.'   14. sūmptus
bellī, 'the expense of war.'   15. pendō.   16. summa.   17. cōnstituō.
18. status.   19. 'that it be decreed (dēcernō) concerning the status,' etc.

EXERCISE 20

To these terms the Turks practically [1] agreed [2]; but they will
probably be modified [3] to this extent, that [4] the boundary line
be drawn from Midia on the Black Sea to Enos on the Aegean,
that the disposition [5] of the Aegean islands shall rest with the
Powers, and that an autonomous [6] state, Albania, shall be
created [7] from [8] territories lying centrally in the Balkan peninsula.   The Powers also strongly object to the payment of
indemnity by Turkey.   Turkey's last hope vanished [9] in the
fall [10] of Adrianople on March 26.   The Powers now demanded
that King Nicholas raise [11] the siege of Scutari, but he boldly
refused, even though the demand was supported [12] by the blockade [13] of Montenegro's port by the warships of the Powers.
His bravery was successful, and Scutari surrendered early in
April.   It seems a cruel trick [14] of Fate [15] that the brave nation
which began the war against the Turk should alone receive no
advantage from it, but be forced by Austria's greed [16] to give
up what she has conquered by her own arms.   There is much
uncertainty [17] about the closing [18] events of the war and the
establishment [19] of peace, for the Allies are very careful [20] that
no news shall reach the outside world.[21]   There are even rumors
that they are quarreling [22] among themselves over the division [19]
of the spoils.[23]   It is said that they have even resorted to arms.
But though peace has not yet been proclaimed, and though
many difficulties to a full settlement [24] still exist, any further
military operations [25] must be considered a new war with new
causes and aims.   The Balkan-Turkish War is over.

1. magnā ex parte. 2. Develop an expression. 3. commūtō. 4. ūsque eō, ut. 5. attribuō or distribuō. 6. suī nōminis. 7. creō. 8. ex. 9. dēficiō. 10. Abl. absol. 11. relinquō. 12. sustineō. 13. obsideō, abl. absol. 14. dolus. 15. Fātum. 16. avāritia. 17. 'it is indeed uncertain' (incertus). 18. ultimus. 19. Gerundive. 20. praecaveō. 21. Devise a phrase to express the facts. 22. 'quarrels (contrōversia) have arisen (existō) among them.' 23. praeda. 24. 'to settling (cōnstituō) everything.' 25. 'whatever military things shall take place (fīō) in the future' (in reliquum tempus).

TABLE OF SYNONYMS

ABANDON (related English words = *desert, leave*): **relinquō** expresses merely the idea of leaving something behind; **dēserō** involves the reproach of leaving what one ought not to leave. The intransitive sense of *leave* is expressed by **exeō, ēgredior**, *to go out from*, and by **discēdō** which emphasizes the idea of parting from.

ABILITY: *see* POWER.

ACCEPT (*receive, take*): **capiō** indicates the act of taking or laying hold on; **accipiō** (ad + capiō), taking to one's self that which is offered or which presents itself ; **recipiō** (re + capiō), taking for protection, also taking what really or rightfully belongs to one.

ACCOMPLISH (*achieve, bring about, cause, do, make*): **gerō** expresses the act of carrying on, having reference to the continuance of the activity; **cōnficiō** (con + faciō), to complete in all detail, leaving no portion of the work undone; **perficiō** (per + faciō), to do thoroughly; **faciō**, to do something tangible, something existing both in space and time, to make; **agō**, to produce an effect existing in time only; **efficiō** (ex + faciō), to bring about as a result.

ACCORDINGLY (*therefore*): **itaque** indicates the ground of an action; **igitur**, the ground of an opinion.

(ON) ACCOUNT OF: *see* BECAUSE OF.

ACHIEVE: *see* ACCOMPLISH.

ADVISE (*command, direct, exhort, order, urge, warn*): **moneō** appeals to the judgment, urging a course of action because it is believed to be advantageous; **hortor** has its source solely in the will of the speaker; **praecipiō** (prae + capiō) indicates the giving of advice in order to forestall an act, and by one in a position of authority; it carries also the idea of instruction; **iubeō** is the general word of commanding; **imperō** implies a command by virtue of vested authority, usually with military reference.

ALLOW (*permit, suffer*): **patior** means merely not to object; **concēdō**, to permit upon request; **permittō** indicates a free or voluntary permission; **licet** simply indicates that there is no objection.

ALMOST (*nearly*): **paene** and **prope** indicate an approach to a limit, *nearly* in the sense of *just short of;* **ferē** is used of loose approximations, chiefly in respect to number or time.

AND: **et** connects words and expressions of equal or indifferent importance; **atque** (**ac**) indicates that the second of the two connected words or expressions is more important or emphatic than the first; **-que** joins closely into one idea or group.

ANNOUNCE (*report, tell*): **nūntiō** expresses the mere giving of information; **renūntiō**, the bringing of information to one expecting it or entitled to receive it.

ARMY: **exercitus** indicates an army as a drilled organization; **agmen**, an army on the march; **aciēs**, an army drawn up for action, a line of battle.

ASK (*ask for, demand, inquire, request*): **rogō** is the general term; **petō** means to seek to obtain; **postulō**, to demand as a right; **quaerō**, to seek detailed or full information.

ASSAULT: *see* ATTACK.

ASSEMBLE: *see* CALL.

ATTACK (*assault, besiege*): **oppugnō**, **expugnō**, **obsideō** are used of places only; **oppugnō** (**ob** + **pugnō**, *fight against*) has reference to the active siege operations; **obsideō** (**ob** + **sedeō**, *sit down against*), to the blockade only; **expugnō** refers to a successful assault; **aggredior** means to attack persons or armies; **impetum facere** refers to the suddenness or violence of the attack.

BATTLE (*fight*): **pugna** is the general term for a fight, whether of individuals or of armies; **proelium**, a military engagement.

BECAUSE OF (*on account of*): **ob** refers to the object in view; **propter** indicates a proximate cause or motive.

BESIEGE: *see* ATTACK.

BRING ABOUT: *see* ACCOMPLISH.

BRING TOGETHER: *see* CALL.

CALL (*assemble, bring together, collect, summon*): **vocō** is used of calling or summoning one person, also in sense of *name;* **convocō**, of summoning more than one person; **colligō** (**con** + **legō**), of bringing together things or persons; **cōgō** carries the additional idea of force or urgency.

CAUSE: *see* ACCOMPLISH.

COLLECT: *see* CALL.

COMMAND: *see* ADVISE.

CONQUER (*defeat, excel, surpass*): **superō** means to rise above, to surpass in general; **antecēdō**, to outstrip or take precedence; **vincō**, usually of military reference, to conquer by active exertion.

CONSIDER: *see* THINK.

CUSTOM: **mōs** is custom based on moral right; **cōnsuētūdō** is custom based on habit or convenience.

DAILY: **cotīdiē** refers to simple daily occurrence; **in diēs**, or **in singulōs diēs**, to daily increase or decrease.

DEEM: *see* THINK.

DEFEAT: *see* CONQUER.

DEMAND: *see* ASK.

DESERT: *see* ABANDON.

DESIRE (*want, wish*): **volō** is the general term of wishing; **cupiō** expresses an ardent desire; **studeō** means to give earnest attention to obtaining the object of desire.

DIRECT: *see* ADVISE.

DO: *see* ACCOMPLISH.

EITHER . . . OR: **aut . . . aut** is used when the alternatives are mutually exclusive; **vel . . . vel** (same root as **volō**), when there is a choice of alternatives; **sīve . . . sīve** lies in the conditional sphere and indicates that it is immaterial which alternative is chosen.

EXCEL: *see* CONQUER.

EXHORT: *see* ADVISE.

FEAR: **timeō** implies a weak or cowardly fear; **vereor**, the fear due to dread or hesitation.

FEEL: *see* FIND.

FIGHT: *see* BATTLE.

FIND (*feel, find out, know, learn, realize, understand*): **inveniō** (**in +
veniō**) means to come upon, to find accidentally; **reperiō**, to find by search; **comperiō**, to find out with certainty; **cōgnōscō**,

to find out by investigation, also to know by marks that appeal to the senses, to become acquainted with; **intellegō**, to find out thoroughly, to understand; **sentiō**, to know by experience; **sciō** is the most general verb of knowing.

HINDER (*prevent, prohibit*): **impediō** places obstacles in the way; **prohibeō** keeps away from the desired goal; **dēterreō** frightens away.

INQUIRE: *see* ASK.

KNOW: *see* FIND.

LABOR (*work*): **labor** refers to the hardship involved; **opera** refers to effort put forth in the aim to assist or serve; **opus** is effective work, and also the result or product of work (**opera**).

LEARN: *see* FIND.

LEAVE: *see* ABANDON.

MAKE: *see* ACCOMPLISH.

MAN: **homō** denotes a human being, in plural often *men, mankind;* **vir** is an individual man, a man of worth or distinction.

MUST (*necessary, ought*): **dēbeō** expresses a subjective duty, duty to one's self; **oportet**, an objective duty, duty to others or to the law; **necesse** refers to a necessity imposed by natural cause; the passive periphrastic is the weakest and most general expression of obligation.

NEARLY: *see* ALMOST.

NECESSARY: *see* MUST.

OPPORTUNITY: *see* POWER.

ORDER: *see* ADVISE.

OTHER: **alius** is another, in general; **alter**, the other (of two only), in plural, the other group; **reliquus** is the one remaining, in plural, the rest; when plural, **reliquī** is often replaced by **cēterī**.

OUGHT: *see* MUST.

PERCEIVE: *see* SEE.

PERMIT: *see* ALLOW.

POWER (*ability, opportunity, strength*): **vīs** is primarily physical strength; **potestās** (**possum**) emphasizes the ability to perform an act, and also refers to official power; **facultās** (**faciō**) emphasizes the performance of an act; **imperium** is military power.

PREVENT: *see* HINDER.

PROHIBIT: *see* HINDER.

REALIZE: *see* FIND.

RECEIVE: *see* ACCEPT.

REFLECT: *see* THINK.

REPORT: *see* ANNOUNCE.

REQUEST: *see* ASK.

SAFE: **tūtus**, secure, out of reach of danger; **salvus**, saved from danger by active exertion or assistance; **incolumis**, having escaped from danger unharmed.

SAY: **dīcō**, to say a thing; **loquor**, to speak or talk.

SEE (*perceive*): **videō** is the general term for seeing, literally or figuratively; **cōnspiciō** is to have in view; **perspiciō**, to see clearly.

STRENGTH: *see* POWER.

SUFFER: *see* ALLOW.

SUMMON: *see* CALL.

SURPASS: *see* CONQUER.

TAKE: *see* ACCEPT.

TELL: *see* ANNOUNCE.

THEREFORE: *see* ACCORDINGLY.

THINK (*consider, deem, reflect*): **putō** is the most general term for forming or holding an opinion; **exīstimō** is to form an opinion by weighing the value of the evidence; **arbitror**, to form an opinion by judging between conflicting evidence; **cōgitō** expresses the act of thinking, pondering, reflecting.

UNDERSTAND: *see* FIND.

URGE: *see* ADVISE.

WANT: *see* DESIRE.

WARN: *see* ADVISE.

WISH: *see* DESIRE.

WORK: *see* LABOR.

APPENDIX

This Appendix furnishes ample verbal material to prepare students to pass any college entrance examination based on the orations of Cicero which are regularly read in secondary schools. Since Caesar and Cicero both wrote Latin, and wrote contemporaneously, the principles of the syntax of the language, as set forth in the lessons of this book, apply equally well to the writings of both. The only important difference between the language of the two authors lies in the vocabulary, for each writer requires for the treatment of his particular subject some words which are not needed by the other. No student should be expected in his writing to imitate personal idiosyncrasies of style.

A. FIFTY IMPORTANT CICERONIAN WORDS [1]

accomplish, **adsequor**, -ī, -secūtus (*in sense of* gaining an end; *also* bring to pass); **perficiō**, -ere, -fēcī, -fectum (*chiefly in sense of* completing an undertaking; *also* bring to pass, finish).

attain, **cōnsequor**, -ī, -secūtus; **attingō**, -ere, -tigī, -tāctum.

break forth, **ērumpō**, -ere, -rūpī, -ruptum.

case (at law), **causa**, -ae, *f.*; **quaestiō**, -ōnis, *f.*; plead a case, **causam dīcere**.

Citizens (*as term of address*), **Quirītēs**, -ium, *m.*

in civil capacity (*acting as a citizen, not as a soldier; used especially of the civil magistrates*), **togātus**, -a, -um.

common people, **plēbs**, **plēbis**, *f.*, or **plēbēs**, -eī (-ī), *f.* (*the* masses, *as socially opposed to the* aristocracy, **optimātēs**, *and to the* senatorial order *or* patricians, **patriciī**); **vulgus**, -ī, *n.* (*the* rabble, mob; *also* common soldiers, rank and file). *The political opponents of the aristocracy are called* **populārēs**.

[1] See Suggestions to Teachers, p. 7.

confess, **cōnfiteor**, -ērī, -fessus.

conspire, **coniūrō**, I; *hence the perf. ptc. as subst.*, **coniūrātus**, -ī, *m.*, conspirator, *occurring only in pl.; and the abstract* **coniūrātiō**, -ōnis, *f.*, conspiracy.

consular, **cōnsulāris**, -e, *adj.; as subst.*, ex-consul.

crime, **facinus**, -oris, *n. (an overt act).*

decree (*v.*), **dēcernō**, -ere, -crēvī, -crētum, *w. acc. dir. obj. or w.* **ut** (**nē**) *and subjunctive; also, w. inf.*, determine.

decree (*n.*), **senātūs cōnsultum**, -ī, *n.*

defendant, **reus**, -ī, *m., w. gen. of the charge.*

destroy, **dēleō**, -ēre,-ēvī, -ētum.

destruction, **perniciēs**, -ēī, *f. (used of persons and governments)*; **ruīna**, -ae, *f. (of material objects, and also figuratively).*

disgraceful, **turpis**, -e, *adj.; hence the abstract* **turpitūdō**, -dinis, *f.*, disgrace.

dishonor, **dēdecus**, -oris, *n.*

efforts, **labōrēs**, -um, *m. pl.*

envy (*v.*), **invideō**, -ēre, -vīdī, -vīsum, *w. dat.; hence perf. ptc.* **invīsus**, -a, -um, hated, detested, *and the abstract* **invidia**, -ae, *f.*, envy, unpopularity.

fame, **fāma**, -ae, *f. (also* notoriety, report, reputation).

Forum, **forum**, -ī, *n.*

hold (*as a formed and expressed opinion*), **cēnseō**, -ēre, cēnsuī, cēnsum.

joy, **laetitia**, -ae, *f. (joy as felt)*; **gaudium**, -ī, *n. (joy as felt and shown).*

judge (*v.*), **iūdicō**, I (*in legal sense and also of forming a personal judgment*).

judge (*n.*), **iūdex**, -icis, *m.; in pl.*, jurymen.

knight, **eques**, -itis, *m.*

lay before, **dēferō**, -re, -tulī, -lātum (*of giving information or making formal report*); **referō** (*of referring to senate for deliberation or vote*).

learning, **doctrīna**, -ae, *f.*

limit, **modus**, -ī, *m. (not of physical limit; also* measure, method).

look out for, **prōspiciō**, -ere, -spēxī, -spectum, *w. dat.;* **prōvideō**, -ēre, -vīdī, -vīsum, *w. dat.*

manage, **administrō**, I; **gerō**, -ere, gessī, gestum.

neglect, **neglegō**, -ere, -lēxī, -lēctum.

old, **vetus, -eris** (*of long standing*); **antīquus, -a, -um** (*ancient, of the remote past*); **senex, senis** (*of men; as subst.*, old man); *hence* **senectūs, tūtis,** *f.*, old age.

pleasure, **voluptās, -tātis,** *f.*

praise (*v.*), **laudō, I.**

praise (*n.*), **laus, laudis,** *f.*

propose (a law, **lēgem**), **rogō, I.**

prosecutor, **quaesītor, -ōris,** *m.*

public, **pūblicus, -a, -um** (*also* official).

punish, **ulcīscor, -ī, ultus** (*with idea of requital rather than of the suffering caused*).

pursuit (in life), **studium, -ī,** *n.* (*also* favorite study, specialty, hobby).

it is a question of, **agitur,** *pass. of* **agō** *used impersonally, w.* **dē** *and abl.* (*also in personal construction,* be at stake, be in peril).

records (*official*), **tabulae, -ārum,** *f. pl.*

relying upon, **frētus, -a, -um,** *w. abl.*

scoundrel, **dēspērātus, -ī,** *m.* ; **improbus, -ī,** *m.* ; **perditus, -ī,** *m.*

sense of honor, **pudor, -ōris,** *m.*

succeed in, **valeō, -ēre, -uī, -itum,** *w.* **ad** *and acc. of gerundive.*

tribute, **vectīgal, -ālis,** *n.* (*also* revenue, *especially in pl.*) ; *hence the adj.* **vectīgālis, -e,** tributary ; *as subst.*, tributary province.

try (a case), **agō, -ere, ēgī, āctum.**

wickedness, **scelus, -eris,** *n.*

worthlessness, **nēquitia, -ae,** *f.* (*as result of lack of ability*) ; **īgnāvia, -ae,** *f.* (*as result of cowardice*) ; **inertia, -ae,** *f.* (*as result of laziness*).

worthy, **dignus, -a, -um,** *in noun constructions w. abl.; in verb constructions w. rel. pronoun and subjunctive: hence the abstract* **dignitās, -tātis,** *f.*, worth, dignity.

B. TWENTY–FIVE CICERONIAN CATCHWORDS AND PHRASES

at home and abroad, **domī mīlitiaeque.**

at last (at length), **tandem aliquandō.**

but (then), *as particle of resumption of argument after digression,* **igitur,** *postpositive.*

but why? **quamquam quid?**

but yet (*as a strong adversative*), **at vērō.**

by land and sea, **terrā marīque.**

come now, **age vērō.**

for certainly, **nam profectō.**

for truly (and indeed, really), **etenim.**

in the first place, **prīmum.**

lastly (finally), **dēnique.**

moreover (nay, indeed), **quīn etiam.**

nay more, **immō vērō.**

now then, **iam vērō, nunc vērō.**

pray (then, will you, *or any word or phrase strengthening a question or command*), **tandem.**

secondly (thirdly, *and so on up to the final topic*), **deinde** (*lit.*, next).

then at last, **tum dēnique.**

therefore (wherefore), **quā rē, quam ob rem.**

to be brief (not to say too much, not to be tiresome), **ac nē longum sit.**

to say the least, **ut levissimē dīcam.**

what! *or* what, then? **quid!** *or* **quid igitur?**

what indeed, **quid vērō.**

what is it (there) that? **quid est quod** . . .? *w. verb in subjunctive.*

what of this, that. . .? **quid, quod. . .?** *w. verb in indicative.*

you say (you claim), **inquis,** *always parenthetical.*

C. FIFTY USEFUL CICERONIAN WORDS

abode, **sēdēs,** -is, *f.* (*lit.*, seat).

accuse, **accūsō,** I; **īnsimulō,** I.

attribute, **attribuō,** -ere, -uī, -ūtum.

beginning (*of an undertaking*), **prīncipium,** -ī, *n.*

blood, **sanguis,** -inis, *m.*

capital (*in financial sense*), **rēs, reī,** *f.*

check, **reprimō,** -ere, -pressī, -pressum (*lit.*, press back); *note the progressive effectiveness and completeness of the checking as indicated by the prefixes in* **comprimō,** crush (*lit.*, press together) *and* **opprimō,** overwhelm (*lit.*, press against).

this city (this government), *often* **haec,** *n. pl.*

credit (*in financial sense*), **fidēs,** -eī, *f.*

culture, hūmānitās, -tātis, *f.*

debt, aes aliēnum (*lit.*, another's money: aes, aeris, *n.*, bronze; *hence* money).

devote, cōnferō, *w.* ad *and acc.*

dignified, moderātus, -a, -um.

distinguished, amplissimus, -a, -um.

do one's duty to, satisfaciō, *w. dat.*

do without, careō, -ēre, -uī, -itum, *w. abl.* (*also* be without, lack).

early (*adj.*), iniēns, -euntis.

elections, comitia, -ōrum, *n. pl.*

end (*of an undertaking*), exitus, -ūs, *m.* (*also* outcome).

equal, pār, paris.

exile, exsul, -is, *m.* (*a person*); exsilium, -ī, *n.* (*a condition of life*).

fault, culpa, -ae, *f.* (*also* blame).

glory, glōria, -ae, *f.*

greed, avāritia, -ae, *f.*; cupiditās, -tātis, *f.* (*the latter also* desire, eagerness).

honor, honor, -ōris, *m.* (*hence adj.* honestus, -a, -um, honorable); decus, -oris, *n.*

income, fructus, -ūs, *m.* (*lit.*, fruit).

influential, gravissimus, -a, -um.

knowledge, scientia, -ae, *f.*; *often* cōnsilium, -ī, *n.*, *especially in sense of* military knowledge, strategy; sapientia, -ae, *f.*, *in sense of* wisdom.

life, vīta, -ae, *f.*

literature, litterae, -ārum, *f. pl.*

merciful, clēmēns, -entis (*showing mercy*); misericors, -cordis (*feeling pity*); *hence the abstracts* clēmentia, -ae, *f.*, mercy, *and* misericordia, -ae, *f.*, compassion.

methodical, modestus, -a, -um.

patriotic, amāns reī pūblicae (amāns, -antis, *ptc. w. obj. gen.*).

pirate, praedō, -ōnis, *m.*

plot (*v., tr.*), cōgitō, I; (*intr.*) īnsidior, -ārī, -ātus, *w. dat. of person against whom the plot is laid.*

plot (*n.*), īnsidiae, -ārum, *f. pl.*

plunder, dīripiō, -ere, -uī, -reptum.

quarrel, dissēnsiō, -ōnis, *f.*

regard (consideration), **rātiō, -ōnis,** *f., w. obj. gen. (the student should familiarize himself with the meanings of this word, which has almost as wide a range of application as* **rēs**).

remedy (*v.*), **medeor, -ērī, ——,** *w. dat.*

remedy (*n.*), **medicīna, -ae,** *f.*

save (preserve), **cōnservō, I** (*also* keep safe).

scatter, **dispergō, -ere, -persī, -persum;** *perf. ptc.* **dispersus, -a, -um,** widespread.

success (*habitual and due to good fortune*), **fēlīcitās, -tātis,** *f.*; (*in general*) **fortūna, -ae,** *f.* (*also* fortune *in all senses*).

sword, *often* **ferrum, -ī,** *n* (*lit.,* iron).

talent (*inborn*), **ingenium, -ī,** *n.*

trial, **iūdicium, -ī,** *n.* (*also* the court; *also* judgment, sentence).

wealthy, **locuplēs, -ētis.**

witness, **testis, -is,** *m.* or *f.*; *hence* **testimōnium, -ī,** *n.,* testimony, evidence.

it is worth while, **operae pretium est** (*lit.,* it is the reward of labor).

yield to, **cēdō, -ere, cessī, cessum.**

youth, **iuventūs, -tūtis,** *f., the period of life, also as coll. subst.,* the young, young men; **iūvenis, -is,** *m.* or *f.,* young person; **adulēscens, -ntis,** *m.,* young man.

VOCABULARY INDEX

The Arabic numerals refer to the lesson in which the word is given. The combined Roman and Arabic numerals refer to the exercises in Part II. If the word is not found in the vocabulary proper, it will appear among the synonyms or in the text of the lesson.

A

abandon 6, 10
able 3, 32
abode 14
about 5, 11, 13
about to 31
above 5, 14
absent 14, II 12
accept 24
access 20
accomplish 8, 16
accordance (in) 5
according to 5
accordingly 5
account of (on) 5
accustomed (be) 18
achieve 8
achievements 13
across 5
act (v.) 32
addition (in) 5
administer 34
adopt 7
advance 11, 17
advance to attack 17
advantage 8
advantageous 8
adverse 10
advice 32
advise 17
afar 28
afraid 23
after (prep.) 5
after (adv.) 14
after (conj.) 24
afterward 28

again 25
against 5, 19
against one's will 35
ago 14
aid 4, 15
alarm 8
all 1, 9, 12
allegiance 10
allow 3
allowed (it is) 32
ally 2
almost 13
alone 12
along 5
already 1
also 14, 32
although 26
always 6
am to 31, 40
ambassador 9
ambush 6
among 5
amount to 13
ancestors 21
and 1
and also 1
and not 9, 27
and so 5
announce 8
annoy 6
another 12
answer 5
anxious for 3
any 9, 12
appearance 13, 34
apprehend II 20
approach (n.) 20

approach (v.) 14
arm (v.) II 19
arms 1
army 1
around 5
arrange 11, 30
arrange for 16
arrangement 7, 12, 26
arrival 4
arrive 5
art of war 13
artillery II 9
as 5, 8, 11, 24, 25, II 4
as far as possible 20
as if 30
as much as 4
ascend 5
ascertain 36
ask 17, 19, 37
ask advice 32
ask for 19
ask permission 32
assault (n.) 4, 19
assault (v.) 1
assemble 16, 17, II 1
assembly 15
assert 36
assign II 17
assistance 4
assure 36
at 5
at all 12
at first 20
at last 13
at least 7, 21, 23, 29
at length 19
at once 10

INDEX OF SUBJECTS

(The references are to paragraphs.)